MW00878500

PRESENTED TO:

ON:

BY:

DEVOTIONAL

MY HEALTHY CHURCH

ISBN: 978-1-62423-108-7 (hardcover)
      978-1-62423-109-4 (softcover)

17 16 15 14 • 1 2 3 4 5

Printed in the United States of America

CONTENTS

INTRODUCTION

Without God's love for us and our love for each other, life would be missing something important. Sort of like French fries without salt or pizza without cheese or a banana split without bananas. Want to hear a good idea? Read one devotion in this book each day to remind you of God's great love. He thinks you're special, and He loves you very much.

Do you want to know how to love God and others? There are 366 devotions in this book to help you do just that. You'll find many different stories, interesting facts, and fun activities to do each day. Are you having a sad day or a bad day? Do you have to make a tough decision? God can help you with that!

Try to set aside a few minutes each day to read the devotion for that day. Think how you can act on what you have read and pray that God would help you do that. These devotions will teach you how God can guide you and how you can serve Him. They will help you grow more like Jesus every day through the power of the Holy Spirit.

FIRE BIBLE FOR KIDS ICONS

Beside many of the Bible verses at the top of each page you will see a word symbol. The symbol points you to a note in the *Fire Bible for Kids* with helpful information about that verse. If you see one of these symbols, simply turn in your *Fire Bible for Kids* to the Scripture reference and look for the note with that symbol. There are four types of word symbols:

 GOD'S PROMISES. Key verses about God's promises. Memorize them and use them to live for God.

 POWER-PACKED WORDS. Definitions of key words in the Bible.

 IDEAS. Awesome ideas about life and facts from the Bible that can help you live for God. Questions and activity suggestions will help you put these ideas into practice.

 POWER FOR LIFE. These notes give added information about the Bible. They help you understand how the Holy Spirit worked in the past and works in the present to give power to God's people.

InTERACTIVE Elements

You can unlock extra Bible knowledge with digitally interactive games and activities. You can access these on the first page of each month and with weekly QR codes. Timeless Bible stories leap from the pages with eye-popping 3D graphics. This is your chance to interact with Augmented Reality versions of ancient Bible artifacts and more!

Go to www.firebibleforkidsdevotional.com to download the App for iOS or Android to bring these daily devotions to life.

JANUARY

You're a Masterpiece

Find It in the Bible

For you created my inmost being; you knit me together in my mother's womb. I praise you because I am fearfully and wonderfully made; your works are wonderful, I know that full well.

PSALM 139:13–14

A masterpiece is the best work a craftsperson can produce. For example, Leonardo da Vinci's painting, *Mona Lisa,* is considered by most to be a masterpiece. It's the most valuable painting in the world, worth a whopping $760 million.

Know what else is a masterpiece? You! This passage from Psalm 139 explains how. David, the second king of Israel and writer of many of the psalms in the Bible, wrote this psalm as an offering of praise to God. David thanked God for creating him. He knew that as God's creation, a human being is a masterpiece.

Even when you were a tiny unborn baby, you were God's masterpiece, seen only by Him. If you're ever tempted to compare yourself to someone else, remember this: God made you exactly the way you are. That means you're a masterpiece!

A POWER NOTE

Grab a piece of paper and trace the shape of your hand. On each finger, write something great about you. Don't forget to include victories in your life. For example: "I'm kind to my friends." "I can sing." "I can run fast." Thank God for making you just the way you are.

GOD IS NUMBER one

Find It in the Bible

You shall have no other gods before me.

EXODUS 20:3

Have you been in a car that uses a Global Positioning System (GPS) to help the driver know where to go? A GPS uses signals from multiple satellites to determine the position of the car and to help the driver get where he wants to go. In this way the satellite gives guidance to the driver. But the GPS is only useful to the driver if he turns it on and listens to it and believes it is telling the truth.

From the moment God created Adam and Eve He wanted people to trust Him and to look to Him for guidance. That's why the first of the Ten Commandments tells us not to worship any other gods.

When God gave this commandment to the people of Israel, He wanted them to know that only He could guide and protect them. He wanted them to love Him more than anyone else or anything else. The people in Egypt worshipped gods made of stone and wood. They thought these "gods" could keep them safe and bring rain from the sky. But this was not possible. There is only one true God who has the power to guide us and care for us.

A POWER NOTE

When we believe in Jesus as our Savior, we have our own GPS (God's Powerful Spirit) to help us and to guide us. Make a paper sign with the letters GPS on it and hang it in your room. It will remind you to depend on the one true God.

GOD'S SPECIAL DAY

Find It in the Bible
Remember the Sabbath day by keeping it holy.

EXODUS 20:8

What's your favorite day of the year? Your birthday? Or maybe a holiday like Christmas or Easter? Besides those days, every year has fifty-two special days—one each week. Can you guess which day it is? That special day is Sunday or the Sabbath day. It's not like other days in the week so in some ways it's sort of like a holiday every week!

God wanted the people of Israel to treat Sunday as a special day, so He told them not to work on that day. He wanted them to take time off from their work to rest and to worship Him.

God is our example about how to treat Sunday. He made the world in six days but rested on the seventh day (Genesis 2:2–3). Just think about that. If the mighty God of the universe stopped creating oceans and mountains to rest, surely we need to spend one day in a quiet and restful way. Take some time to think about ways you can make Sundays special. Perhaps you can go to church and Sunday school, and you might take time to read some books that will teach you about Jesus.

A POWER NOTE

If you have a calendar, circle the Sunday of each week. Write the name of one person you will pray for on that day.

THE FRUIT OF THE SPIRIT

Find It in the Bible

But the fruit of the Spirit is love, joy, peace, forbearance, kindness,
goodness, faithfulness, gentleness and self-control.
Against such things there is no law.

GALATIANS 5:22–23

How many fruits can you name? Apples, bananas, cherries, oranges, pears, strawberries . . . the list goes on and on! Did you know there's a fruit called the donut peach? It looks like a donut and tastes sweet like a donut but it's not a donut! It's a peach! This kind of peach was first grown in China.

Hundreds of different fruits grow in countries around the world. These are fruits we can see and touch and taste. The Bible describes a different kind of fruit called "the fruit of the Spirit." This fruit refers to actions and attitudes that please God, things like kindness and patience.

When our hearts are filled with God's Holy Spirit, He helps us to show love to others. He helps us to be joyful and patient even in difficult situations. When we do these things, other people can see the fruit of the Spirit in our lives.

A POWER NOTE

On a piece of paper, draw nine pieces of fruit. Under each fruit write the name of a fruit of the Spirit. You can trust the Holy Spirit to help you live the fruit of the Spirit each day. He will help you be kind to kids at school or be gentle with your little brother or sister.

DO GOOD INSTEAD

Find It in the Bible

I will not look with approval on anything that is vile.
I hate what faithless people do; I will have no part in it.

PSALM 101:3

Think about the kids in your class at school. Do you know students who talk when the teacher is talking or say mean things to other students? These students aren't being respectful. When they talk out of turn or bully other students, they're doing what God doesn't like, and that makes Him sad. It also makes other people sad.

Sometimes you may feel tempted to laugh when kids do things that don't show respect. You might even want to join them and make fun of other people. The person who wrote this psalm felt that way, but he didn't join in the bad activities. Instead, he told God that he would ignore what the bad people were doing and wouldn't be a part of it. He chose to turn away from wrong to do what was right.

That was a good choice, and God wants you to do the same. Make a promise to yourself that you will always choose to do what is right.

A POWER NOTE

The next time you see a kid do something mean, think how you can do something nice instead. Then do it. Say kind words to other kids or raise your hand to help when your teacher asks for a volunteer.

GOD IS BIGGER THAN YOUR FEARS

Find It in the Bible

Do not be anxious about anything, but in every situation,
by prayer and petition, with thanksgiving,
present your requests to God.

PHILIPPIANS 4:6

It really isn't much fun to worry about things in life, is it? And the reason is because you can't be worried and happy at the same time! What do you worry about? Do you worry about tests and grades at school? Or having friends and being popular? Maybe you worry that your family doesn't have enough money to pay the bills. But worry doesn't fix a single thing!

Worry doesn't help, it doesn't make us happy, and it doesn't make God happy. Why? Because when we worry we show we don't trust Him to take care of us.

No matter what problem causes you to worry, God is bigger than that problem. The Bible says we don't have to worry because God wants to take care of us. He's more powerful and mighty than anything or anyone in the world. No matter what makes you worried, He wants you to tell Him about it. He loves you and is always with you. When you talk to Him about your worries, the Holy Spirit will give you peace.

A POWER NOTE

The next time you feel worried or afraid, find a piece of paper and write down the verse at the top of this page. Under the verse write down all the things you are worried about. Draw a line through every one of them to remind you that God will take care of them for you.

LIGHT IN THE DARKNESS

Find It in the Bible

In the beginning God created the heavens and the earth.

GENESIS 1:1

You've been in your room when it's very dark and the bedroom door is shut. The only light you see comes from the moon shining down through tree branches. But you know that all you have to do is flip a switch and your whole room will light up. That's thanks to Thomas Edison who invented the light bulb. He tested his first light bulb in 1879, and the bulb lasted for over thirteen hours. It was many, many experiments later before he invented a bulb that would last as long as the ones that you have in your lamp.

But back when God created the heavens and the earth, it was completely dark because not even the sun or moon had been created yet! Everything was blackness.

But it wasn't too dark for God. In the darkness, He spoke and created light. Then He created the sun, moon, and stars. And then, of course, He created everything else, including you.

The King of the universe created light and life for the whole world. That was the beginning of everything. That was the first light in the darkness.

A POWER NOTE

The next time you get ready for bed, turn off all the lights and see how dark it is. Then turn on your light and thank God for creating light in the darkness. Thank Him for creating life in you!

CLEAN UP YOUR ROOM!

Find It in the Bible

The next day John saw Jesus coming toward him and said, "Look, the Lamb of God, who takes away the sin of the world!"

JOHN 1:29

What happens when you leave your laundry sitting on your bedroom floor for days, or you don't pick up your books and magazines and put them away, or you don't empty your waste basket? Pretty soon, you can't find anything, you lose your homework papers, and your bedroom is a mess! You need to get organized, put the laundry in the hamper, and throw out the trash.

Imagine that your life is like your bedroom. You have great memories and many good people and things in your life, just like you have nice things in your room. But when you let sins or other bad attitudes or actions accumulate, they clutter up your life and make it hard to do good things and to think good thoughts.

That's what sin does—it makes a mess of your life. So how do you stay clean? You let Jesus help you! He took away the sin of the world when He died on the cross. You stay clean by confessing your sins to Him every day and asking Him to help keep you clean from the inside out. When the Holy Spirit speaks to your heart about a sin, repent of it that very moment.

A POWER NOTE

Do you need to get some clutter out of your room? As you throw away trash or put pieces of laundry in the hamper, pray about one thing in your life that you want God to help you with.

FORGIVE AND FORGET

Find It in the Bible

Be kind and compassionate to one another, forgiving each other,
just as in Christ God forgave you.

EPHESIANS 4:32

When two objects rub against each other this causes friction. Rough surfaces like sandpaper have lots of friction. Smooth surfaces like glass have less. When two surfaces are covered with oil or water there is little friction between the two surfaces. That's why snails make slippery slime to help them slither along the ground.

Have you had an argument with a friend? Have you rubbed against each other and created friction in your relationship? Pour on the oil of forgiveness and get along.

In the letter Paul wrote to the Ephesians, he taught us to forgive others just as God forgave us. That means we should always be willing to forgive those who hurt us. At times, we feel as if the other person is at fault and should apologize first—*then* we'll say we're sorry.

But that isn't God's way. Jesus told His disciples to forgive their enemies—not just seven times, but seventy times seven! In other words, He told them to forgive time after time after time . . . and not to keep count! After all, God doesn't keep count—He keeps on forgiving.

A POWER NOTE

Ask an adult to help you find a piece of sand-paper and a small mirror. Rub your fingers over each one. Which surface will produce the most friction? Which do you want to be like?

THE GREATEST COMMANDMENT

Find It in the Bible

Love the Lord your God with all your heart and
with all your soul and with all your
mind and with all your strength.

MARK 12:30

What does it mean to love God with your heart, soul, mind, and strength? It means to put God first in everything you do. When Jesus said these words, He was talking to some people who wanted to know what laws they should obey. They asked Jesus what was the most important law of all.

Jesus said it was to love God with everything they felt, cared about, thought, and did. He reminded them that if they loved God that way, they wouldn't break any of God's laws because they would live in a way that pleased Him.

So how do you put God first? You think about Him the moment you wake up in the morning. You pray and ask Him to guide you through your day. Then with every situation that happens, every person you talk to, everything you think about, you first think about Him and how He wants you to act.

When we put God first, we love Him the way we should.

A POWER NOTE

On a piece of paper, write the words *heart, soul, mind,* and *strength*. Draw something next to each word that helps you remember this verse. Hang it somewhere where you will see it every day.

THE SECOND-GREATEST COMMANDMENT

Find It in the Bible

The second is this: "Love your neighbor as yourself."
There is no commandment greater than these.

MARK 12:31

If you could visit a tunnel town built beneath the prairie, you would find that prairie dogs have quite a variety of neighbors. A burrowing owl lays her eggs in an empty tunnel hole to keep them safe. A snake sleeps in one of the tunnels during the winter. Sometimes mice or rabbits dart into a tunnel to escape a coyote. All these neighbors get along just fine.

When Jesus said to love your neighbor, He wasn't just talking about the person who lives next door. He was talking about all kinds of people—the ones in your family, your friends, the people who live next door, the kids down the street, the cashier at the grocery store, or the bus driver. Anyone you meet, even a person across the world, can be your neighbor.

So how do you love them in the same way that you love yourself? You treat them in the same way you want others to treat you. Smile and say hello. Say kind words. Help them if they need help. Play fair. Offer to share your snack. Invite them to Sunday school. Pray for them.

A POWER NOTE

See if you can find a map of your city. Ask an adult to help you mark an X on the place where some people you know live. Draw a line from each X to the edge of the map and write one thing you can do for each person to show that you love them.

GOD IS WITH YOU

Find It in the Bible

And we know that in all things God works for the good of those who love him, who have been called according to his purpose.

ROMANS 8:28

Think of a time you went through a difficult experience—a grandparent died, you had to move to a new school, or someone was mean to you. We all go through things that hurt and don't make sense to us.

The world is a difficult place and bad things happen. When we get hurt, it's easy to feel like we just want to give up because we don't understand. We might even wonder if God cares.

The Bible promises that God does care, all the time in every situation. In fact, He takes those difficult circumstances and brings good out of them. He can work to bring good out of *all things* (no matter how difficult). It may not seem possible right now, but don't focus on what seems impossible to you or what is hard. Instead, focus on God's promise in the Bible.

You know you can trust God to keep His promises. They are as sure as the sun that rises every morning and sets every night.

A POWER NOTE

Find a photo you like in a magazine. Glue it to a large piece of paper. Beneath the photo write these words: "God always works for my good!" Cut the photo into several pieces like a puzzle. When you put the puzzle together, it will remind you that God is working to put things together for you.

THE KINDEST ACT

Find It in the Bible

Whoever is kind to the poor lends to the LORD, and he will reward them for what they have done.

PROVERBS 19:17

If you suddenly had one million dollars, what would you do with it? Would you give some away? A million is a mind-blowing number. If you were counting a million one-dollar bills at the rate of sixty a minute for eight hours a day five days a week, it would take you nearly seven weeks to complete the task. At the same rate it would take over 133 years to count a billion dollars.

You may not have a million dollars to share with others, but you can share what you have. A small act of kindness can make a big difference to a person who doesn't have much food or money.

Solomon, one of Israel's kings, wrote and collected many proverbs. Here, and in other places in the Bible, is advice about the poor. Widows and orphans were part of that group. They were the ones people often forgot about. They had the least and needed help to survive. Giving to the poor was the kindest act anyone could do.

Want to make God glad? Give to someone in need.

A POWER NOTE

Talk with your mom or dad about how you can help needy people in your area. Perhaps your family could serve in a soup kitchen or pack school supplies for a ministry. You can help a kid at school with his or her homework or with a project. You can always offer a smile or a kind word.

YOU'VE GOT SKILLS!

Find It in the Bible

I have given ability to all the skilled workers to make
everything I have commanded you.

EXODUS 31:6

What do you think you're good at? Perhaps someone has told you that you draw really well. Someone probably said that to Michelangelo Buonarroti (1475–1564). He was a painter and a sculptor who is best known for his frescoes in Rome's Sistine Chapel (he had to lie on his back on a scaffold to paint the ceiling) and his sculpture of David (carved out of pure marble). Michelangelo is still considered one of the greatest artists of all time.

When the people of Israel left Egypt, they wandered in a wilderness. While there, God wanted them to make a place to worship Him. This place would be called the tabernacle—a tent they could carry with them as they traveled. He chose several men to do the job—men who were especially skilled in working in gold, sewing, cutting stones, and working in wood. Bezelel and Oholiab were experts at what they did. They were the Michelangelos of their day. But they didn't depend only on their skill. The Holy Spirit helped them do what God wanted done.

God has given you that special skill you have. Be sure to use it to honor Him.

A POWER NOTE

Make a list of things you're good at. Then ask a parent to pray with you. Ask God to show you what you can do for Him.

HONORING PARENTS

Find It in the Bible

Honor your father and your mother, so that you may live long
in the land the LORD your God is giving you.

EXODUS 20:12

Has anyone ever told you that you act like one or both of your
parents—or maybe like one of your brothers or sisters?
Speaking of brothers and sisters, a woman married to a man
named Feodor Vassilyev in Shuya, Russia, in the eighteenth
century holds the record for having the most children. She had
sixty-nine! Imagine having sixty-eight brothers and sisters!

While God's people were camped in the wilderness after they
escaped from Egypt, He gave them the Ten Commandments. He
wanted them to have a set of rules that would help them become
a strong nation that honored Him. One of these commandments
says that children are to honor their parents. "Honor your
father and your mother" means that you respect them by being
obedient when you're young and kind and helpful when you're
older.

At times you may get mad at your parents or want them to do what
you want. But God's way is for you to obey and honor. You can
honor a parent by listening instead of talking back or complaining.

A POWER NOTE

Today, when your mom or dad ask you to do something, give
honor by answering kindly, saying you'll do it right away, and
then *doing* it. When you do that every time, you show that you
honor your parents.

FALLING SHORT

Find It in the Bible

For all have sinned and fall short of the glory of God.

ROMANS 3:23

How are your grades in school? Do you get 100 percent correct papers all the time? If you're a gymnast, do you always get a perfect ten when you compete? Probably not. In fact, no one got a perfect score in Olympic gymnastics until Nadia Comaneci received a score of ten on the uneven bars in 1976. But even she wasn't perfect all the time in every event.

The Bible says that we aren't perfect. We all have sinned. This means we are guilty and separated from God. We deserve His punishment. The only way to get rid of our guilt was for a perfect person to die in our place and take our punishment. God knew that—and so He sent His Son, Jesus, to die for us.

Jesus gets that perfect ten in everything He does. His death paid for sin for all time for those who trust in Him.

A POWER NOTE

On a piece of paper, draw a cliff on one side (label it "me") and a cliff on the other side (label it "God"). Make sure there is a big chasm in between the cliffs and label it "sin." Now draw Jesus' cross in the middle of the chasm with the two sides of the cross connecting the two cliffs like a bridge. That's what Jesus' death did—it closed up the chasm between God and your sin.

WHILe We WeRe STILL SINNERS

Find It in the Bible

But God demonstrates his own love for us in this: While we
were still sinners, Christ died for us.

ROMANS 5:8

What if you had to have a perfect score on every test in every
class before you could move up to the next grade? Or what
if you couldn't be on the baseball team unless you hit a home run
every time at bat? It's impossible to do everything perfectly all
the time.

The good news is God doesn't expect us to be perfect before He'll
accept us as His children. We'd never be able to do it! Instead,
He knows we're not perfect, but that's what makes this verse so
wonderful. God showed His love for us by sending Jesus to die for
us even when we were sinners.

You don't have to be perfect to come to Jesus and ask Him to
be the ruler of your life. He knows that even when we try our
hardest to be perfect, we still make mistakes and mess up. But
when we confess our sins to Him and ask Him to forgive us, the
record is wiped clean. He doesn't see us in our sin, He sees us
clean through the sacrifice of Jesus.

A POWER NOTE

Make a list of some things you have done wrong this week. Write
it in pencil on a paper. Now use a big eraser to erase a cross shape
in the middle of the list. Let this remind you that Jesus died for us
even when we were sinners. He came to save sinners.

One Special Sacrifice

Find It in the Bible

But he was pierced for our transgressions, he was crushed
for our iniquities; the punishment that brought us peace
was on him, and by his wounds we are healed.

ISAIAH 53:5

Here is an amazing fact about human bodies: one person can sacrifice parts of his or her body to help heal someone who is ill. An adult who donates one pint of blood can have that blood transfused into someone's body who has lost blood and the sick person will grow stronger. If someone is battling bone cancer, a person who is well and is compatible can donate marrow from his bones and allow it to be infused into the sick person's bones, and it will cause healing. Corneas from a dying person can be transplanted to a blind person who then can see.

There is one sacrifice that no human can make. That is the sacrifice for sin. Only Jesus, who lived a sinless and pure life, was worthy to be the sacrifice for the sins of the world. He gave His life so that we could gain forgiveness from God. All we have to do is accept His sacrifice as payment for our sins.

A POWER NOTE

In a library or on the Internet, find information about the ways people can donate their organs to others. Thank Jesus for the sacrifice He made for your salvation.

YOUR BFF

Find It in the Bible

For to us a child is born, to us a son is given, and the government will be on his shoulders. And he will be called Wonderful Counselor, Mighty God, Everlasting Father, Prince of Peace.

Isaiah 9:6

Sometimes you just need friends to help you get through rough times. Maybe you had a science fair project that was taking too much time, and then your friend came over and helped you finish it. Or maybe you had to clean the garage before you could go ride your bike, and your brother came out and helped you get the job done. Wow, what a relief!

Well, imagine having a friend who is *always* there to help you. Someone who gives you good advice, provides peace when you are upset, and helps you be strong when you feel weak. You already have that friend. His name is Jesus.

That's just what the prophet Isaiah foresaw when he gave this prophecy. He said "to us a child is born," meaning that child who would grow up to be the Messiah, our Savior, was born for *us*. He was born to become our Wonderful Counselor, our Mighty God, our Everlasting Father, and our Prince of Peace.

He promises to be your BFF.

A POWER NOTE

Have you ever thought about Jesus as your BFF? Make yourself a special sign to put where you can see it at all times. Write on it, "Jesus is my BFF!"

GOD'S POWER SOURCE

Find It in the Bible

So he said to me, "This is the word of the LORD to Zerubbabel: 'Not by might nor by power, but by my Spirit,' says the LORD Almighty."

ZECHARIAH 4:6

Just think of all the machines that people use for their work. Farmers use tractors, gardeners use lawn mowers, carpenters use electric saws, and dentists use drills. (That's probably not your favorite machine!) These machines are helpful tools but only when they are turned on. Each one needs a power source, whether gasoline or electricity, to run the motor. If the farmer wants to plow his field, he must first turn on his tractor. If a carpenter wants to cut a piece of lumber, he must turn on his electric saw. The engines in these machines provide the power.

If we want to live for God, we also need a power source. And we have one! God has given us the Holy Spirit to help us win victories against sin and selfishness. We don't have to rely on our own strength or wisdom. The Holy Spirit will help us if we ask Him. Why try to live by your own might when God has given you His mighty power? Every day, you can decide to rely on God's power source.

A POWER NOTE

Read stories in your Bible about people who were victors with the help of God's Spirit. Read about David, Joshua, and Gideon.

THE NEW KID

Find It in the Bible

So in everything, do to others what you would have them do to you, for this sums up the Law and the Prophets.

MATTHEW 7:12

There was a new kid at school today," Joey told his mom. "His name is Brian."

Mom handed Joey an after-school snack. "Oh?" she said. "Did you talk to Brian?"

"Not really," Joey replied. "Brian was really shy. He didn't really talk to anybody."

"Don't you think Brian wants a friend?" asked Mom.

Joey shrugged and munched on his snack. "I guess. But if I talked to Brian, I wouldn't get to hang out with my other friends. They would just go play without me. But I know that Brian must be lonely."

Mom smiled and asked, "If you were the new kid, how would you want the other boys to treat you?"

He thought for a minute and then grinned. "I'll ask Brian if he wants to play with me and my friends tomorrow at recess."

A POWER NOTE

Who is the new kid in your class at school or at church? Since Jesus says you should treat others the way you want to be treated, what can you do to make the new kid feel comfortable?

FINISHING THE JOB

Find It in the Bible

He who began a good work in you will carry it on to
completion until the day of Christ Jesus.

PHILIPPIANS 1:6

Have you ever started a project and quit before you finished it? If beavers did that, they wouldn't have a place to live or food to eat in winter. Before the pond freezes over they must work for many months to cut down dozens of trees with their large front teeth. They work day after day to drag these trees to the water to build their lodge. Then they have to gnaw on many smaller, tender branches and pile them up inside the house to eat in winter. They can't give up on their project or they will be cold and hungry!

When you believe in Jesus as your Savior, you become God's project. He keeps working to help you become more and more like Jesus, and He doesn't give up on you. Sometimes you might not pray as much as you should. At times you may do what you shouldn't. Other times you may disappoint God by the way you act. But His Holy Spirit will speak to you about the things you need to change or repent of.

A POWER NOTE

Look around your room and find a project or task you began and never finished. Set a goal for yourself to finish that task—remind yourself that you are finishing the work you began, just as God will finish the work He began in you.

LITTLE WORDS AND DEEDS

Find It in the Bible

And let us consider how we may spur one another on toward love and
good deeds, not giving up meeting together, as some are in the
habit of doing, but encouraging one another—and all the
more as you see the Day approaching.

HEBREWS 10:24–25

Once, a little girl who was very poor won a prize at a flower show. She entered a flowering plant in an old cracked teapot that she had grown in a small attic window. When people asked how she could raise such a lovely flower in that dark and dreary place, she replied that she took care each day to move it so it was always in the sunlight.

Kind words and deeds are like rays of sunshine. They make people feel good, and everyone needs them once in a while. When we encourage others our heavenly Father smiles on us because we are showing love to those He loves.

So how can you do it? Sometimes encouraging a person means giving a compliment. Other times it can be a hug or spending a few minutes quietly listening to someone who is hurting. You can ask the Holy Spirit to show you how to encourage people.

A POWER NOTE

Be on the lookout today for someone who looks sad or discouraged. Then do something to bring a smile to their face. Give them a hug or say encouraging words.

THOUGHTS AND ATTITUDES

Find It in the Bible

For the word of God is living and active. Sharper than any double-edged sword, it penetrates even to dividing soul and spirit, joints and marrow; it judges the thoughts and attitudes of the heart.

HEBREWS 4:12

When you help your mom or dad cook in the kitchen, you probably don't get to use the sharp knife. They know that can be dangerous, so *they* work with the knife to cut the meat for dinner. They cut away bad parts from vegetables and chop the rest for cooking. A good sharp knife slices easily through the food, but it can also cut your finger just as easily!

God says His word is sharp like that knife. It can cut right to the middle of what you do and what you think. Just like a sharp kitchen knife, it can separate what's good and what's bad.

In fact, God's Word can slice right through your actions to see what's going on in your thoughts and attitudes. Have you ever obeyed your parents when you didn't want to? Did you pout or grumble about it? God knows—and He wants you to both *do good* and *have good thoughts and attitudes.*

How can you do that? You can read God's Word, the Bible. It will help you understand how to act in ways that please Him.

A POWER NOTE

Write the word *attitude* vertically on a piece of paper. By each letter, write something that describes a good thought or attitude. For example, by the letter A, you might write, "always thankful."

TELL PEOPLE ABOUT JESUS

Find It in the Bible

He said to them, "Go into all the world and preach
the gospel to all creation."

MARK 16:15

So you're just a kid. How do you do what Jesus said and "go into all the world" to preach the gospel? Perhaps you don't think you want to be a preacher when you grow up. Maybe, instead, you want to be a doctor or a teacher or a chef.

You can still work toward that goal—in fact, if you like something and are really good at it, that's probably what God has in mind for you to do. The thing is, you don't have to be a preacher to "preach the gospel." You don't have to be a missionary to "go into all the world."

In fact, right now as a student, you can tell people how Jesus died for their sins and rose again to give them eternal life.

Sometimes the best way to "preach the gospel" is to live in a way that pleases Jesus. Then, when the opportunity arises, you can tell others how much Jesus means to you and what He has done for you. This can be scary at first, but after a while, it will be natural for you to talk to others about what you believe.

A POWER NOTE

Today, when someone says hello or asks you how you're doing, try to say something about Jesus and share one thing you're thankful for.

Team Jesus

Find It in the Bible

So in Christ we, though many, form one body, and
each member belongs to all the others.

ROMANS 12:5

Meerkats are frisky little animals with black patches of fur around their eyes. They live in desert regions of Africa in groups that take care of each other. One meerkat will stand guard and watch for enemies. When he purrs, the other meerkats know they are safe. A young female meerkat will babysit the young meerkats while their parents are busy looking for food. When meerkats return from hunting, they bring food for everyone— beetles, snakes, and scorpions. Meerkats can teach us how to work together as a team.

When you're part of a sports team, you spend a lot of time together. You practice, run drills, scrimmage, and try out new plays. Everyone works toward a single goal—winning for the team!

Everyone who believes in Jesus is part of God's team. Even though there are millions and millions of Christians in many lands, speaking many languages and dressing in different types of clothing, we're still one big team. We're all working for the same goal—to help other people know about Jesus and to live to please Him.

A POWER NOTE

Support your teammates! Ask your pastor for the name and email address of a missionary who works in another country. Then email that person and ask them to tell you about the people on Team Jesus in that country.

No Need For Fear

Find It in the Bible

Even though I walk through the darkest valley, I will fear no evil,
for you are with me; your rod and your staff, they comfort me.

PSALM 23:4

A shepherd guides and comforts his flock of sheep by using his staff (a long stick). During daylight he carries the staff across his shoulders. The sheep can see the staff, so it reassures them of his presence and protection. If the shepherd is out with his sheep after dark, he walks slowly in front of them and taps his staff on the ground. The sheep can't see the staff, but they can hear the tapping and will follow the sound to a safe resting spot for the night.

When you feel hurt or afraid you probably feel like you are walking in a dark valley. Maybe you feel as though no one is around to help you. But God says that He is always with His children. He is the Good Shepherd who promises to comfort you and guide you.

Every once in a while you'll be frightened. When that happens, call out to Jesus. He hears you when you call, and He will comfort you and guide you by His Holy Spirit and by the Bible. You never have to fear any kind of evil. God has already defeated anything that could make you afraid.

A POWER NOTE

The next time you feel afraid, read these verses aloud: Psalm 27:1; Psalm 56:3; Psalm 118:6; Proverbs 3:24. Then go tell someone about your worries or fears, and ask that person to pray with you.

WALK ON GOD'S PATH

Find It in the Bible

Blessed is the one who does not walk in step with the wicked or stand in the way that sinners take or sit in the company of mockers.

PSALM 1:1

Have you been in a situation when someone tried to get you to do something you knew you shouldn't do? How did it make you feel? When that happens, we usually have to make a tough choice. Are we going to follow that person's bad example, or are we going to choose to be a good example?

The book of Psalms talks about the difference between a godly example and an ungodly one. The person who follows what the Bible says is much happier than the person who follows what ungodly people say. When you do what you know is right, God blesses you. That means you get to enjoy His promises and all the privileges that come with being His child.

Choosing to walk on God's path can be difficult, especially when people you want to have as friends tell you to follow a sinful path. But when all is said and done, your life will be much better when you do what God wants, not what ungodly people want. Most important, this pleases God.

A POWER NOTE

Write the word *blessed* on a piece of paper vertically or put it on the computer screen. Beside each letter in the word, write a blessing from God that begins with that letter. For example, the blessing of the letter B might be "beautiful creation." This will help you remember to walk in God's way.

Seek First

Find It in the Bible

But seek first his kingdom and his righteousness, and all
these things will be given to you as well.

MATTHEW 6:33

Have you ever wanted something so badly that you saved some of your money for months? How did you feel when you could finally buy it and have it for yourself? Maybe it took a long time to save up for that bike or tablet computer or new pair of running shoes. Even though it took a while to save the money, when you finally had enough and could buy what you wanted, you probably felt awesome. Waiting for what you want is always worth it.

But Jesus talks about something we should want more than anything else—God's kingdom and His righteousness. This means looking forward to the day when God will bring His kingdom to earth. And in the meantime, we seek God's righteousness by acting right, being fair, and living in a moral way. Jesus says that when we do this, He will give us peace in everything else in our lives.

Now that's worth working and waiting for!

A POWER NOTE

What can you do today to "seek first" God's kingdom and His righteousness? How might you act right or be fair or make a good choice to live for God? At the end of today, go back to these questions and write down what you did to seek God's kingdom.

GOD'S LETTER TO YOU

Find It in the Bible

Heaven and earth will pass away, but my words will never pass away.

MATTHEW 24:35

In this day of emails and texting, few people write and send paper letters anymore. But it can be very nice to receive an envelope with your name and address on it sent from a friend or relative. It could be a thank-you note, a birthday card, or a letter telling the latest news about that person's life.

God wrote a letter to you called the Bible. It's a really long letter— you probably won't read it in one sitting! The Bible is more like a library with sixty-six books, including history books and laws and prophecies in the Old Testament. The New Testament has books about Jesus (the Gospels). Most of the other New Testament books were written originally as letters.

Jesus quoted from the Old Testament during His time on earth. He told everyone that, no matter what might disappear, His words would never, ever disappear. Early on, people carefully copied the Bible by hand. And do you know what was the first book ever printed on a printing press? The Bible!

Thousands of years after those Bible books were written, we still have God's words. Jesus promises that we always will!

A POWER NOTE

Get a piece of stationery, an envelope, and a stamp. Write a letter to someone special telling that person what you're learning about how God's words will never disappear.

THE HIDING PLACE

Find It in the Bible

I have hidden your word in my heart that
I might not sin against you.

PSALM 119:11

When you have a special treasure, you want to hide it to keep it safe. To a mother kangaroo, her babies are a treasure. That's why she hides them in a furry pouch on her belly. One bird, the hornbill, keeps her babies safe in a nest she builds inside a tree. No one can find her treasure because the father bird closes the opening to the nest with mud, except for a feeding hole.

God teaches us to hide His Word in our hearts, not to keep it from others but because it is a valuable treasure. So how do we hide it in our hearts?

You hide something in your heart by using your memory. When you remember something nice done for you, that memory stays in your heart. Kind words from Mom and Dad stay in your heart because you remember them.

When you memorize parts of the Bible, you hide God's Word in your heart. Knowing what makes God happy helps you keep from doing things that will make Him unhappy.

A POWER NOTE

Memorize the Bible verse at the top of the page. When you think you have hidden it in your heart, recite it to someone. Ask a parent or children's leader to help you pick out other Bible verses to hide in your heart.

YOU'RE GLOWING!

Find It in the Bible

You, LORD, are my lamp; the LORD turns my darkness into light.

2 SAMUEL 22:29

A new study has been released with actual proof that humans do glow. We are called *bioluminescent,* which means that the reactions between our cells produce a light source or a glow. Scientists were able to capture this light in photographs showing our bodies glowing at different levels throughout the day.

Imagine how much more we glow spiritually with the Holy Spirit inside of us! When we invite Jesus to be our Savior, the Holy Spirit comes to dwell in our hearts. He changes us from the inside out. He helps us live better lives and grow to be more like Jesus by showing more love, joy, peace, forbearance, kindness, goodness, faithfulness, gentleness, and self-control (the fruit of the Spirit, Galatians 5:22–23). You could say that the Spirit makes us shine like lights in a dark world.

Want to make a difference in your world? Let your light shine! The Holy Spirit will make you glow like a light in a dark and sinful world.

A POWER NOTE

Purchase some glow-in-the-dark stickers. You have to put them under the light for a while so that, when you turn off the light, they'll glow. Likewise, you will glow for God, but only when you've spent time in the light of His presence.

STAY IN SHAPE

Find It in the Bible

The LORD makes firm the steps of the one who delights in him; though he may stumble, he will not fall, for the LORD upholds him with his hand.

PSALM 37:23–24

Every February, the Empire State Building in New York City hosts a popular race, and only four hundred people per year are allowed to run it. Runners ("climbers") race up the tower's 1,576 steps. The Run-Up, completed by the winners in around ten minutes, leaves most entrants with wobbly knees and burning lungs.

For the winners of the race, this is just another gut-busting workout. It's not easy, but they've trained for it. They can rely on their muscles to do what they've been trained to do. They might stumble every now and then, but they won't fall.

As Christians, we can rely on God, His Word, and the faith He gives us, to keep us from falling during the race of life. There will be times when we stumble—no one is perfect. But like a child reaching up to grab a parent's hand, you can reach out and grab God's hand. He promises to hold you, keep your steps firm, and pick you up when you fall.

A POWER NOTE

How do you stay spiritually in shape? Do you pray often and read your Bible every day? Knowing why you believe what you believe will help you answer when someone asks. Ask the Lord to help your steps of faith always be firm in Him.

BLINK OF AN EYE

Find It in the Bible

The LORD is my light and my salvation—whom shall I fear? The LORD is the stronghold of my life—of whom shall I be afraid?

PSALM 27:1

Blink your eyes once. Feel how it takes little to no effort? You do this simple act hundreds of times every day without even thinking. In fact, the average person blinks sixteen times every minute!

Now think of the sun and its light. Did you know that in the blink of an eye, light from the sun circles the earth seven times? Light travels extremely fast; you can't outrun it! And whenever you're in a dark room, all you have to do is flip a switch to instantly flood the room with light.

Light may be faster than a blink of an eye, but you don't even need to blink or flip a switch for God to be with you. Whenever you are worried or nervous about something, your heavenly Father is already at your side. He promises to be your light so you have nothing to fear. All you have to do is trust Him.

A POWER NOTE

Next time you feel afraid or worried about something, blink. There. God is already with you. He was with you before you even blinked. Now, say a prayer for God's strength and comfort. Your heavenly Father will hear you and warm your heart with the light of His presence.

NOT-SO-STINKY FEET

Find It in the Bible

How beautiful on the mountains are the feet of those who bring good news, who proclaim peace, who bring good tidings, who proclaim salvation, who say to Zion, "Your God reigns!"

ISAIAH 52:7

Feet can be funny. They're super ticklish when someone pokes them. Parents play "piggy went to market" with their baby's toes. And if you kick your shoes off your feet after a long day of walking, somebody might yell, "Ew! What stinks?!"

Even though feet seem funny and even smelly at times, did you know that your feet can also be beautiful? It all depends on how you use them (not just painting your toenails or dancing).

God thinks your feet are special because they can take you to people and places where you can share His love with others. You can use your feet to help your parents carry groceries, visit a sick person in the hospital, or hang out with someone who needs a friend. You can even use your feet to go tell someone about Jesus Christ.

So get up on those beautiful feet of yours! You have great news to share!

A POWER NOTE

Think of someone with whom you'd like to share God's love. Maybe he or she could use a surprise batch of cookies or help with a project. Pick something to do for that person, and then let your feet take you there!

NOT PERFECT, BUT FORGIVEN

Find It in the Bible

On hearing this, Jesus said to them, "It is not the healthy who need a doctor, but the sick. I have not come to call the righteous, but sinners."

MARK 2:17

When do you go to the doctor? You probably don't go when you feel great, but when you are sick. Your mom takes your temperature and, if it's high, she may take you to the doctor. Your body temperature is supposed to be 98.6 degrees. So if your temperature goes up above 99 degrees, it shows that your body is trying to fight an infection.

Jesus was sitting with people who were considered to be the worst of sinners. Some religious leaders (who didn't like Jesus much and didn't believe in Him) asked why He would be with such sinful people. Jesus said He didn't need to tell people about God who already thought they were good. Instead, He needed to talk to people who knew they were sinners but didn't want to sin anymore.

You don't have to be perfect before Jesus will love you. He didn't die for perfect people but for sinful people. That includes you and me. The Bible says that while we were still sinners, He loved us. You're not perfect, but you can be forgiven!

A POWER NOTE

When you feel frustrated because you want to do right but you sin instead, remember that Jesus knew you wouldn't be perfect and He still died for you. Try to unscramble this sentence to remind you:

I ma tno cetrfpe, tub I ma nivefrog!

(I am not perfect, but I am forgiven.)

LIKE A CHILD

Find It in the Bible

And he said: "Truly I tell you, unless you change and become like little children, you will never enter the kingdom of heaven. Therefore, whoever takes the lowly position of this child is the greatest in the kingdom of heaven."

MATTHEW 18:3–4

Little kids can be a lot of fun to play with, or they can be very annoying. They can be sweet or mean, crazy or calm.

One cool thing about younger kids is how they trust the people around them. They accept what their parents tell them without questioning. If Mom, Dad, or another adult says something, young children will often accept it because they trust them.

That's what Jesus is talking about in this verse. People who have faith like little children will get into heaven because they trust God completely in all situations.

When it comes to faith in God, we need to be like little kids. He wants us to read His Word, listen to Him, and accept what He says because we trust Him. He wants us to trust Him like children in the times when life is scary or sad. He wants us to trust Him no matter what.

A POWER NOTE

Ask your parents to help you find a picture of you when you were little. Glue the picture to a piece of construction paper. Write this verse on the paper, then use glitter or stickers or whatever you want to decorate it. Hang the picture in your room as a reminder to have faith like a little child.

GOING Home

Find It in the Bible

For the Lord himself will come down from heaven, with a loud command, with the voice of the archangel and with the trumpet call of God, and the dead in Christ will rise first. After that, we who are still alive and are left will be caught up together with them in the clouds to meet with the Lord in the air. And so we will be with the Lord forever.

1 THESSALONIANS 4:16–17

What happens when the bell rings at the end of the school day? You probably jump up to leave because you are excited to talk to your friends and go home for the night.

Just as the bell signals the end of the school day, the Bible tells us that a loud voice and a trumpet blast will signal the end of our time on earth. But instead of us all going to our different houses, everyone who believes in Jesus will rise up into heaven. We will get to meet with all the other Christians, including the people who have died before us. You could see your great-grandparents, your friends, and even people from long ago like Moses and Noah.

Best of all, you will get to see Jesus face to face! On that day, heaven will become our new home, the place where we will live forever with Jesus. What an exciting day!

A POWER NOTE

Make a list of the Bible people you are excited to see in heaven and what questions you would like to ask them. Then draw a picture of what you think heaven will look like.

GREAT JOB!

Find It in the Bible
The crucible for silver and the furnace for gold,
but people are tested by their praise.

PROVERBS 27:21

The heat of fire is used to purify and soften gold and silver so the metal can be shaped into useful items. A crucible is a pot made of metal that can withstand very high heat. When silver is put into it, the silver melts and impurities are skimmed off the top. This leaves pure metal that can become household items or jewelry.

Another definition of *crucible* is a difficult time or a severe test or challenge. And that's what this verse means. Silver and gold get heated to very high temperatures to purify them. People also go through crucibles (difficult times), and these help make them stronger, wiser, and kinder. Their lives become more pleasing to God.

But the crucible doesn't always have to be a hard time—it can be something positive and nice, like praise. Everyone loves to be praised for good work. But praise can make some people prideful.

How do you react to praise? Instead of becoming prideful, it should make you humble and thankful to God for giving you the ability to do well. If you do that, you pass the test!

A POWER NOTE

Do you have some medals or certificates or prizes for doing something well? Put them all in one special place and make a sign to put with them that says, "Thank You, God, for helping me do well. I want to honor You in everything I do."

WAKE-UP CALL

Find It in the Bible

In the morning, LORD, you hear my voice; in the morning
I lay my requests before you and wait expectantly.

PSALM 5:3

How do you begin your day? Most people have a specific routine they follow each morning. They might take a shower and get dressed before eating breakfast. Some have specific foods they eat for breakfast, while others skip breakfast entirely. How the day begins for you sometimes lets you know how the rest of the day will go.

How you start the day isn't all about you, though. Sometimes the things that happen to your mom or dad in the morning will affect you. If they woke up late, you might be late to school. If they are grumpy, you might feel grumpy as well.

There is Someone waiting to make your morning better. God is always listening to you. He hears the things you want and need before you even say them. God is a part of your morning, whether you are making time for Him or not.

Start your day by talking with God and remember that He is with you through the whole day!

A POWER NOTE

Ask your parents for a calendar or small daily planner. Each day for one month, make a plan to start the day with God. Pray as soon as you wake up, then write on that day in the calendar "I met with God today."

An Undivided Heart

Find It in the Bible

Teach me your way, LORD, that I may rely on your faithfulness;
give me an undivided heart, that I may fear your name.

PSALM 86:11

In your science class you will learn that the human heart has four chambers, two on each side: the right atrium and right ventricle and the left atrium and left ventricle. Two sides, four chambers, blood vessels running in and out, yet they all work together as one. If one part of the heart decided to do something different, to not work in harmony with the other parts, serious health problems and even death would occur.

When the Bible talks about the heart, it doesn't mean the physical beating heart inside your body, but the spiritual part of you. Your spiritual heart works very much like the physical heart. If your desires and hopes and dreams are selfish, or if you know the right decision to make or action to take but don't do it, your heart becomes divided. Divided, the heart fails.

If you follow God's advice in His Word, your heart will be undivided and strong.

A POWER NOTE

Cut out a heart of red construction paper. Then cut the heart into four parts. Label them with the correct names. The two upper portions are the right and left atriums, and the two bottom parts are the right and left ventricles. Then tape all of the parts back together and write "An Undivided Heart" across the entire heart. Keep your heart focused on God.

Messy Heart? Clean It Up!

Find It in the Bible

Create in me a pure heart, O God, and
renew a steadfast spirit within me.

PSALM 51:10

In the Bible, the word *heart* almost always refers to the innermost part of a human being—not the actual beating heart, but the part deep inside you where you keep your hopes and dreams. The word *pure* is an adjective that means "not mixed with any other substance or material." (You didn't know you were going to get a vocabulary lesson!)

A pure heart stays so close to God that all of your hopes and dreams—everything that's important to you—has God at the center. You always want to please Him.

So how does a heart become impure? When you envy someone else's stuff, or hold a grudge, those things get into your heart and dirty it up. It's kind of like letting a gorilla into a grocery store—things are going to get messy!

Asking God to clean up a messy heart is only the start. Having a "steadfast spirit" means you are going to do your best to keep the dirt from making its way back inside your heart.

A POWER NOTE

With a pencil, draw a heart on a sheet of paper and write inside it the kinds of things that could make a heart impure (like "jealousy" or "gossip"). Then, erase those words and use a pen to write words that could keep your heart pure (like "forgiving others" and "showing love").

HEART HEALTH

Find It in the Bible

Above all else, guard your heart, for everything
you do flows from it.

PROVERBS 4:23

Your heart is like the engine that runs your body. It beats about 100,000 times a day—and you don't even have to remind it to! The heart does everything all on its own, even when you're sleeping. It keeps blood flowing through the 60,000 miles of blood vessels that take care of your muscles and organs.

But the heart is more than just a muscle that pumps blood. It is also a symbol of love. That is why guarding your heart is so important. You want to be careful what you love—what you spend time with, what you think about all the time, what matters most to you. If you don't guard your heart by staying close to God and His desires for you, you can easily be led to love things or people that aren't God's best for you.

The Bible says that we should keep away from evil so we won't stumble. To guard our hearts means to love and obey the Lord's commands.

A POWER NOTE

Make a heart booklet. Cut out six hearts. Glue or staple them together at the top. On the first heart print "I will guard my heart." On each of the remaining hearts, write one of these verses that tell how to guard your heart: Psalm 31:24; Psalm 119:11; Psalm 136:1; 1 Corinthians 13:4; Ephesians 4:32.

THE HEART OF THE MATTER

Find It in the Bible

The LORD said to Samuel, "The LORD does not look at the things people
look at. People look at the outward appearance,
but the LORD looks at the heart."

1 SAMUEL 16:7

Is the way you look important? Well, it sure is for many animals.
The Surinam toad looks exactly like the red leaves that cover
the riverbed where it lives. When it floats on one of these leaves, it
can hide from both its enemies and the insects it wants to catch.

Sometimes people care too much about the way a person looks. This
was true in Bible times. Israel's first king, Saul, was tall and handsome.
But he didn't always behave handsomely by obeying God. So when
God decided to choose someone else, He sent the prophet Samuel
to anoint the new king. After Samuel went to the home of Jesse, he
expected God to choose one of Jesse's tall, handsome sons to be the
next king. After all, looks count, right? But God chose the youngest
son—David—who wasn't the most noticeable. God looked for
a man after His own heart (see 1 Samuel 13:14). This meant God
wanted a person who would love Him and obey Him.

God reminded Samuel that what is on the inside of a person is
more important than what is on the outside.

A POWER NOTE

Create a valentine for God. Find some heavy paper and draw a
heart. Now look through the book of Psalms and find a verse that
describes how wonderful God is. Write that verse in the middle
of the heart. Now cut out the heart and decorate it to look like a
valentine. Let God know your heart belongs to Him!

BE MY VALENTINE

Find It in the Bible

By this everyone will know that you are my disciples,
if you love one another.

JOHN 13:35

One Valentine's Day, students at a Bexar County middle school in San Antonio, Texas, surprised their teachers at a school assembly. The teachers thought the assembly was to give awards to students. Instead, the students wanted to show their appreciation for their teachers in a special way: through letters. These letters expressed what the students learned from these wise teachers.

Teachers in Bible times were called rabbis. A disciple was a student or follower of a rabbi. Others in the community would know which teacher the disciple followed by the way the disciple acted or the words he used. Good disciples imitated their teachers.

Jesus wanted His disciples to put into practice what He taught them. He showed love for people. One way He did that was to wash His disciples' feet before the Last Supper. Jesus wanted His disciples to imitate Him by serving others.

If you are a disciple of Jesus, you will act the way He acts. Loving others is the best way to honor Jesus and to show what you have learned from Him.

A POWER NOTE

How can you show your love to others? One good way is to write a thank-you note to the people who help you. Maybe you could thank a teacher or coach, or even your parents or grandparents.

DEAD AND ALIVE!

Find It in the Bible

I have been crucified with Christ and I no longer live, but Christ lives in me. The life I now live in the body, I live by faith in the Son of God, who loved me and gave himself for me.

GALATIANS 2:20

In February 2014, Walter Williams, a man from Mississippi, had been pronounced dead by the Holmes County coroner. Walter had no pulse, so they placed him in a body bag and took him to a funeral home. Then, suddenly, Mr. Williams started moving as he tried to get out of the bag! He was alive!

But guess what? In a way, you are like Walter Williams. As far as God is concerned, you were pronounced dead. How is that possible? Because of Jesus. Those who trust Jesus as Savior are considered dead to sin. This means that Christ's death on the cross in payment for your sins was your death, too. You have been crucified with Christ, and you no longer live as your old sinful self. Instead, because of Jesus, you live by faith in the Son of God.

You are dead and alive at the same time. Amazing!

A POWER NOTE

Ask an adult to help you plant some flower or vegetable seeds in a paper cup filled with dirt. Put it in a warm spot near the window and keep it watered. After a few days you will see tiny new plants spring up. The seeds seem to be dead, but when they are planted and watered they grow to new life.

WHO IS MY NEIGHBOR?

Find It in the Bible

"Which of these three do you think was a neighbor to the man who fell into the hands of robbers?" The expert in the law replied, "The one who had mercy on him." Jesus told him, "Go and do likewise."

Luke 10:36–37

Think about a time when you saw someone who needed help. Maybe that person needed a friend or needed help with homework. Did you help that person? Have you ever not helped someone and later wished you had helped? Sometimes the need looks too big, and you don't think you can help with the whole thing. That shouldn't stop you from doing what you *can* do.

In Luke, Jesus told the story of the Good Samaritan. This man saw someone in need, someone who many would say was his enemy. Instead of moving on because he didn't like him or because he thought he couldn't help, he stopped and helped the man. He was a better neighbor than the "good people" who saw the man but refused to help him.

Jesus taught us to treat our "neighbors" well. The word *neighbor* in this verse doesn't just mean the people who live next door, it means everyone. He wants us to look around and see people in need and have mercy on them. We must do our best to help people in need, even people we may not like.

A POWER NOTE

Keep your eyes open to look for people in need. Think how you can help someone and do it. This pleases your heavenly Father.

THE TRUTH

Find It in the Bible

To the Jews who had believed him, Jesus said, "If you hold to my teaching, you are really my disciples. Then you will know the truth, and the truth will set you free."

JOHN 8:31–32

This expression, "the truth will set you free," is on the wall at the entrance to the CIA headquarters. That is the agency in the United States government that collects information around the world to keep American citizens safe. It wouldn't help much if the agency gathered false information. The information must be true.

The "truth" in this verse refers to Jesus and the truth found in Him. We believe in His message of salvation because it is true. Jesus actually lived, died, and rose again. And everything He taught is completely true.

Jesus can be trusted. We can always know that He is telling the truth because everything He has ever said has come true. And when you know the truth, you are set free.

If you obey what Jesus taught in the Bible, people will be able to tell that you are His disciple. The truth Jesus tells you in His Word helps you live the Christian life. How can you know God's truth? By reading your Bible every day.

A POWER NOTE

Using this devotional every day is a good way to remind you of the truth in God's Word. Find some verses that you want to memorize so that the truth is always in your mind. Start with these verses!

A Good Good-Bye

Find It in the Bible

May the grace of the Lord Jesus Christ, and the love of God, and the fellowship of the Holy Spirit be with you all.

2 CORINTHIANS 13:14

The apostle Paul wrote many letters. In fact, most of the books in the New Testament were letters that he wrote. He always greeted his readers and told them exactly why he was writing the letter. At the end of the letter, in his good-bye, he always wished them well.

Paul's good-byes were his way of ending on a high note. He hoped that his readers would remember the *grace of Jesus Christ* (meaning the undeserved mercy He gave us by taking our sin), the *love of God* (He loves us so much He sent Jesus to die for us), and *the fellowship of the Holy Spirit* (meaning the constant presence of the Holy Spirit). No matter what the letter was about, Paul wanted his readers to feel hopeful about grace, love, and the constant presence of the Spirit.

You can be glad that you have grace, love, and the fellowship of the Holy Spirit.

A POWER NOTE

The next time you write a letter or an email, think about the end of your note. How can you say good-bye and remind the person of your faith and how much God has done for you?

REST WITH JESUS

Find It in the Bible

Come to me, all you who are weary and burdened,
and I will give you rest.

MATTHEW 11:28

When a load is too heavy for people to carry, there are animals to help. The people of Tibet use yaks to carry their loads because the yak is strong and its thick fur keeps it warm in the cold and snow. In areas where heavy monsoons flood the rivers and boatmen are afraid to cross, elephants help to ferry loads and people across the river. Because the elephants are so huge and tall, they can withstand the strong currents and can drift diagonally to the other side of the river.

When difficult things happen to you in life, it can feel like you are carrying a heavy load or a big burden. It is not a load on your back but in your heart. It isn't easy to carry a burden of sorrow or fear or anxiety. And you don't have to!

Jesus wants you to tell Him about the things that feel like burdens to you—things that make your heart heavy. He promises that He will hear your prayers and will give you rest in your heart and mind. He will help you find answers.

A POWER NOTE

Ask your parents if you can have an empty envelope. Now tear a sheet of paper into several pieces and write something that is a burden for you on each piece. Put these pieces of paper in the envelope. On the front of the envelope write "God bears my burdens." Thank Him for loving you and caring for you.

CELEBRATE GOD'S PROTECTION

Find It in the Bible

The LORD is my strength and my shield; my heart trusts in him,
and he helps me. My heart leaps for joy, and
with my song I praise him.

PSALM 28:7

What does a shield look like? People all over the ancient world used them—Egyptians, Romans, Persians, and many other countries all had shields for their armies. The shields could be round, square, or any shape in between, and they were made out of everything from animal skin to metal. All these different kinds of shields had one purpose: to keep the soldiers safe. The shield was one of the most important parts of a soldier's armor because it could stop an enemy's weapon.

God gives armor to His followers. This armor is not bulletproof vests and shields of metal or wood, but attitudes and beliefs that help God's children live the Christian life. Paul describes one piece as the "shield of faith." "Take up the shield of faith, with which you can extinguish all the flaming arrows of the evil one" (Ephesians 6:16).

When you have faith and believe in the truth of God's Word, no matter what lies Satan tries to shoot at you, you can hold up your shield and the lies can't hurt you.

A POWER NOTE

Look for images of shields in a book or on the Internet. Read information about how they helped to protect soldiers. Think what kind of shield you would design to remind yourself that God is your protection.

GLORIFYING GOD WITH VERBS

Find It in the Bible

So whether you eat or drink or whatever you do,
do it all for the glory of God.

1 CORINTHIANS 10:31

You have probably learned that a verb is the part of speech that represents an action. A verb can be a simple action like *walk* or it could be something more complex, like *calculate*. We use verbs to describe daily activities, such as *run*, *talk*, *learn*, *play*, *climb*, or *eat*. We do a lot of actions in a day!

What actions in your life please God? Actions such as *reading* the Bible, *obeying* parents, *speaking* kindly to a little brother, and *praying* all glorify God. But you can also *cook*, and *clean* your room and *take out* the garbage and *do* your homework to the glory of God. That is, you don't just have to read your Bible to glorify God. When you read your homework or a helpful book, that can also bring glory to God.

Paul says we should do *everything* "for the glory of God." This means that you think about God and His presence with you no matter what you are doing. It means you want everything you do to please Him. By living this way, you will create a life full of "verbs" that glorify God and make Him happy.

A POWER NOTE

Make a list of action verbs that you think would please and glorify God. You can include things like "*Help* Mom with chores" or "*Share* my toys with my siblings." Try to do a few of the actions on the list each day.

SPIRITUAL WATER

Find It in the Bible

Jesus answered, "Everyone who drinks this water will be thirsty again,
but whoever drinks the water I give them will never thirst.
Indeed the water I give them will become in them a
spring of water welling up to eternal life."

JOHN 4:13–14

More than half of your body is made up of water. This life-giving substance is important for almost every bodily function. It helps your body make saliva, digest food, keep a stable body temperature, and protect your brain. When you feel thirsty your body is telling you it needs water. Not having enough water in your body can lead to dizziness, exhaustion, sleepiness, and more. It's important to drink lots of water every day.

Just as our bodies need water for physical life, so our souls need salvation in order to have spiritual life. Jesus said that the salvation He came to provide is like water from a spring that brings eternal life. Our souls are parched and dry until we choose to believe in Jesus as our Savior. Then He washes away our sins and fills our hearts with the Holy Spirit. This refreshes our hearts and our souls. It gives us good spiritual health.

A POWER NOTE

Find a container that holds a quart of liquid. Use a drinking cup to fill the container with water, and count how many cups it takes. That's how much water you should drink each day to be healthy. To keep your spirit healthy, read one Bible verse for each cup of water you drink.

PUPPY PUDDLES

Find It in the Bible

The LORD is gracious and compassionate,
slow to anger and rich in love.

PSALM 145:8

Puppies sometimes go to the bathroom on carpets. It's what they do until they are properly housebroken. Often we can tell when a puppy has done something bad in the house. With its head down and tail between its legs, the puppy doesn't want anyone to see the mess it made.

A wise owner won't hate the puppy because of a potty training accident. Instead, a wise owner will scold the puppy to help it learn not to go to the bathroom in the house. Then the owner will clean up the mess and cuddle the puppy to show it is still loved.

God has so much more love and goodness than a puppy trainer. When you do something wrong, you may feel embarrassed or ashamed, but God wants you to talk to Him about it. God may gently show you what you did wrong so you know how to become like His Son, Jesus Christ. But He is rich in love and will draw you into His arms so you feel His grace and compassion. All you have to do is go to God—even when you have done something wrong—and trust His love for you.

A POWER NOTE

God wants to hear about what you've done. Go to Him and let your heavenly Father know you trust Him with everything, including your mistakes and sins.

SALTY FOR THE SAVIOR

Find It in the Bible

You are the salt of the earth. But if the salt loses its saltiness,
how can it be made salty again? It is no longer good for anything,
except to be thrown out and trampled underfoot.

MATTHEW 5:13

The aroma of baking bread slowly filled the house. Finally, the oven timer dinged. After they let the bread cool, Jeremy and his dad tried a slice. But then . . .

"Ew!" Jeremy exclaimed. "That doesn't taste right!"

Dad's face was scrunched. "You're right!" Dad grabbed the recipe card. "Oh no," he said. "We forgot to add the salt."

"But it's only a little bit of salt. How come missing that little bit makes such a difference?" asked Jeremy.

"Salt makes the bread dough less sticky and adds flavor," Dad explained.

"In Sunday school," said Jeremy. "We learned Christians are like salt. If the world doesn't have Christians sharing the love and name of Jesus, it will be less beautiful, and people will be lost to Satan."

Dad nodded. "That's why we need to share Christ with others." He winked. "And add salt to our bread."

A POWER NOTE

Pick a recipe with salt in it and make that food with a parent— once with salt and once without salt. Does the version *with* salt taste better? Think about how you can be salt today, whether this means talking to someone about Jesus or showing God's love to them!

PAID IN FULL

Find It in the Bible

Do not think that I have come to abolish the Law or the Prophets;
I have not come to abolish them but to fulfill them.

MATTHEW 5:17

Everything written about sin and salvation in the Old Testament points to Jesus. He is the fulfillment of all of God's plans for salvation!

Here's what you need to know. The Old Testament sets the stage for the New Testament. In the Old Testament, God gave His people laws to help them live well, but also laws about worshiping Him. Some of those laws had to do with sacrificing animals. That may seem kind of gross, but God wanted His people to understand how bad sin is—it's deadly. And instead of the people dying for their own sins, they could sacrifice an animal.

Then Jesus came. Sin is still deadly, but Jesus provided the very last blood sacrifice. Jesus never sinned, so His death (sacrifice) paid for all sins. God looks at Jesus' sacrifice and it covers everyone's sins—those who believed before Jesus came and everyone who has believed since then. He took everyone's sins and stamped "Paid in full" over them. That's how Jesus came to "fulfill" the Law and the Prophets, as the verse says.

A POWER NOTE

Find a Bible (the *Fire Bible for Kids* is a really good one!) and spend some time over the next few weeks reading the book introductions to every book in the Bible. This will help you understand what is in each book and how all the books fit together.

Peace!

Find It in the Bible

Peace I leave with you; my peace I give you. I do not give to you
as the world gives. Do not let your hearts be
troubled and do not be afraid.

JOHN 14:27

You probably have days when you just can't stop worrying. Maybe a big test is coming up, or you had a fight with your best friend. Feeling that way certainly isn't enjoyable. In fact, all the worry and sadness make you feel just plain rotten.

But then your mom and dad help you study, or you and your friend apologize to each other. Isn't that a great feeling? It feels peaceful because you aren't worried about the problem anymore.

Jesus offers that kind of peace *all the time.* When we pray, God hears us and lets us know that He has everything in control. Jesus' peace isn't the same peace that we get from talking to someone. His peace is *everlasting.* It doesn't change or go away . . . ever.

While we can't be totally worry-free, praying always helps. When we pray, the Holy Spirit helps us feel better and reminds us that God is in control of everything.

A POWER NOTE

Make a Prayer Box! Cover an empty facial tissue box with bright papers, stickers, and whatever else you want. Write "Prayers" on the top of the box. Whenever you feel worried about something, write your prayer on a slip of paper and put it in the box.

one Little Sheep

Find It in the Bible

And when he finds it, he joyfully puts it on
his shoulders and goes home.

LUKE 15:5–6

This verse is at the end of a passage where a shepherd has been looking for a lost sheep (Luke 15:1–7). It's just one sheep. The shepherd has ninety-nine more, and many lambs are sure to be born in the spring. So no big deal, right?

Wrong. The shepherd loves that little sheep so much that he leaves the others in safety and searches until he finds the sheep. When the shepherd finds the sheep, he takes it home and celebrates. He tells all of his friends so they can celebrate with him, too.

That's what happens when a sinner comes to Jesus. No matter how many people already believe, Jesus is joyful when one person repents. God and all of the angels celebrate because *one person* has accepted Christ.

When you decided to follow Jesus, heaven had a party! That's why you want to keep talking about Jesus to your friends—so they can make heaven happy, too!

A POWER NOTE

Find a notebook that has pictures on it that remind you of a party (if you can't find one, make your own). Keep it beside your bed and write down the names of family members and friends whom you want to come to know Jesus. Call it your Party Notebook! And when someone responds and comes to Christ, celebrate (with the angels).

TAKe HeART

Find It in the Bible

I have told you these things, so that in me you may have peace.
In this world you will have trouble. But take heart!
I have overcome the world.

JOHN 16:33

A swiftly flowing river doesn't seem like a safe place for a spider. But that is exactly where the water spider lives most happily. How? It spins a strong circular web of silk, round and round, kind of like a waterproof basket. It anchors the web to a plant and then fills it with an air bubble from the surface of the river. This unusual bubble of protection provides a safe and cozy home for the spider in a dangerous environment.

Many things can happen to you each day that hurt you or make you afraid or worried. You might feel sort of like that little spider in the middle of a raging river. But God promises that even in the middle of trouble, He will give you peace. You can survive the troubles of life by wrapping yourself in God's bubble of protection. Study the Bible, pray, listen to the Holy Spirit, and obey God's Word every day.

Becoming a Christian doesn't eliminate all our problems and troubles. The difference is that we get to face our problems *with* Jesus!

A POWER NOTE

Memorize John 16:33. The next time you are in the middle of a whole lot of trouble, remind yourself that Jesus has told you to take heart.

THE SUN STOOD STILL!

Find It in the Bible

So the sun stood still, and the moon stopped,
till the nation avenged itself on its enemies.

JOSHUA 10:13

The earth revolves around the sun once every 365.242199 days. That extra .242199 days means that every four years we have what is called Leap Year—and we add February 29 to the calendar. That allows the earth an extra day to catch up.

The earth orbits the sun at a speed of 67,000 miles per hour, and it rotates on its own axis once every twenty-four hours.

The book of Joshua describes a great battle between the Amorites and the Israelites. To help the Israelites win the battle, God gave them more daylight by actually causing the sun to stand still. Essentially, God paused time, and the Israelites were victorious!

The Bible says that if God is for us, who can stand against us? (Romans 8:31) Remember that in the middle of your battles, God is more powerful than time itself. The God who can stop the sun cares about you.

A POWER NOTE

If you had one extra day this year and could do anything you wanted to do on that day, what would you do? Make a list of some of the things you would like to do or the places you would like to visit. Be thankful you serve a God who is mightier than the sun!

MARCH

TO THE ENDS OF THE EARTH

Find It in the Bible

But you will receive power when the Holy Spirit comes on you;
and you will be my witnesses in Jerusalem, and in all
Judea and Samaria, and to the ends of the earth.

ACTS 1:8

Can a fish live on the sand? No. Its natural habitat is water. Can a polar bear live in the rain forests of Brazil or the deserts of Egypt? No. Its natural habitat is an iceberg. The Holy Spirit wants to dwell inside your heart. That is His natural habitat.

Jesus promised to baptize His followers with the Holy Spirit to give them power to be witnesses. When He told His followers that they would be witnesses in "Jerusalem," He meant right there, where they lived. Jerusalem was in Judea, but Samaria was a next-door country, and the "ends of the earth" was everywhere else. Today, the world has about 196 countries—and all of them have people who need to hear about Jesus.

When you are baptized in the Holy Spirit, He will give you the power to tell people about Jesus everywhere you go.

A POWER NOTE

Draw a circle in the center of a sheet of paper. Draw a bigger circle around that circle, and then a bigger circle around the other two circles. In the center circle print the name of your town. In the next circle, print the name of your state. In the biggest circle, print the names of as many countries as you can think of. Pray for the Holy Spirit to help you share about Jesus, starting right where you are.

Jesus, the Storyteller

Find It in the Bible

But these are written that you may believe that Jesus is the Messiah, the Son of God, and that by believing you may have life in his name.

JOHN 20:31

What's your favorite story? Maybe you like *The Cat in the Hat* by Dr. Seuss. It's a simple story with a lot of rhymes about the adventures of Thing 1 and Thing 2 and the cat who wears—obviously—a hat. But did you know that it took Dr. Seuss a year and a half to write that story? A simple story can sometimes be the most difficult for the author to write.

Jesus told stories, too. These stories were called "parables." That's a word that means stories with meanings. His stories were about seeds, farmers, travelers, a runaway son, and lost sheep. They might seem like simple stories, but they always had important lessons in them. Some stories tell how much God loves you, while others tell how strong He is!

If you pay attention to the stories Jesus told, you can learn what God is like and what He wants you to do to live for Him.

A POWER NOTE

Read Luke 10:25–37. This is a story Jesus told called "The Good Samaritan." Find some friends who will help you act out this story. If you can dress up like people in Bible times it will be even more fun. Afterwards, discuss how each of you can show kindness to another person.

WIND OF FAITH

Find It in the Bible

Now faith is confidence in what we hope for and
assurance about what we do not see.

HEBREWS 11:1

On a trip to the park on a windy March afternoon, you may decide to fly a kite. You get your kite and your ball of twine. You make sure you have a tail on the kite because, without a tail, the kite doesn't stay balanced and can't fly.

You find a big open space so your kite won't get tangled in trees or wires. The wind is strong enough, so you run, pulling the kite behind you until the wind draws it up higher and higher. Then you can stand still and hold onto the string while the wind keeps it flying.

You cannot see the wind, yet you know it's there. You feel it blowing your hair and jacket. You see it making your kite bounce and its tail flow back and forth. The wind isn't visible, but you know it's there by what it does.

Having faith means believing in something that you can't see. You can have faith in God even though you can't see Him with your eyes. Just as you know the wind is there by what it does, you have faith that God is there because you see His work in your life.

A POWER NOTE

Go fly a kite! You can purchase one from the store to put together, or use some instructions online or in a book to make one. The next windy day, take your kite for a flight! Thank God for the wind of His Spirit!

LOVE OF LEARNING

Find It in the Bible

Blessed are those who have learned to acclaim you,
who walk in the light of your presence, LORD.

PSALM 89:15

The Bible sure says a lot about teaching and learning! You might be thinking, "Wow, I go to school enough already!" But this kind of learning is what you do when you meet a person you like, someone who could become a good friend.

When you meet someone new, you first find out the person's name. Next you get to know that person—their interests, family, likes and dislikes, and more. The more time you spend with that person, the better you understand him or her and the better friends you become. Then comes the really cool part. When you have the chance to introduce your friend to someone else, you get to tell others how awesome your friend is.

When you talk about God, the verse above says that you are blessed if you "acclaim" the Lord. *Acclaim* is a fancy word for *praising with enthusiasm*. Can you praise God if you don't know anything about Him? Of course not! But you can praise God if you have taken the time to learn about Him and what He has done for you. Tell others what you have learned about God.

A POWER NOTE

Want to know more about God? Write out each of these three verses and beside each write what it says about God: Deuteronomy 10:17; Psalm 52:8; Daniel 9:4. Thank Him for being so awesome!

ISSUMAGIJOUJUNGNIANERMIK

Find It in the Bible

As far as the east is from the west, so far has he
removed our transgressions from us.

PSALM 103:12

Issumagijoujungnianermik might just be the craziest-looking word you've ever seen. You could chip a tooth trying to pronounce it! But it's a real word with an amazing definition. The word is from the Eskimo language, and it describes a special kind of forgiveness. It means "not being able to think about it or remember it anymore."

If you've ever been hurt by someone, you probably didn't want to forgive that person. But when you refuse to forgive, you only hurt yourself. Why? Because you keep thinking about how that person hurt you and how unfair it was. Then you just get mad all over again.

That's not how God acts toward us. When God forgives, He throws our sins away as far as the east is from the west. They're never, ever coming back.

When you stop thinking about how people have hurt you, your mind is free. When God forgives you, your soul is free.

A POWER NOTE

The next time someone does something to hurt you, write it down on a piece of paper in pencil. Now erase what you have written and imagine that you are also erasing the grudge from your thoughts.

A LIGHT IN THE DARKNESS

Find It in the Bible
Your word is a lamp for my feet, a light on my path.

PSALM 119:105

The Luray Caverns in the Shenandoah Valley of Virginia are a natural wonder. The caves extend for over one and a quarter miles into the earth where spaces just large enough to crawl through give way to enormous caverns. The caverns were discovered in 1878 when Andrew Campbell felt cold air rushing from a sinkhole on the side of a hill. He and some of his friends investigated and found the caves—one of the largest series of caverns in the eastern United States.

Taking that first step into the darkness of an unexplored cave must have been frightening at first, but Andrew and his friends carried lanterns with them. They knew that a light would make the path far less dangerous and would keep them safe.

God's Word, the Bible, is a light for all Christians as we walk the path of life. Stepping into the unknown can be a little frightening. Whether it's a new school, an illness, or a thunderstorm, we know that God is with us because His Word says that He is.

A POWER NOTE

Ask a parent to help you create a Bible light. Around the outside of an empty glass jar, paste some pictures of Bibles from old magazines. Now place a tea-light candle in the bottom of the jar and light it with adult supervision. Let it remind you of the light of God's Word.

BLAMELESS IN HIS SIGHT

Find It in the Bible

For the LORD God is a sun and shield; the LORD bestows
favor and honor; no good thing does he withhold
from those whose walk is blameless.

PSALM 84:11

The sun provides light and warmth—without it, every living thing on the planet would wither and die. The sun is essential to life. A shield provides protection. A warrior of old wouldn't think of entering battle without a shield. Even if he lost his sword, he still would be able to protect himself from injury.

When the psalmist wrote this verse, he wanted to remind us that we can't live without the Lord God. We need Him to help us live, and we need Him to help us in the battles that we face in a sinful world.

The verse also says, "The LORD bestows favor and honor." He doesn't hold back anything good from those who are *blameless*. The Bible also tells us that we have all sinned (Romans 3:23). So how can anyone be blameless? Is that even possible?

Yes, it is. When you admit your sin to God, tell Him you're sorry (and mean it), and ask for His forgiveness, you become blameless in His sight. When you do that, the Lord promises to give you life and protection, favor and honor.

A POWER NOTE

Logos are designs that companies create to help people recognize their products. McDonald's has arches; Nike has a swoosh. Try to design a logo for your life—and include an image of the sun and a shield. Let your logo remind you to walk blameless before God.

A FIRM FOUNDATION

Find It in the Bible

If you do not stand firm in your faith, you will not stand at all.

ISAIAH 7:9

The tallest building in the world (right now) is the Burj Dubai, a skyscraper that reaches 2,684 feet (almost exactly a half a mile high!). But that building doesn't just sit on the ground. Its foundations reach down 164 feet into the soil. The tallest buildings in the world require the deepest foundations in order for them to stand tall and strong.

In the same way, to build a strong life, you need to reach down and make sure you have a solid foundation. You'll find that as you grow up, lots of things will try to chip away at your faith foundation. Right now, as you're building your life, you want to make sure that your foundation is solid. That means, you want to make sure of your faith in Jesus. People will ask you *why* you believe *what* you believe. "It's what my parents believe," or, "It's what I was always taught," is not a firm foundation. "I believe because of what Jesus has done for me, because of what I read in the Bible, because I have faith"—those are words that reveal a solid foundation.

Decide to study the Bible every day. Memorize verses. Learn from your parents and pastor. As you lay a strong foundation, you will be able to stand firm in defense of your faith.

A POWER NOTE

Start building your firm foundation by memorizing Psalm 18:2 and Matthew 7:24.

SHARE THE GOOD NEWS

Find It in the Bible

Therefore go and make disciples of all nations, baptizing them
in the name of the Father and of the Son
and of the Holy Spirit.

MATTHEW 28:19

The dictionary defines *disciple* as "one who accepts and assists in spreading the doctrines of another." Most people know that Jesus had twelve disciples. They went with Him from town to town as He taught people about His Father. When Judas betrayed Jesus, the number of disciples dropped by one. (Later, Matthias was chosen to replace Judas. See Acts 1:12–26). So what did Jesus mean when He told His disciples to go and make more disciples?

Jesus gave this command to His disciples who saw Him after His resurrection. He wanted them to go into all parts of the world and tell people about the salvation that comes only by believing in Jesus. They had to share the good news!

Jesus wants us to share this good news as well. Far more people live on earth today than two thousand years ago. Jesus asks us to share the good news with anyone who is willing to listen. But no one can hear about Him unless someone tells them (Romans 10:14). Perhaps that someone is you!

A POWER NOTE

Search in a library or on the Internet to discover the languages that are spoken in ten foreign countries. Write down the ten countries and beside each write the language that is spoken there. Remember, people all over the world need to hear about Jesus.

THE SWEET LIFE

Find It in the Bible

Give, and it will be given to you. A good measure, pressed down,
shaken together and running over, will be poured into your lap.
For with the measure you use, it will be measured to you.

LUKE 6:38

Have you ever helped your mom make a batch of chocolate chip cookies? Most recipes call for "packed brown sugar." *Packed* brown sugar isn't a brand name, it's an instruction. It means you don't just scoop the brown sugar into a measuring cup—you scoop and pack it down, scoop again and pack it down again. You do this until the sugar is level with the top of the cup. If you don't use that much sugar and don't pack it down, the cookies won't be sweet enough.

In today's verse, Jesus wants us to see that when we give, we need to give without being stingy. We need to give in the same way we pack brown sugar into a measuring cup. We can even give over the top so that our giving spills out all over. Jesus tells us that when we give that way, we will receive in the same way. A few verses before this one, He also tells us to give without expecting to be paid back (verse 35).

Of course, we can't forget that when we give, we should do so with a cheerful heart (2 Corinthians 9:7). When we give cheerfully and abundantly, life is sweet.

A POWER NOTE

Ask your mom or dad to help you make some chocolate chip cookies! And don't forget to *pack* the brown sugar!

CHOOSE PEACE

Find It in the Bible

Make every effort to live in peace with everyone and to be holy;
without holiness no one will see the Lord.

HEBREWS 12:14

The famous artist Paul Gustave Doré (1832–1883) was traveling in Europe when he lost his passport. He came to a border crossing but could not pass. He told the border guard that he was Paul Doré, the famous artist, but the guard thought he was just saying that to cross the border.

Finally, the guard said he would test the artist to see if what he claimed was true. He handed Doré a pencil and paper and told him to sketch some people standing nearby. Within a few minutes, Doré had sketched an amazing drawing of the people. Now the guard knew that the man in front of him truly was the great artist, and the guard let him cross the border.

The artist's actions proved who he was. Do your actions prove that you are a child of God? The writer of Hebrews encouraged believers to make peace part of their lives. God can help you do what is right "to live at peace with everyone." Sometimes people around you will *not* be peaceful; in fact, they may seem like they *want* to start a fight. You can choose how you react. Let peace begin with you.

A POWER NOTE

What efforts can you make "to live in peace with everyone"? Need some suggestions? Here are a few: Do your assigned chores before anyone has to nag you about them. Be quick to forgive others and to ask others to forgive you.

ANGELIC JOY

Find It in the Bible

In the same way, I tell you, there is rejoicing in the presence
of the angels of God over one sinner who repents.

LUKE 15:10

A ngels are mentioned 108 times in Old Testament, and 165 times in the New Testament. Genesis 3:24 is the first time the Bible mentions an angel. That angel with a flaming sword was sent to guard the Tree of Life in the Garden of Eden.

Angels are God's creations. They were with Him before He created Adam and Eve. They saw His disappointment when Adam and Eve sinned. They watched Him destroy the earth with the flood and start over with only Noah's family. They were present when He looked away from Jesus as He hung on the cross, and they celebrated when Jesus rose from the grave.

Angels know God's awesome power and love for His creation, so when one person recognizes his sin, asks for God's forgiveness, and accepts God's love, the angels rejoice! Someday, all who believe in Jesus will have the opportunity to meet God's angels in heaven. And in heaven, angels probably won't have to tell us, "Don't be afraid!"

A POWER NOTE

Read Revelation 22:8–9. What happened when John tried to worship the angel? Why did the angel tell John not to worship him? Like us, angels love, serve, and worship God. Someday we will worship God with them in heaven.

WHAT AND WHY

Find It in the Bible

For God so loved the world that he gave his one and only Son,
that whoever believes in him shall not perish but have eternal life.
For God did not send his Son into the world to condemn
the world, but to save the world through him.

JOHN 3:16–17

Almost every Christian knows John 3:16 and has probably memorized it. Many people see it as the most important verse in the whole Bible. But sometimes people forget to keep reading.

John 3:16 tells us what God did. He sent His Son, Jesus, as a sacrifice for our sins. That gives us hope. It also tells us what we need to do to have eternal life—we need to believe in Jesus. But verse 17 tells us why God sent His Son.

God could have sent Jesus to judge each person on earth. If He had done that, everyone would have been condemned forever (pronounced guilty and punished). But God didn't want to do that. Instead, He gave us the option of believing in His Son for salvation.

God loves us so much that He provided a way out of eternal punishment and a way into eternal life. Jesus offered Himself to take our punishment so we could be saved.

A POWER NOTE

You might have John 3:16 memorized already. If not, take some time today to memorize it, but also memorize verse 17. Both verses help you understand what Jesus did and why He did it.

ENDLESS LOVE

Find It in the Bible

I am the Alpha and the Omega, the First and the Last,
the Beginning and the End.

REVELATION 22:13

Today is called "Pi Day" (pronounced "pie") because the mathematical value pi (π—you'll learn about it in geometry class) begins with the number 3.14, and today is 3/14, March 14. But pi is actually a number that never ends. After the .14, the numbers keep on going without ever settling into a repeating pattern. It's a problem that has puzzled mathematicians for centuries. It's a math equation that has no end.

Here's something else that will never end: God and His love for you. God never had a beginning and He will never have an end. He just always was and is and will be. He was here before the universe began, and He'll be here forever after the world ends. This means He knows everything that has ever happened and ever will happen. The future is in His hands.

The Bible says that God is the Alpha and the Omega (those are the first and last letters of the Greek alphabet—kind of like saying He's the A and the Z). He's the First and the Last, the Beginning and the End. The Bible also tells us that God is Love. He is always here to care for us no matter what the future holds. God never ends and His love never ends.

A POWER NOTE

Eat a piece of pie to celebrate Pi Day! While you're eating, think about how God's love for you never ends.

An Official Seal

Find It in the Bible

When you believed, you were marked in him with a seal, the promised
Holy Spirit, who is a deposit guaranteeing our inheritance until
the redemption of those who are God's possession—
to the praise of his glory.

EPHESIANS 1:13–14

In times past, a signet ring was used to seal important documents or to secure the tie around a package. The seal meant something of great importance was within. The seal was usually made of warm wax impressed by the signet ring. No one else had the same ring, so the seal was instantly recognizable.

The Bible tells us that from the very moment you believed in Jesus, a seal, much like the seal of a signet ring, is placed upon your heart. It marks you as someone very important to the King of kings. That seal is the Holy Spirit.

So what is the purpose of this seal to those who believe in Jesus for salvation? The verse tells us that it is a deposit guaranteeing our inheritance as a child of God. When you believed in Jesus, you were adopted into God's family. The Holy Spirit's seal shows your relationship with God.

A POWER NOTE

Find some modeling clay. Press something (like a coin) into its surface, then pull it out and see the image left in the clay. It will look something like an official seal.

A LIVING TEMPLE

Find It in the Bible

Don't you know that you yourselves are God's temple and
that God's Spirit dwells in your midst?

1 CORINTHIANS 3:16

Since the great Exodus of the nation of Israel from Egypt, God has always lived with His people. At first His house was called the tabernacle. This was a large, portable tent. It was made with large poles with long sheets of fabric for walls on the outside and rooms on the inside.

King Solomon built a more permanent temple in Jerusalem about a thousand years before Christ's birth. The Bible gives details about the size of that temple and its contents in 1 Kings 6. With all of the gold and precious stones used in its construction, scholars estimate that to build the same temple today would cost nearly six billion dollars!

Sadly, that temple was destroyed. But after the death of Jesus on the cross, God said He would dwell in brand new temples! Did you know that each Christian is one of those temples? *You* are God's temple! He lives inside you through His Holy Spirit.

Paul is making the point in this verse that because God lives in us, we should live differently from the rest of the world.

A POWER NOTE

Ask your mom or dad for an old sheet or blanket that you can use to build a tent. Hang it over some chairs or a piece of rope. Sit inside the tent and think how God once dwelled inside a tent on earth but now He dwells inside of you by His Holy Spirit.

THRee-LeAF CLOVeR

Find It in the Bible

[God] saved us through the washing of rebirth and renewal by
the Holy Spirit, whom he poured out on us generously
through Jesus Christ our Savior.

TITUS 3:5–6

In these two verses, we see all three parts of the Trinity—the name that describes that God is three persons in one. *God* saved us by washing and renewing us by the *Holy Spirit* who comes into our hearts because of what *Jesus Christ* did for us on the cross. All three members of the Trinity are involved in saving us.

But trying to understand how God can be three-in-one is very difficult. That's why St. Patrick used a three-leaf clover to try to illustrate the concept. St. Patrick lived in the fifth century (that's the 400s!) and was a missionary to Ireland. The three leaves of the clover helped him to explain the Trinity. That's why the clover is the symbol of St. Patrick's Day and why it's tradition to wear green on that day.

St. Patrick wanted to help people understand all that God did to save them. The same is true today. God loves you so much that He gave His Son, Jesus, to pay for your sins. When you accept forgiveness through Jesus' death on the cross, the Holy Spirit cleanses you from the inside out.

A POWER NOTE

Wear green today—not just to keep from getting pinched but to honor St. Patrick and what he did to help people understand more about the Trinity. If you get the chance, tell someone the story of St. Patrick and the three-leaf clover.

Be An overcomer

Find It in the Bible

Do not be overcome by evil, but overcome evil with good.

ROMANS 12:21

Billy and Colten are great friends, but it wasn't always that way. In fact, in junior high, you might have called them enemies. Colten was a pretty good kid, but Billy was a troublemaker. And he constantly tried to get Colten into trouble.

One day at the end of seventh grade, their math teacher told Billy that if he didn't pass the next test, he would fail. Billy was upset. Colten went up to Billy after class. "I don't want you to fail. I understand this math section really well and could help you if you want." It took Billy a minute, but then he smiled.

"Yeah, I could really use the help." And the rest, as they say, is history. Billy and Colten have been friends ever since.

When someone is mean, it's natural to want to get back at the person or to be happy when that person is in trouble. Colten might have been glad to see Billy fail because Billy was always so mean to him. But Colten overcame evil with good.

A POWER NOTE

Do you know someone who could use a little kindness or compassion, even though that person is mean to others? How can you help that person? With the help of a trusted adult, make a plan to do something good for them this week. In this way you can overcome evil with good.

An Audience of One

Find It in the Bible

And as for you, brothers and sisters, never tire of doing what is good.

2 THESSALONIANS 3:13

Sometimes you just get tired of being good, don't you? Some days you may just feel like being good is hard work, being kind to others is exhausting, standing up for what's right is overwhelming, trying to overcome evil with good can be discouraging.

Paul understood this—and that's why he encouraged the believers to "never tire of doing what is good." Sure, it's tough sometimes. You may not get thanked, or honored, or win any prizes. People may not treat you any better. In fact, they may treat you worse.

But here's the good part. God knows. He sees every time you make a right choice, every time you're an overcomer, every time you're kind, every time you try to do the right thing. And He's the only one who really matters.

So don't get tired! Get inspired! God is your audience of one. He sees and applauds!

A POWER NOTE

Challenge yourself. Today, be aware of every action you take and the fact that God is watching. Do you want God to be sad or happy about what you do? Of course, you want Him to be happy. Make the choices that you know He'll applaud.

GOD IS LOVE

Find It in the Bible

We love because he first loved us.

1 JOHN 4:19

Who do you love the most? You might think of your parents, siblings, best friend, or your favorite teacher. You may not be able to choose. Truthfully, it doesn't matter. What matters is that you *love* others. God loves, too. The Bible tells us that God loves everyone, including you—and that He loved us all before we were even born. He loved us first.

And because God loves, we can love others. That doesn't mean that we have to be "in love" with everyone (that would be impossible—and not a good idea). It also doesn't mean that we have to feel mushy feelings about everyone. Love isn't a feeling; it's a choice.

Love is a decision to act with care and compassion toward others. It's being kind when we don't want to be. It's being thoughtful even when we don't feel like it. It's helping out when we'd rather do something else.

It may seem difficult, but it isn't. God gives us the ability to love others because He loved us first.

A POWER NOTE

Make your favorite sandwich. With the help of a grownup, cut the sandwich into the shape of a heart. As you enjoy your sandwich, think of one thing you can do today to show love to someone.

WALKING IN LOVE

Find It in the Bible

And this is love: that we walk in obedience to His commands.
As you have heard from the beginning, His command
is that you walk in love.

2 JOHN 6

Have you ever thought how complicated it is to walk? Each step requires around two hundred muscles to work together perfectly. Some keep you balanced. Some bend your knees. Others make sure your foot lands the right way. No wonder babies take so long to figure it out!

The "walking" in this verse is to "walk in love." But how do we do that? Think of it as walking down a path, and then you get to a fork in the road. You could take one path. That is to go your own way and do whatever it takes to make you happy—even if it hurts other people. The other path is the path of love. It means being kind (even when it hurts), serving and helping others, and thinking of others before yourself.

God wants us to walk in love. That means taking the path that puts others before ourselves. But you know what's really cool? *That* path will help you walk closer to God!

A POWER NOTE

Take some construction paper and put your foot on it. Draw around your foot (don't forget between your toes!) and then cut it out. Make two more cut-outs of your feet. Then write "Walk In Love" on the footprints—one word on each footprint. Tape the prints to your wall to remind you to walk as God wants you to walk.

FLAWLESS

Find It in the Bible

As for God, his way is perfect: The LORD's word is flawless;
he shields all who take refuge in him.

2 SAMUEL 22:31

The word *flawless* means "without any defects." The largest flawless diamond ever to be auctioned is a pear-shaped gem weighing over 101 carats. It's considered flawless because of its perfect clarity, clear color, rare brilliance, and perfect symmetry (meaning the cuts are completely perfect and equal on all sides). Something so flawless is extremely rare.

Except when you talk about God! As this verse says, His way is perfect, and His Word is flawless. The Bible says that when God promises something, He always means it. He always tells the whole truth. He doesn't tell little lies. Nor does He forget what He says, the way you might forget about promising to clean your room because you got distracted by a TV show. Because God is perfect, He will always fulfill His promises.

When the Bible says that He will care for anyone who trusts and relies on Him, it really means it! God's promises are perfect and flawless. When you read His Word and follow it, you will do great things for God!

A POWER NOTE

See if you can unscramble this phrase. Write it on a card and put it in your Bible to remind you of God's flawless Word.

ehT drwso of dGo ear reepftc dan wallsesf.

(The words of God are perfect and flawless.)

THE WALLS CAME TUMBLING DOWN

Find It in the Bible

When the trumpets sounded, the army shouted, and at the sound of
the trumpet, when the men gave a loud shout, the wall collapsed;
so everyone charged straight in, and they took the city.

JOSHUA 6:20

After the Israelites wandered in the desert for forty years, the time had finally come for God to give them the Promised Land. But right after they entered the land, they came to the city of Jericho. Its walls were tall and thick. How was God going to get them into the city?

God told them to march silently in a circle around the city, once a day for six days. That probably seemed a little weird—it was probably even weird to the soldiers of Jericho who watched from up high on the walls: *What are these people doing?*

But on the seventh day the Israelites marched around the city seven times, blew their trumpets, and shouted. And you know what happened! That gigantic wall just crumbled and fell! The Israelites learned that if they trusted in God and obeyed Him, He would do amazing things.

It's always best to trust God and follow what He says in His Word, even if it seems hard or downright silly. Why? Because God does amazing things when we trust Him!

A POWER NOTE

Walk around your house or apartment silently seven times. Pretend you are walking around Jericho. Think how powerful God is, and remember that He will help you if you trust and obey Him.

YOU COUNT!

Find It in the Bible

Indeed, the very hairs of your head are all numbered. Don't be afraid;
you are worth more than many sparrows.

LUKE 12:7

How many hairs do you think you have on your head? Take a guess. The total is a lot more than 100. It's more than 1,000, or even 10,000. The average person has about 100,000 hairs! That's too big a number to even think about clearly—for example, try to imagine 100,000 jumping frogs. It's just too many. And here's an even bigger number: seven billion, which is approximately the number of people living on earth. Imagine trying to count each and every hair on each and every person's head!

God already knows about all those hairs—and He knows about yours! He loves you so much that He knows every little detail about you, down to the number of hairs in your scalp. He knows about your family. He knows about your worries. He knows your favorite food and your favorite book.

And get this . . . He even knows your future! And knowing everything about you, He still loves you! He has amazing plans for your life. Trust Him to lead you and guide you.

A POWER NOTE

Write down everything you know about someone you love, like your best friend or a family member. What does that person look like? What's their favorite food? Think about the way God knows them even better than you do. He even knows you better than you know yourself! Trust Him with your future.

FACING FEAR

Find It in the Bible

I tell you, whoever publicly acknowledges me before others,
the Son of Man will also acknowledge before the angels of God.
But whoever disowns me before others will be
disowned before the angels of God.

LUKE 12:8–9

You and your family are praying together one night. Suddenly, the door bursts open and soldiers rush in. They haul you off and throw you in a jail cell with other people. All the people in the cell are Christians, because where you live it is against the law. The officials give you a choice: Either say that Jesus isn't God and give up your faith or be killed. What do you choose?

This is the hard choice many Christians around the world face. And many Christians throughout history faced that choice, chose to keep their faith, and were put to death. You will most likely never have something like that happen to you, but God tells us that even in the face of bullying or teasing, we need to keep believing in Him and telling others the good news.

That sounds scary, but don't worry. You are never alone. God promises to give you strength and help. He even promises to give you the words to say when people question you about your faith. Pray that God will give you courage and wisdom when you face people who do and say hurtful things to you because you believe in Him.

A POWER NOTE

Write a story about someone who is mistreated because of his or her faith in Jesus. What does he or she do and say in response?

WORLD RECORD

Find It in the Bible

Praise the LORD, all you nations; extol him, all you peoples.
For great is his love toward us, and the faithfulness
of the LORD endures forever.

PSALM 117:1–2

On March 26, 2014, a world record in chorus national anthem singing was set when about 300,000 people in Bangladesh gathered in the capital to sing the Bangladeshi National Anthem. That's a really big chorus! They wanted to celebrate their independence day as well as to show the unity of their people.

Today's verse says, "Praise the LORD, all you nations." One thing that brings Christians around the world together is the common language of music and praise. What would the sound be like if every Christian on earth began singing praises to God at the same time? Would we be heard across continents? Across oceans? Would the earth shake from the vibrations of all those vocal cords?

Maybe you feel like you're just one small voice—but one small voice multiplied over and over and over can shake the world! Add your voice of praise to the chorus of praise for God.

A POWER NOTE

No matter how big or small you are, your voice matters. Find a Christian friend who speaks another language or contact some missionaries your church supports. Ask for help learning how to sing a praise chorus in another language.

No Greater Love

Find It in the Bible

Greater love has no one than this: to lay down
one's life for one's friends.

JOHN 15:13

How do you show love for others? One teen showed his love in an amazing way. Mateus Moore, a teen from Marysville, California, saved the life of his girlfriend Mickayla by pushing her out of the way of an oncoming train. He died saving her life.

Imagine the courage and love needed to sacrifice one's life to save another's! During the Last Supper with His disciples, Jesus talked about this kind of love. Very soon after the meal, Jesus would lay down His life not just for His disciples but for all those who would believe in Him in the whole world—including you. He willingly did that because of His love.

You may never have to lay down your life for a friend or a family member. But if you trust Jesus as your Savior, He will give you the courage to love others boldly, the way Jesus loves people.

A POWER NOTE

What are you willing to do for a friend? Perhaps you might lay down your pride by saying you're sorry if you hurt a friend. Or, you might defend a friend, even if doing so makes you unpopular.

A TRUE SERVANT

Find It in the Bible

Now that I, your Lord and Teacher, have washed your feet,
you also should wash one another's feet. I have
set you an example that you should
do as I have done for you.

JOHN 13:14–15

The world has many types of roads. Some are paved, like the ones in neighborhoods and cities; some are gravel, like the ones in the country; and some are made only of dirt. In Israel when Jesus was on earth, most of the roads He traveled were dirt.

Jesus and His disciples wore sandals, so walking on dirt paths and roads meant their feet got really dirty. A custom at the time was that a visitor in someone's home would take off his sandals and a servant would wash his feet. (Seems like a yucky job, huh?)

During the Last Supper, Jesus washed His disciples' feet. Even though this was normally the job of the lowest servant in the house, Jesus wanted to give His disciples an example of what serving others means. He was their Lord and Teacher, yet He willingly stooped to wash their dirty feet.

A true servant doesn't try to be more important or get more power or fame than others. A true servant is humble enough to serve others, even those he leads.

A POWER NOTE

Do you have a leadership role? Do you help your teachers as a leader at church or at school? Whatever it is, how might you follow Jesus' example to be a humble, serving leader?

THE SIGN OF LOVE

Find It in the Bible

If you love me, keep my commands.

JOHN 14:15

In sign language you form the sign for *love* by making two fists and crossing your arms over your heart. In a way, this sign also points to the ultimate sign of love—Jesus' death on the cross. Another sign that can remind you of what Jesus did is the sign for *Jesus*. If you're right-handed, you place the tip of your middle finger against the palm of your left hand, then place the tip of the middle finger of your left hand against your right hand. Reverse the order if you're left-handed. This sign is a reminder of the scars in Jesus' hands from when He was nailed to the cross.

Jesus had one last meal with His disciples before He was arrested. Because He was about to die, He wanted to remind them to obey what He taught them. Obedience was the sign of their love for Jesus.

Have you ever heard the phrase, "all talk and no action"? This saying refers to people who talk about what they will do, but they never do it. Jesus wants His followers to talk *and* act. Don't just say you love Jesus. Act like it!

A POWER NOTE

In order to keep Jesus' commands, you have to know them. Can you name one of them? If you need some help, check out these verses: Matthew 5:43–45; 7:1–2; 22:37–40; Luke 6:31. Memorize Jesus' commands.

He Took Your Sin

Find It in the Bible
For he bore the sin of many, and made
intercession for the transgressors.

ISAIAH 53:12

The prophet Isaiah gave an important prophecy here. Chapter 53 is all about Jesus! Isaiah was describing Someone who would come as a Savior—Jesus—and the sacrifice He would make for all people.

That's what this verse means—Jesus "bore the sin of many and made intercession for the transgressors" (meaning He asked that we not be punished for our sins). The chapter predicts that a Man would take our pain and suffering. He would be punished for our sins. He would be hurt because God would take all of the world's sin and put it on Him.

Imagine that! This would be like your brother coming along, just before you get punished, and saying that he will take the punishment for you.

That's what Jesus did. It's not easy to understand, but you accept it by faith. Then, when you accept the sacrifice Jesus made for you, He comes into your life and makes you certain of all He has done for you.

A POWER NOTE

During the Easter season this year, read Isaiah 53. It may be difficult to understand, but underline the words that make you think of the story you know about Jesus dying on the cross. Thank Jesus for taking the punishment for your sins.

He HAS RISen!

Find It in the Bible

The angel said to the women, "Do not be afraid, for I know that
you are looking for Jesus, who was crucified.
He is not here; he has risen, just as he said."

MATTHEW 28:5–6

The women who followed Jesus were with Him at the cross
when He died that horrible Friday. Afterward, they went
home and sat quietly because that was the law for the Sabbath.
From sundown on Friday to sundown on Saturday, the people
were to rest and do no work. Then, as soon as it was light on
Sunday morning, the women went to the place where Jesus had
been buried.

Jesus wasn't buried in a casket in the ground. His body was laid
in a small cave that had been cut out of a hillside. A big stone was
rolled in front of the entrance.

Imagine the surprise of these women when they got to the tomb,
only to find the stone rolled back and an angel sitting on it! They
must have been frightened because the angel told them not to be
afraid. And then, the angel said the best words of all, "He is not
here; he has risen, just as he said."

Jesus was alive. Jesus *is* alive!

A POWER NOTE

Find a stone with a smooth surface that you can write on. Put
these words on the stone with paint or markers: "Jesus is alive!"
Put it in your room to remind you that you serve a living Savior.

NOT JUST APRIL FOOLS

Find It in the Bible

Walk with the wise and become wise,
for a companion of fools suffers harm.

PROVERBS 13:20

You've probably heard of April Fools' Day—a day when people play pranks on one another. Did you know that on April 1 in France, people try to pin paper fish on each other's backs? When the paper is discovered, the person who pinned it says "*Poisson d'avril!*" which means "April fish." Candy shops in France even sell chocolate candy shaped like fish for this special day. People all over the world enjoy a day for jokes and foolishness.

It's one thing to play pranks and have a few laughs, but the Bible takes the topic of fools and foolishness seriously. And it's no laughing matter. The Bible says that you should be careful not to be a foolish person. That means you should be careful who you choose as your best friends. If your close friends are wise, you'll be wise, too. If your close friends always do things that get them into trouble, then you'll find yourself in trouble as well.

So think about your friends. Are they helping you be a wise person? Are you helping your friends be wise?

A POWER NOTE

Have an "April Friends" Day! Write "Friend" on some sticky tabs and stick them to your good friends. Then tell them how much you like being friends with them.

THE GREATEST IS LOVE

Find It in the Bible

And now these three remain: faith, hope and love.
But the greatest of these is love.

1 CORINTHIANS 13:13

*F*aith is what helps us believe in Jesus as our Savior. *Hope* is what we have because we believe in Jesus. *Love* is what Jesus showed us by dying for us on a cross and rising again on Easter morning.

Why is love the greatest of all? Without love, God wouldn't have sent Jesus, His only Son, to earth to die for our sins. Without love, the Holy Spirit wouldn't have come to comfort and help us after Jesus returned to heaven.

Without God's love for us and our love for one another, life would be missing something important. Sort of like French fries without salt or pizza without cheese or a banana split without bananas.

The Bible says that we are able to love because God loved us first (1 John 4:19). Without God, we would have no faith, no hope, and no love.

A POWER NOTE

Read all of 1 Corinthians 13. Write down four things you learned about love. Beside each of these, write how you will show someone that kind of love this coming week.

A BAG OF BRICKS

Find It in the Bible

Even to your old age and gray hairs I am he,
I am he who will sustain you. I have made you and I will
carry you; I will sustain you and I will rescue you.

ISAIAH 46:4

Did you know that the *Guinness Book of World Records* includes one entry for carrying a brick? It's true! As of April 2014, Paddy Doyle from the United Kingdom holds the record for carrying a ten-pound brick over eighteen hours nonstop!

That's a lot of walking with that extra weight! It can be tiring just thinking about carrying a ten-pound weight of any kind for eighteen minutes, much less eighteen hours. And what if Paddy didn't just have to carry a ten-pound brick? What if he had to carry another person? How about you?

Thankfully, Someone can do this much longer than eighteen hours. Your heavenly Father can carry you your entire life and never get tired. He promises to bring you through all of life's trials, each new experience, each exciting victory, and each loss—all the way until you're old. If you ever need comfort and encouragement, all you need to do is ask God for strength. His Holy Spirit will help you. That's a record-breaking promise!

A POWER NOTE

Go outside and find a stone that you can fit in your pocket or backpack. Then carry that stone around with you. Whenever you feel or look at that stone, it will help you remember that God carries you in the same way you carry the stone.

GOD OF TIME

Find It in the Bible

As long as the earth endures, seedtime and harvest,
cold and heat, summer and winter, day and night will never cease.

GENESIS 8:22

What if the seasons weren't dependable? What if you couldn't know for sure that winter would eventually end and spring would come? Or what if something went wrong with time so that morning didn't come one day, and night just kept going for weeks at a time? How confusing that would be!

Fortunately, the Bible tells us that God controls everything, including the seasons and time itself. Both are entirely out of our control but completely dependable because God made them that way! He promises that cycles like the seasons or day and night will keep going until the end of the world. He makes sure the sun rises and sets each day. He brings snow in winter and flowers in spring.

To know our God is so big and powerful is comforting. Because God is big enough to control time, you can be sure He is also big enough to take care of you!

A POWER NOTE

Get some green onions (your mom probably has some in the kitchen). Cut the white root parts off the bottoms of these onions and put the roots in a glass of water. Keep an eye on them for a few days—they should start growing! Just as plants have natural cycles for growth, the earth has natural cycles of time and seasons. When you look at your green onions, remember that God is in control of all times and seasons!

GOOD BUILDING

Find It in the Bible

Therefore everyone who hears these words of mine and puts them into practice is like a wise man who built his house on the rock.

MATTHEW 7:24

People make birdhouses out of all kinds of materials in all kinds of shapes. You can find apartment-building birdhouses, trailer-shaped birdhouses, even birdhouses that look like cupcakes!

To build a basic birdhouse, you need boards, a saw, a measuring tape, a hammer, and nails. Even if you have collected all the materials and tools you need, without instructions or someone to help you, the birdhouse probably won't come out right. What you build may still look like a birdhouse, but it will probably fall apart sooner than if you had followed instructions.

People often try to build their lives on their own, too. They may think they don't need any instructions. But without guidance, getting it right is impossible. Try that and your life will end up crooked and will fall apart as easily as the birdhouse.

Thankfully, we have an instruction manual, an example, and even a Helper—the Holy Spirit! The Bible is our instruction manual, full of good advice. Jesus is our example. We should try to live like Him. The Holy Spirit helps us live to please God.

A POWER NOTE

With a parent's help, purchase a kit for building a birdhouse. Follow the instructions step-by-step, then hang it up and watch the birds. Remind yourself to use God's instruction book for your life.

IGNORE THE BULLIES

Find It in the Bible

For I am not ashamed of the gospel, because it is the power of God
that brings salvation to everyone who believes: first to
the Jew, then to the Gentile.

ROMANS 1:16

Jonas Hanway lived 200 years ago in England. He traveled a lot, and on one trip he discovered people using something called an "umbrella." He thought it would be most useful to have in England, so he bought one and was eager to show it to his friends. But most people just made fun of him. When he used his umbrella, young boys often threw cabbages and rotten eggs at him because they thought he was strange. Hanway never let this stop him. He was ridiculed for thirty years as "the umbrella man," but he never stopped using his umbrella. Eventually people did recognize the usefulness of the umbrella.

Have people ever made fun of you because of something you said or did? Did they make fun of you when you told them about Jesus?

People may make fun of you because you believe in Jesus as your Savior—but don't be ashamed. Stand tall. Think of the sacrifice Jesus made on the cross for you. You are in great company!

A POWER NOTE

Ask your parents or your pastor about some places in the world where Christians are persecuted. Read more about that country and pray for the Christians who live there that they will stand strong against persecution.

A Promise in the Sky

Find It in the Bible

I have set my rainbow in the clouds, and it will be
the sign of the covenant between me and the earth.

GENESIS 9:13

Have you ever seen a rainbow after a storm? Rainbows appear when rain is falling in one part of the sky and the sun is shining through in another. The sun's light is reflected and refracted (or bent) through the raindrops like light through a prism. The white light is then broken up into all the colors of the rainbow—red, orange, yellow, green, blue, indigo, and violet. The millions of little raindrops in the sky refract the light and turn it into the colors you see.

After the water from the flood dried, God promised never to destroy all life on the earth with a flood again. He set the rainbow in the clouds to remind Himself and all people on the earth of His promise or covenant. Imagine what Noah and his family must have thought when the first beautiful rainbow appeared in the blue sky! They were probably amazed!

The rainbow is a symbol of a promise that God made to Noah. Whenever you see one, it is a reminder of the God who keeps His promises. That means that all of God's promises will come true.

A POWER NOTE

Draw a picture of a rainbow. Put the colors in the order of the color spectrum. Start with red, then below that do an arc of orange, then yellow, green, blue, indigo (dark purple), and violet. In the arc of the rainbow write these words: God keeps His promises.

TALKING WITH GOD

Find It in the Bible

I always thank my God as I remember you in my prayers, because I hear about your love for all his holy people and your faith in the Lord Jesus.

PHILEMON 4–5

What do you talk about with God? Maybe you pray about the things you need or people you're concerned about. Perhaps you have a big test coming up, and you want God to give you focus as you study and, during the test, to help you remember what you learned. God is pleased when you bring your needs to Him. But He also likes to hear more than just requests. Paul told Philemon that he always thanked God for him because of all the good Philemon was doing for God.

An easy outline for prayer uses three phrases. First, say, "Thank you," and tell God how much you appreciate who He is and all He has done for you. Next, say, "I'm sorry," and confess all your wrong actions and attitudes to Him. The last phrase is simply one word: "Please." Now ask Him to take action (for example, heal someone who is sick, help you get along with a friend, bring your parent home safely from a trip, and so forth).

Then take a few minutes just to listen quietly. Give God a chance to bring to mind something He wants to tell you. Prayer is a conversation with your very best Friend!

A POWER NOTE

Make a poster with the three prayer phrases on it to remind you how to pray: "Thank you" and "I'm sorry" and "Please." Decorate it and hang it in a place where you can see it when you pray.

Seek His Face

Find It in the Bible

Look to the LORD and his strength; seek his face always.

1 CHRONICLES 16:11

Newborn babies can see, but not very well. Did you know they can only focus on objects that are close? The best distance for them to focus is about eight to twelve inches from the object—and that happens to be the distance from the baby's eyes to the mother's face when she is cradling and feeding the baby. You have probably seen a baby stare contentedly into his mother's face. The mother's face is comforting and familiar.

As a child of God, you constantly want to seek God's face, just like a baby seeks his mother's face. When you look into God's face, He will comfort you. No, you can't actually "see" God—your focus isn't set to see Him yet. But you can sense His presence with you when you think about Him, read His Word, and worship Him.

When you seek God's face, you will find strength and comfort.

A POWER NOTE

The next time you see a mother holding her baby, notice how the baby looks into the mother's face. Think about having that same kind of focus on God.

SPEAK UP!

Find It in the Bible

For if you remain silent at this time, relief and deliverance for the Jews will arise from another place, but you and your father's family will perish. And who knows but that you have come to your royal position for such a time as this?

ESTHER 4:14

Esther was a little girl when her parents died. Her cousin, Mordecai, adopted her and raised her. They were Jewish people—an important point. Esther grew up and was very beautiful. When the king decided he needed a new queen, he had all the beautiful, young single women in his kingdom come to his palace. He wanted to choose one of them to be his queen. He chose Esther.

Mordecai was devoted to God and refused to bow before Haman, the king's right-hand man. This made Haman super angry, but instead of punishing only Mordecai, Haman decided to punish all of the Jewish people. Mordecai called on Esther to help her people, but she was afraid at first. He reminded her that perhaps God had allowed her to become queen for the exact purpose of saving the Jewish people from the evil plans of Haman.

Esther didn't remain silent, and God used her to save the Jewish people.

A POWER NOTE

Read the first four chapters of Esther in your Bible. It won't take you very long. Find out what Esther did. Wherever you read about her being brave, put a B next to the verse. Determine to be brave, like Esther.

STAND UP!

Find It in the Bible

Go, gather together all the Jews who are in Susa, and fast for me.
Do not eat or drink for three days, night or day.
I and my attendants will fast as you do. When this is done,
I will go to the king, even though it is against the law.
And if I perish, I perish.

ESTHER 4:16

Esther knew that to help save her Jewish people, she needed to talk to her husband, the king. The law of the land, however, said that she was not allowed to enter the king's court without being invited. To disobey the law meant she could be killed . . . unless her husband held out his scepter to her.

When Mordecai asked Esther to go to the king on behalf of her people, she was terrified. Still, she knew it was the right thing to do. She asked others to fast and pray for her. She wanted to be especially brave, and she wanted God to allow the king to let her speak to him.

Sometimes standing up for what is right can be scary, especially if no one else stands with you. Remember that you can count on other Christians to pray for you. When you know you need to stand up for what is right, ask people to pray for you so you have the courage you need.

A POWER NOTE

Fasting is going without food in order to pray. Ask your mom or dad if you could skip one meal to fast and pray so that you can understand what it means. Spend the meal time reading your Bible and praying. You will feel hungry, but let that remind you to keep on praying.

GOOD THINGS

Find It in the Bible

How abundant are the good things that you have stored up
for those who fear you, that you bestow in the
sight of all, on those who take refuge in you.

PSALM 31:19

Right now, look around you. Where are you sitting? In your bedroom? In your yard? At the lunch table at school?

Make a list of all the good things you see. Blue sky. Clouds. Good food (maybe you're eating your favorite food right now!). Friends. Mom or dad. Brother or sister. Warm blankets on your bed. Soft pillows. A favorite book or video game. A stuffed animal.

Get the idea? Like the psalm writer, you're noting the abundance of good things God has given you. Everything you see came from Him. Everything is a gift from His hands.

And with all the beauty you see, imagine what God has stored up for you in heaven!

A POWER NOTE

Start a Blessing List in a journal or notebook. Every time you think of a good thing that God has given you, write it down. Pretty soon you'll have a big list. Be sure to thank God every day for those good things!

LET GOD LEAD

Find It in the Bible

Show me your ways, LORD, teach me your paths. Guide me
in your truth and teach me, for you are
God my Savior, and my hope is in you all day long.

PSALM 25:4–5

Have you ever seen a blind person being led by a dog? Guide dogs provide their blind masters with safety, comfort, and friendship. The dogs need about five months of training to be ready to help blind people. During that time they practice constantly to learn things like walking right or left, steering around obstacles, and refusing to move if a situation is unsafe. The dog leads the way, stops when danger appears (like a red light at a crosswalk), and stays close beside the blind person at all times.

In some ways, all human beings seem blind at times. Sometimes we don't know which way to go, we confuse right and wrong, and we don't see the danger ahead. We need a friend who will lead us, guide us around obstacles, and stop us when we're heading into unsafe situations.

It's good to have a parent or friend to rely on, but don't forget you can always rely on God to lead you. He guides you through His Word and by speaking to your heart through the Holy Spirit.

A POWER NOTE

Check out some books from the library about training guide dogs or find information on the Internet. Learn what the dogs are trained to do and how they are trained. Blind people also need to be trained to work with their guide dogs. As you read, think how you can learn to rely on God to guide you.

Be Humble

Find It in the Bible

Good and upright is the LORD; therefore he instructs
sinners in his ways. He guides the humble in what is
right and teaches them his way.

PSALM 25:8–9

God loves us so much that He is willing to take the time to teach us. The first verse for today tells us that (1) God is good and upright, and (2) God instructs sinners in His ways. That's good news! Do you know why? Because we are all sinners (Romans 3:23), and we all need instruction.

Now for today's second verse, which tells us that (1) God guides the humble, and (2) God teaches them His way. The verse has a hint that tells us how we should behave if we are going to learn anything the Lord wants to teach us. Did you catch it? We have to be *humble*. Being humble doesn't mean being a weakling or letting people walk all over you. Being humble means being modest about your strengths and showing respect toward others.

If we are respectful to God and don't boast about ourselves, He can teach, guide, and instruct us in His ways. You don't have to be perfect in order for the Lord to teach you.

A POWER NOTE

Write the word *humble* vertically. Try to think of one word for each letter that describes how you should act in order to be humble. For example, the letter *H* could be "honor others above myself." Write a word or phrase beside each of the six letters. Think how you can put those words into action.

GOD'S PLANS ARE BEST

Find It in the Bible

Many are the plans in a person's heart, but it is the
LORD's purpose that prevails.

PROVERBS 19:21

You've probably heard about the *Titanic*. It was a huge passenger ship sailing from England to New York. Reverend J. Stuart Holden had a ticket to ride on that ship. He was a pastor, and he was supposed to speak at a large Christian convention in America. One day before the *Titanic* sailed, his wife got sick. Reverend Holden decided to stay with his wife until she got better. He was probably very disappointed about missing his trip! But if you know about the *Titanic*, you might also know that on April 15, 1912, it hit an iceberg and sank. Reverend Holden believed that God had saved him from sailing on that ship.

God has a purpose for everything—even for you! His plans are a lot bigger than yours. He makes sure that whatever happens works with His plans. No matter how good your plans are, His are always better. When you're disappointed about a change in plans, trust God. He knows what He's doing.

A POWER NOTE

Make a boat ticket! You could use construction paper and markers. On the front, write one thing that you wanted to do but didn't get to. On the back, write a prayer. You can thank God for always having the best plans and tell Him that you trust Him to take care of you.

Money Matters

Find It in the Bible

For the love of money is a root of all kinds of evil.
Some people, eager for money, have wandered from the
faith and pierced themselves with many griefs.

1 TIMOTHY 6:10

People need money to live—to purchase food, clothes, and other necessities. In the United States, we have dollars, but money in other countries has different names and looks different. If you went to China, you would buy things with *yuan.* In Denmark, you would need *krones.* In Vietnam, you would spend *dong,* and in Thailand, you'd need *baht.*

This verse says that "the love of money is a root of all kinds of evil." It's important for people to earn money to live, but if they start to *love* money, then they might do all kinds of wrong or illegal things to get it. They might cheat people or steal from them. Loving money leads to greed, and being greedy means people care too much about what they want. That doesn't honor God.

So no matter how much money you earn, always remember that everything you own comes from God—even money.

A POWER NOTE

To help you remember to love God and not money, determine that you will always give 10 percent of everything you earn in the offering at church (this is called *tithing*). If you don't know how to figure out what 10 percent is, ask an adult to help you. It may not seem like much, but God is honored when you give, and you will always remember what is most important.

Hometown Hero?

Find It in the Bible

He came to that which was his own, but his own did not
receive him. Yet to all who did receive him, to those who
believed in his name, he gave the right to
become children of God.

JOHN 1:11–12

Jesus was born and raised in the Jewish culture. He lived in the little town of Nazareth that had only about 500 people. Do you know what living in a small town is like—going to a small school and a small church? In a place like that, everyone knows everyone else. Everyone knows what other people do well and what they do wrong. And because of that, everyone thinks they know what everyone else is and isn't capable of doing.

When Jesus left Nazareth to begin His ministry, He went first to His own Jewish people. Most of them didn't believe He was the Son of God. When Jesus went to His own hometown, He was almost pushed over a cliff! His former friends and neighbors, who had known Him when He was little, refused to believe that Mary's son could be the Messiah.

Some Jews did believe in Him and became His disciples. If you had been in Nazareth when Jesus was teaching, would you have believed in Him? Or would you have gone along with the crowd?

A POWER NOTE

Do you know of anyone from your community who has become famous? Talk to your parents or others about how people react to this celebrity. How would you like to be treated if you were famous? How can you show that Jesus is famous to you?

A KID FOR A KING

Find It in the Bible

Joash was seven years old when he became king. . . . Joash
did what was right in the eyes of the LORD.

2 CHRONICLES 24:1–2

After the reign of King Solomon, Israel divided into two
nations: north and south. Judah was the southern kingdom,
and Joash became its king at an age when kids in our country enter
second grade. Being king was a dangerous job. His grandmother,
Athaliah, had other members of the royal family put to death so
that she could rule the country as queen. But God helped Joash's
aunt and uncle keep him safe.

What would you do if you were king? The world's youngest ruler
is King Oyo of Toro, Uganda, who became king at the age of three.
Imagine being king or queen at that age! Like Joash, King Oyo has
advisors who help steer him to make good decisions so he can
rule wisely.

You may not be a king or queen, but God wants to help you make
good decisions. Do you trust Him? Ask Him to guide you as you
read His Word and listen when the Holy Spirit speaks to your
heart.

A POWER NOTE

Are you ready for more responsibility? Ask your mom or dad
if you can have another chore at home that will show how
responsible you are. Follow Joash's example by doing what is
"right in the eyes of the LORD." Follow the rules and do the work
given to you. In this way, you earn the trust of others.

GOD IS STRONGER

Find It in the Bible

"With him is only the arm of flesh, but with us is the
LORD our God to help us and to fight our battles."
And the people gained confidence from what
Hezekiah the king of Judah said.

2 CHRONICLES 32:8

Take a look at your arm. It has three bones: the ulna and radius are in the lower part of your arm and the humerus (sounds like *humorous*) is in the upper part. Skin and muscles cover those bones. In the Bible, the arm is often a symbol—a word picture—for strength.

Sennacherib, the king of Assyria, had a huge army and he threatened to attack Judah—a much smaller nation. The "arm of flesh" mentioned in the verse above is a word picture for the army of Assyria. They were super tough warriors. Though his army was outnumbered, Hezekiah, the king of Judah, trusted that God was stronger than any army and could defeat Judah's enemies. You can read what happened in 2 Chronicles 32:21. You'll see just how strong God is.

Are you facing a huge challenge? You can't win in your own strength. But God has the strength you need to face any challenge.

A POWER NOTE

Draw an arm and on top of it write the people or things you think can help you. For example, your parents, friends, good grades, etc. Then write "God" across all the others words. Other people can help you, but God wants you to have confidence that He will help you.

THE GOOD KIND OF FEAR

Find It in the Bible

And he said to the human race, "The fear of the LORD—
that is wisdom, and to shun evil is understanding."

JOB 28:28

No one wants to feel afraid—that's a bad feeling. But a certain kind of fear can be good. This verse talks about the "fear of the LORD." In this case, the word *fear* means "respect." It means knowing that God is all-powerful, can do what seems to be impossible, and has the right to tell you what to do! You're not *afraid* of God, but you respect Him. You live in awe of Him, and you don't want to disappoint Him. That's why you also want to "shun evil." To shun something means to keep away from it or to avoid it.

It's not always easy to fear the Lord and shun evil. Job was a man who experienced this. In just a few days, all of his children died, and he lost everything he owned. But Job still respected God and shunned evil. He didn't blame God for his suffering. That showed his respect, or fear, of God. He didn't say bad things about God. That was shunning evil.

As you grow older, certain things may happen that won't make sense to you. You may wonder what is happening. But be like Job. Keep on trusting God. Fear Him and shun evil. Then you'll have wisdom and understanding no matter what life holds.

A POWER NOTE

Write Job 28:28 on a card. Put the card up near your mirror so you will see it every day. Remember to honor (or fear) God and shun evil each day.

FOREVER IS REAL

Find It in the Bible

Trust in the LORD forever, for the LORD,
the LORD himself, is the Rock eternal.

ISAIAH 26:4

Some animals live a really long time—longer than most humans. In fact, some live for centuries. A Galapagos tortoise can live for 175 years. The rougheye rockfish can live for 200 years. And the ocean quahog, a kind of clam, can live for 400 years! But none of them live forever. Nothing lasts forever. Nothing except God. And you.

When you believed in Jesus as your Savior, He immediately gave you a new life—eternal life. You will die physically one day, but then your spirit and soul will be in the presence of God. And one day, the day of the Rapture, your body will become like Jesus' resurrected body. You will spend forever in heaven.

Unlike even the ocean quahog, you will live forever and ever and ever . . . and it will be wonderful because you will be with Jesus! Take time to thank God for eternal life through Christ.

A POWER NOTE

Look up the words to the hymn *Amazing Grace*. You can find them in a hymnal at church or look for them on the Internet. Read all of the verses and write down three things that you look forward to asking Jesus when you get to heaven.

QUIET STRENGTH

Find It in the Bible

This is what the Sovereign LORD, the Holy One
of Israel, says: "In repentance and rest is your salvation,
in quietness and trust is your strength,
but you would have none of it."

ISAIAH 30:15

What's the quietest you've ever been? (And no, being asleep doesn't count.) The Anechoic Test Chamber at Orfield Laboratories in south Minneapolis is the quietest room in the world. It absorbs 99.99 percent of all noise. Some of the scientists who tested it couldn't stand to be in it longer than forty-five minutes. It was too quiet! Do you think you could stand the quiet longer than that?

This verse in Isaiah explains that strength is found in "quietness and trust." The people of Judah were afraid of tough nations like Assyria. They decided to seek the help of countries like Egypt instead of trusting God to protect them. God told the prophet Isaiah that if His people trusted Him and waited for Him to act, instead of grumbling and doing things their way, He would gladly help them.

Being quiet doesn't mean you don't ask for help when you need it. It means your heart is peaceful as you trust God and are willing to wait on Him to act.

A POWER NOTE

See how long you can go without talking or making noise of any kind. While you are being quiet, write a list of ways you can show others that you trust God.

I KNOW YOU!

Find It in the Bible

Before I formed you in the womb I knew you,
before you were born I set you apart.

JEREMIAH 1:5

When you were a baby inside your mother, no one knew much about you. Your parents knew you were there, but they didn't know what you would look like or what color your hair or eyes would be.

But God knows! Even before you were born, God knew all about you—your shoe size and hair color, even what is happening in your life today. God told Jeremiah that He knew all about him before he was born. God had a special purpose for Jeremiah: to deliver His messages to the people of Judah.

God knows all about you too, and He wants you to join His family. He has great plans for you! When you're scared or lonely or feeling unnoticed, remember that God knows all about you. Nothing takes Him by surprise.

Like Jeremiah, God has set you apart to do something special for Him. Stay close to Him and let Him guide you. He will be with you every day of your life!

A POWER NOTE

Create a collage about *you*! Find some old magazines and cut out small pictures of things that you like, activities you like to do, or things that mean a lot to you. Now write your name in the middle of a piece of paper. Glue all the magazine pictures around your name. Thank God that He knows everything about you, and He loves you.

IT'S GOOD TO BE KING

Find It in the Bible

Josiah was eight years old when he became king . . .
He did what was right in the eyes of the LORD and
followed the ways of his father David.

2 CHRONICLES 34:1–2

Are you good at math? Could you pass a university-level math test? Many eight year olds are just learning how to multiply. A pair of eight-year-old Nigerian twins, Peter and Paula Imafidon, who live in England, broke the world record for passing the University of Cambridge's advanced mathematics test. This is a test that most adults would fail! The twins beat their own sister's record. She was nine when she passed that test!

Think that's amazing? Check this out: Josiah was an eight year old who did what most kids only dream of—he ruled a country as its king!

When Josiah grew up, he brought changes to Judah after a priest found a copy of God's Law in the temple. Josiah wanted the people to be right with God. For a long time they had not obeyed God.

You don't have to rule a country or be a super genius to make a difference for God. When you do what's right, people notice and this pleases God.

A POWER NOTE

You can do great things for God just the way you are. On a piece of paper, draw a circle. Write your name in the circle. Then draw lines coming out of the circle. On each line, write the name of someone you know. These are the people you can tell about Jesus.

LOST AND FOUND

Find It in the Bible

He went up to the temple of the LORD with the people of Judah,
the inhabitants of Jerusalem, the priests and the prophets—
all the people from the least to the greatest. He read
in their hearing all the words of the Book of the Covenant,
which had been found in the temple of the LORD.

2 KINGS 23:2

Wʜat if you lost something really, really important . . . but didn't realize it was missing? "That can't happen," you might say. If you lost something you use every day, like your backpack, you'd notice. It might take you a little longer to miss a treasured possession that you keep put away safely. But soon you would realize that it was missing. We keep things that are important near to us, and we look at them often.

And that was the problem for the people of Israel. You see, they lost the Book of the Covenant (God's laws, the first few books of our Bibles) because they didn't use it anymore. This probably happened slowly. The priests stopped reading from the book for teaching and for festivals. The kings no longer turned to it for advice. And soon, everyone forgot about it.

That is, until Josiah became king. This young man realized the importance of the book he had found, like a buried treasure. He treated it with honor and respect. He read the book aloud to the people so they could follow what was in the book.

A POWER NOTE

What about you? Do you treat your Bible like a newly discovered treasure? Or would it take you a long time to miss it if it got lost?

FAMILY TIES

Find It in the Bible

But Ruth replied, "Don't urge me to leave you or to turn back from you.
Where you go I will go, and where you stay I will stay. Your people
will be my people and your God my God."

RUTH 1:16

What makes up a family? A mom and dad with kids, brothers and sisters, grandpas and grandmas—all of these people are family. In the animal kingdom, baby animals have special names. For instance, a baby swan is called a cygnet (*sig-net*), a baby platypus is a puggle, and a baby fox is a kit. And those parents care for their families, similar to what human parents do. Families are very important.

Tragedy struck Naomi and her daughters-in-law, Orpah and Ruth. All three of their husbands died. When that happened, Naomi decided to return to her homeland of Israel. She told Ruth and Orpah they should return to their families. But because Ruth loved her mother-in-law so much, she told Naomi that she would go with her wherever she went. Naomi's family would become her family. Ruth even said she would believe in Naomi's God.

Ruth chose to leave behind the idol worship of her homeland to follow the one true God.

When you believe in Jesus as your Savior, you become part of God's family. You become His child.

A POWER NOTE

Want to know what eventually happened to Ruth and Naomi? Keep reading the book of Ruth.

No Separation

Find It in the Bible

For I am convinced that neither death nor life, neither angels
nor demons, neither the present nor the future, nor any powers,
neither height nor depth, nor anything else in all creation,
will be able to separate us from the love of God
that is in Christ Jesus our Lord.

ROMANS 8:38-39

Lake Baikal, in the southern region of Siberia, Russia, is one of the oldest and largest lakes in the world. It has twenty-seven islands, the longest being forty-five miles long. Over 300 rivers pour water into Lake Baikal, and it is drained by one river, the Angara River. It is the deepest lake in the world. In fact, parts of the lake bottom are actually below sea level. Now that's deep!

God promises us that nothing in the universe, the farthest star or the deepest lake, can separate us from His love. Things can happen to separate us from people we care about. The separation may be small—going to school removes you from people you love. It might also be bigger. Someone you love might move away or even die. Being away from someone you care about can be difficult. You feel the loss of that person's love.

But God promises that we can never be separated from His love. No matter what happens, He loves you and cares about you.

A POWER NOTE

Pour some salt into a glass of water and stir it. Now try to separate the salt from the water. You can't do it. Taste the water—can you taste the salt in it? Even though you can't see the salt, it's still there, and there's no way you can separate it, just like you can never separate yourself from God's love.

SLEEPING SOUNDLY

Find It in the Bible

In peace I will lie down and sleep, for you alone,
LORD, make me dwell in safety.

PSALM 4:8

You probably sleep eight or nine hours every night. Some animals sleep a whole lot more than that! The sleepiest animal of all is the koala bear, which sleeps twenty to twenty-two hours every day. Even your cat is a pretty sleepy animal, as most cats sleep about eleven to twelve hours a day.

Sleep is good for you, as it gives your body the rest it needs. But sometimes falling asleep can be difficult. Maybe you feel a little worried, or you can't stop feeling afraid.

When David wrote this psalm, he knew that God would be with him wherever he went and wherever he slept. David grew up as a shepherd, sleeping in the fields with his sheep. Later in his life, David had to run away into the desert to escape from someone who wanted to hurt him. Even when he was running for his life and not in a familiar place, David slept peacefully each night. How? He trusted God to protect him and keep him safe.

No matter what you are thinking about when you go to bed, know that God is watching over you. He can keep you safe. So close your eyes and sleep!

A POWER NOTE

Tonight, when you go to bed, say a prayer out loud before you fall asleep. Thank God for watching over you every night and for protecting you while you sleep. Remember that no matter where you are, He is with you.

A New Day

Find It in the Bible

Because of the LORD's great love we are not consumed,
for his compassions never fail. They are new every morning;
great is your faithfulness.

LAMENTATIONS 3:22–23

While you slept last night, the earth rotated on its axis (the imaginary line down the center that it turns around). Did you know that the earth is rotating at about 1,000 miles per hour? When the area where you live turns away from the sun, it looks like the sun "sets" and it gets dark. While you sleep, the world keeps on spinning and when your area turns back to face the sun, it is morning! Now the sun rises.

Every morning is a new day. Was yesterday a bad day? Today is a new day. Did you do some things that you are ashamed of yesterday? Today is a new day. Did someone say something mean to you yesterday? Forget about it. Today is a new day.

Whatever happened yesterday is yesterday's news. If you have to ask God (or someone else) for forgiveness, do it today. Otherwise, leave what happened yesterday in yesterday. God's compassion and His grace are new every morning. You can't wear Him out or wear Him down or use Him up. Every day begins anew.

A POWER NOTE

Draw a picture of a big sun peeking up over the horizon at sunrise. Beneath the picture write, "God loves me today and every day." Put the drawing in a place you will see it every morning and be reminded of God's great love each day.

GOD'S ARMOR

Find It in the Bible

Finally, be strong in the Lord and in his mighty power.
Put on the full armor of God, so that you can take your
stand against the devil's schemes.

EPHESIANS 6:10–11

When soldiers go into battle, they need to be protected. You've probably seen pictures of medieval knights wearing armor. Sometimes they wore chain mail, which is body armor made of thousands of small metal rings linked together. They also carried a weapon (often a sword) and a shield. The armor had to fit perfectly so that the knight could fight while wearing it. Even the lightest suit of armor would have weighed about fifty pounds! That weight would have been like carrying a child piggyback on the battlefield!

You aren't a knight, but you have a battle to fight, too. God says that the devil fights against you. He attacks you by discouraging you, tempting you to disobey God, and tempting you to hurt other people. But God gives you armor to protect you from the devil!

He gives you the belt of truth, the breastplate of righteousness, shoes to prepare you to tell people about Him, the shield of faith, the helmet of salvation, and the sword of the Spirit.

A POWER NOTE

Make a shield! Cut the shape of a shield out of a large piece of cardboard and glue cardboard handles onto it. Color the front of the shield, and write "faith" on it somewhere to remind you that God's armor protects you.

Secret Keeper

Find It in the Bible

A gossip betrays a confidence, but a trustworthy person keeps a secret.

PROVERBS 11:13

Trust is the basis of any friendship. If you have a friend you can trust, you tell that person your little secrets—like your thoughts about someone or your fears. You know your friend won't make fun of you by gossiping and telling anyone else.

You also know that some people *can't* be trusted. How can you identify those people? Well, if you're with someone who is talking about a classmate and shares that person's secrets, then you know that your secrets won't be safe with that person either. You can't trust that person.

Being trustworthy is closely related to being honest. When someone tells you a secret, you know how tempting it can be to share that secret with other people. But a good friend keeps the secret and does not gossip. A true friend is trustworthy!

A POWER NOTE

Ask yourself if you are someone who keeps your promises, or someone who likes to share gossip with others. Sometimes it makes people feel important to talk about other people. Commit to being a trustworthy friend and list what you can do to show that you can be trusted.

GOD'S TENT

Find It in the Bible

For in the day of trouble he will keep me safe in his dwelling;
he will hide me in the shelter of his sacred tent
and set me high upon a rock.

PSALM 27:5

Have you ever been chased by a bully? What did you want most? Chances are you wanted a safe place to hide or you wanted someone strong who could protect you from the bully. You wanted protection.

David, who wrote this psalm, often needed protection against his enemies. To stay safe, David spent years hiding from his enemies. Sometimes he camped in the wilderness where his enemies had a hard time finding him. Sometimes he stayed in caves or in fortresses so he could fight if his enemies came near.

But David knew that his real source of protection was always God. God was David's safe house, his high rock above his enemies. God was always strong enough for David. He always provided for all of David's needs.

Like David you, too, can turn to God in your times of need. Whenever you get scared, lonely, sad, or upset you can go to God and He will help you with your problems.

A POWER NOTE

The next time you have a big problem and feel all alone, remember God is always with you. Read Psalm 27 slowly to yourself and imagine God sitting next to you, reading it with you. Underline words or verses that give you courage.

DON'T JUDGE OTHERS

Find It in the Bible

Do not judge, or you too will be judged.

MATTHEW 7:1

Sometimes we are tempted to look at other people and pick out things about them that we would change if we could. Whether it's their habits or the way they dress or act, we can judge them on lots of things. But just as other people have qualities to judge, we also have qualities by which other people might judge us. In fact, God will judge us the same way we judge others.

Part of the reason we are told not to judge other people is that we are not perfect either. To think others need to change when we have a lot we need to change in ourselves is not fair. We are also told not to judge because, as Mother Teresa said, "If you judge people, you have no time to love them." Mother Teresa was a nun who served the poorest of the poor in Calcutta, India. She didn't judge. She loved.

Each time you judge someone, you are focusing on that person's negative qualities. We can't love people when we only see their negative traits. On the other hand, if we resist the urge to judge others and instead focus on their good qualities, we are better able to love them.

A POWER NOTE

The next time you are tempted to judge someone, take out a piece of paper instead and write down three or more qualities about that person that you like, whether it is kindness, being funny, singing well, being a great goalie, or another quality.

GOD'S CLASSROOM

Find It in the Bible

I am the LORD your God, who teaches you what is
best for you, who directs you in the way you should go.

ISAIAH 48:17

You have probably had a lot of teachers in your life so far—
parents, school teachers, tutors, Sunday school teachers,
music teachers, coaches. Who were your favorite teachers? What
did you learn from them? Why did you like them?

Imagine having God as your teacher! But wait! You don't have to
imagine because He already *is* your teacher! This verse says that
He teaches you every day. He teaches you what is best for you and
what direction you should go! Human teachers can't do that for
you, but God can!

God has given us the Bible to teach us how to live. The Bible tells
us what to do and what not to do to please God. It teaches us who
God is and how much He loves us.

No one teaches like God. Not only does He teach you through the
Bible, but He stays by your side to guide you out of the wrong way
and into the right way. His precious Holy Spirit whispers to your
heart and guides your life. If you listen and obey God's voice, you
will find the joy and peace He wants to give you.

A POWER NOTE

Think of one important lesson you have learned from the Bible.
Write a letter to God and tell Him why you liked that lesson and
what you learned from it! Then thank Him for being the best
teacher ever!

UNDIVIDED ATTENTION

Find It in the Bible

I will give them an undivided heart and put a new spirit in them; I will remove from them their heart of stone and give them a heart of flesh.

 Ezekiel 11:19

Imagine that today is your birthday, and your mom brings you a cupcake at school—your favorite! But just as you're about to take a bite, she says, "Wait! You have to share it with everyone in the class."

One cupcake split twenty ways wouldn't leave very much for you, would it? You'd probably say it wasn't even worth it. Some things just weren't meant to be divided.

The same thing is true of our hearts. God doesn't want us to give a little bit of our hearts to Him—just a few crumbs of our leftover time and energy here and there. He wants all of us.

What does that mean? Well, it means that we should love God more than anything else in our lives. It means we should go to Him in prayer first when we have a problem. It means that if something is distracting us from loving God, we need to get rid of it. The Holy Spirit will help you love God with everything you have. He deserves it!

A POWER NOTE

Write Ezekiel 11:19 on a piece of paper, then divide it by cutting or tearing it into ten pieces. Give one piece to a parent or sibling and ask them to guess what the whole verse says. Can they do it? Now arrange the divided pieces back together again and read the verse out loud.

RADIANT COMMANDS

Find It in the Bible

The precepts of the LORD are right, giving joy to the heart.
The commands of the LORD are radiant, giving light to the eyes.

PSALM 19:8

Did you know that you have cones and rods in your eyes? These are microscopic parts of your eye that process light to make your sight possible. Guess how many cones and rods are in one eye. Five? Ten? How about 120 million rods and 7 million cones in just one eye! That's right; all of those parts work every time you see something.

Cones and rods are necessary because they use light to tell your brain about the shapes and colors your eyes are seeing. Without them, you wouldn't be able to tell the shape of a hamburger from the shape of a building or the color orange from the color green.

The Bible says that God's commandments are radiant and give light to our eyes. When we follow His commandments, we see and appreciate the beauty around us. Without the light of His Word, we wouldn't be able to tell what is lovely from what is gross or what is good from what is bad. God's commandments shine light on our lives and help us see the world the way that He created us to see it.

A POWER NOTE

Cut photos out of an old magazine of objects that are similar in shape. Paste objects that are circular on one page. On another paste objects that are triangular. Thank God that you can learn the difference between right and wrong through the light of His Word.

HeaR, HeaR!

Find It in the Bible

Whether you turn to the right or to the left, your ears will hear a
voice behind you, saying, "This is the way; walk in it."

ISAIAH 30:21

Owls have very sensitive ears. As the owl flies high in the sky
above, it can hear the faintest movement of a small animal
on the ground far below. How? The feathers around its face act
like a radar screen and collect even the tiniest sound signals from
the air. Then the feathers focus the sound into the owl's ears, and
it takes action.

When you hear good news, what action do you take? You
probably pass it on. But when you hear bad news, what do you
do? The prophet Isaiah had prophecies for Judah and many
other nations. Many times, he had bad news of God's judgment
for the wrongs the people did. He also knew that they ignored
or complained about what they heard. But this time, Isaiah had
good news.

This chapter in Isaiah is a prophecy about the Savior to come.
That Savior didn't come in Isaiah's lifetime. But He came! His life
is the good news Christians share all over the world.

A POWER NOTE

Ask your mom or dad if you can look at a newspaper. If your
parents don't receive a daily newspaper, you can find newspapers
in the library and even on the Internet. Read through some of
the articles and notice whether they tell good news or bad news.
Think how wonderful it is that God's salvation is the best good
news in the whole universe.

Keep Your Balance

Find It in the Bible

Be very strong; be careful to obey all that is written in
the Book of the Law of Moses, without turning aside
to the right or to the left.

JOSHUA 23:6

If you've ever crashed your bike or fallen off of a skateboard, you know how it hurts. Whether you were going too fast or hit an obstacle, you usually fall from a bike or a skateboard because your balance is thrown off for one reason or another. When that happens, you end up leaning too far right or left, and you fall.

Temptation is the obstacle that tries to get us off balance as we live. If we give in and do something we shouldn't, we fall—and suffer. Sin not only hurts us; it also hurts God!

That's why Joshua told the people of Israel to obey the Book of the Law of Moses. If they obeyed God and did not turn aside and follow temptation, they would remain strong.

God gives us rules to follow so that we don't fall into temptation and hurt ourselves. He loves us and wants us to keep on balance by living His way. If we fall, however, we know God will help us get up and get back on balance to live for Him.

A POWER NOTE

Fill a plastic cup with water. Now go outside and try to balance the cup on two fingers of your left hand while you walk. It is pretty hard to balance the cup. Now try to balance it in the palm of your hand. That is much easier. Keep your life on balance by staying in the palm of God's hand.

LARGER THAN LIFE

Find It in the Bible

But will God really dwell on earth? The heavens, even the
highest heaven, cannot contain you. How much less
this temple I have built!

1 KINGS 8:27

What is the largest building you've ever been in? A museum? A skyscraper? A huge cathedral? Imagine how many people can fit in that building. The temple King Solomon built in Jerusalem was huge. Hundreds of people would come into it every day to worship God and ask for forgiveness for their sins. The entire temple was 2,700 square feet, which is about the size of a four-bedroom house. The roof was forty-five feet high, which means it was a little taller than a four-story building. And yet, Solomon said that the highest skies can't hold God, let alone a temple, even one as big as the one in Jerusalem! God is so big that nothing can contain Him. We can't imagine something that big.

The next time you are scared or lonely or sad, remember how big God is. He is bigger than you can imagine, which means He is also bigger than any problem or situation that you can imagine. When you are going through tough times, don't ever forget that God cares deeply about you and is big enough to overcome all of your worries and problems.

A POWER NOTE

Use dish soap or shampoo to create a large bubble. Try to hold it in your hand. After a while the bubble will pop! Just like air is everywhere and can't be contained by the bubble, God is everywhere and can't be contained by anything.

WHAT'S ON THE MENU?

Find It in the Bible

Live such good lives among the pagans that, though they
accuse you of doing wrong, they may see your good deeds and
glorify God on the day he visits us.

1 PETER 2:12

Quick: What is your favorite restaurant? Why do you like
that restaurant? Maybe it has a certain food you enjoy. Or
maybe the inside looks super cool. Either way, when you hear
that restaurant's name, you have good thoughts.

Now think about a restaurant you don't like because the food
is terrible and the service is slow. You'd rather not ever go there
again. The name of that restaurant brings up bad memories.

Think about your life as though you were a restaurant. When
you tell people you are a Christian, you are putting God's name
on the front. But what do you serve at your restaurant? Acts of
kindness and encouraging words? Or do you serve gossip and
unkind actions?

As a Christian, you have God's name on your life, so you should
live in a way that even if people don't like you because you serve
God, they will see all the good you do and end up glorifying Him.

A POWER NOTE

Make a menu for your restaurant. Take out a piece of paper and
write God's name on top. Then list the "food items" that you will
serve at your restaurant—attitudes and actions that please God.
You can write things like "help around the house" or "say kind
words to others." Then serve some up today!

ALWAYS Be READY

Find It in the Bible

Always be prepared to give an answer to everyone who
asks you to give the reason for the hope that you have.
But do this with gentleness and respect.

1 PETER 3:15

Mike's friend asked him about why he believed in Jesus. Mike stuttered a little bit and coughed a couple times. He said some Bible verses talk about how everyone sins, how Jesus died for our sins, and how people just have to accept Jesus to be saved. Mike pulled out his Bible, but he couldn't remember where the verses were. Mike had a chance to tell his friend more about Jesus from God's Word, but he wasn't ready.

That's just the kind of situation the apostle Peter wanted people to avoid. That's why he said we should always be prepared to answer anyone who asks us about why we have hope in Jesus.

How can you be prepared? You need to know God's Word and memorize verses that are important for telling others about Jesus. Memorize your personal story about how you came to believe in Christ. That way you'll always be ready to tell your story.

A POWER NOTE

Write out your faith-story. It doesn't have to be exciting or wild— just true and genuine. Put in some Bible verses that you think are important to share, such as Romans 3:23, 6:23, 5:8, 10:9–10, and 10:13. Now you are prepared to tell others about your hope in Christ.

BLESSINGS FROM SETBACKS

Find It in the Bible

The LORD restored his fortunes and gave him twice as much as he had before. All his brothers and sisters and everyone who had known him before came and ate with him in his house.

JOB 42:10–11

Certain species of plants only thrive after nature has suffered a serious disaster. In Alaska, a lovely plant with tall stems and beautiful purple flowers thrives. It is called a fireweed. This is because its seeds stay deep in the soil until a forest fire occurs. Once the fire has cleared the land of all trees and bushes, the sun can shine through and provide direct heat and light to the soil, which germinates the seeds of the fireweed. Within a couple of weeks, massive acres of previously scorched land are suddenly overflowing with gorgeous flowers.

Many biblical heroes—Moses, Job, David, Esther—suffered terrible hardships before finding peace and success in life. Their setbacks were often what made them stronger, and wiser for the remaining years of their lives. You, too, may be going through some hard times. Remember that God will use the "fire" of hard times in your life to help you bloom even more abundantly in the future. Trust in His goodness and perfect timing.

A POWER NOTE

Read chapters 1, 2, and 42 in the book of Job to see how people who trust in God can also flourish after disasters.

UNSEEN REWARDS AWAIT

Find It in the Bible

And Elisha prayed, "Open his eyes, LORD, so that he may see." Then the LORD opened the servant's eyes, and he looked and saw the hills full of horses and chariots of fire all around Elisha.

2 KINGS 6:17

Elisha's servant was terrified. The Aramean army had surrounded the city of Dothan just for the purpose of capturing his master, Elisha. As the troops, chariots, and horses set up camp encircling the city, the situation seemed hopeless. But Elisha wasn't worried, and he prayed that God would allow his servant to see that another army was also encamped—God's army. God allowed the servant to see that horses and chariots of fire were surrounding the enemy army!

Then, just for good measure, God blinded the entire Aramean army. Elisha led them all right to the king, who captured them.

At every moment, angels are all around God's people, protecting them. Although you can't see them, always trust that they are there. You can trust God to take care of you.

A POWER NOTE

God promises that His angels watch over His people here on earth. You can't see them, but you can know they are there. Look up Psalm 91:11, write it on an index card, and put it somewhere that you'll see it every day as a reminder that God watches over you.

Seeking a Genuine Master

Find It in the Bible

If you seek him, he will be found by you; but if you
forsake him, he will reject you forever.

1 CHRONICLES 28:9

In the classic children's novel, *The Wizard of Oz*, Dorothy is told that the only one who can show her how to leave Oz and return to Kansas is the Wizard who lives in a distant palace. Thus, Dorothy sets out to find the Wizard. Along the way she is challenged by magical trees, a lion, a scarecrow, a tin man, a witch, and flying monkeys. However, Dorothy refuses to be deterred, and, ultimately, she comes before the Wizard. But, the so-called All-Powerful Wizard turns out to be a fake. He has no mystical powers, and Dorothy and her new friends learn they need to rely only on themselves.

This is very different from our Savior, who, indeed, is all powerful and the Ruler of the universe. When we diligently seek Him, He gladly shares His wisdom, love, care, and protection. If we turn our backs to Him, however, He will not force Himself on us. If we are wise, we will seek Him, serve Him, and obey Him.

A POWER NOTE

The Bible tells us that the streets of heaven are paved in gold. Make a drawing of a golden road leading to God. Why do you want to follow that road?

DAY OF PENTECOST

Find It in the Bible

All of them were filled with the Holy Spirit and began to speak
in other tongues as the Spirit enabled them.

ACTS 2:4

What language do you speak? You probably speak English, and maybe you're also able to speak Spanish or German or Chinese because your family speaks one of those languages. Well, did you know that about 6,500 different languages are spoken in the world? No one would ever be able to learn them all!

After Jesus rose and went to heaven, He left His followers to tell others about His death and resurrection. Jesus knew they couldn't do that without His power, so He filled His followers with the Holy Spirit. This happened on the Day of Pentecost. They began to speak in other languages as the Holy Spirit gave them those languages. A big crowd gathered and those people heard Jesus' followers praising God in many different languages. It was a miracle!

Do you want power to tell others about Jesus? Ask Him to fill you with the Holy Spirit. He has promised to give this gift to every Christian who asks. When you are baptized in the Holy Spirit, you will be filled with God's power to tell others about Him.

A POWER NOTE

Find out how to say, "Jesus loves you," in three different languages. Write the phrases down, practice saying them, and then pray for the people in the world who speak that language that they might know that Jesus loves them.

THE GIFT OF THE SPIRIT

Find It in the Bible

Repent and be baptized, every one of you, in the name of
Jesus Christ for the forgiveness of your sins.
And you will receive the gift of the Holy Spirit.

ACTS 2:38

Imagine a gift that could make you a better person, give you joy, guide your life, convict you when you do wrong, help you do right, and even comfort you in bad times!

Well, what if you learned that such a gift was all wrapped up waiting for you—for free? That gift is the Holy Spirit, and God wants to give Him to you. How do you get the gift? If you are a Christian, you pray and ask Jesus to fill you with His Holy Spirit just like He filled His followers on the Day of Pentecost.

When you ask Jesus to fill you with the Holy Spirit, He will. After the Holy Spirit fills you, He will give you power to do the things He teaches you. He'll guide and comfort and protect you.

A POWER NOTE

On one piece of paper draw a heart and write "My Heart" in big red letters. On another piece of paper draw a heart about the same size and write "The Holy Spirit" in big gold letters. Cut out the gold heart and paste it on top of the red heart. This will help you think about what happens when the Holy Spirit fills your life.

BILLIONS AND BILLIONS

Find It in the Bible

The promise is for you and your children and for all who are
far off—for all whom the Lord our God will call.

ACTS 2:39

The Waltons, who own Walmart, are one of the richest families in the world. They're worth about $136 billion. What would you buy if your family had that much money? Of course, all of that money could still not buy the things that are most important. Money can't buy happiness, people who love you, or a right relationship with God.

But, if you have asked Jesus to forgive your sins, you are part of the truly richest family in the world. You are part of God's family. One important part of your inheritance as a member of God's family is the baptism in the Holy Spirit.

So what is the baptism in the Holy Spirit? It is God the Holy Spirit coming to live in a Christian's life in a special way. He comes to give you power to live for God and power to tell others about Jesus. He comes to live in you as your helper and teacher. He helps you understand God's Word and God's plans for your life. Isn't that an amazing inheritance?

A POWER NOTE

Look up Acts 2:1–4, Acts 10:24,44–48, and Acts 19:1–6. These are three accounts about the baptism in the Holy Spirit. What one thing happened in each of these three accounts? Now read Acts 2:39 again. Is the gift of the baptism in the Holy Spirit for you? Don't leave your family inheritance unclaimed.

WHAT'S IN A NAME?

Find It in the Bible

A good name is more desirable than great riches;
to be esteemed is better than silver or gold.

PROVERBS 22:1

Everyone knows you by your name. Sometimes certain names are popular. If you had been born in 1890, for example, you might have been named Florence or Harry. In 1900, you might have been named Ethel or Henry. The name John seems to be one of the most popular names of all time! If that's your name, you're in good company!

No matter what name you received at birth, you want it to be a "good name"—meaning you want people to know you are a person of good character. You want to be "esteemed." You want people to hear your name and think good things about you because you have proven to be kind, honest, and trustworthy.

King Solomon, the wisest man to ever live, knew a good name was more valuable than any riches or precious gems. Why? Riches and gems can be replaced if they are lost, but a good name is difficult to get back once it is lost. Decide today that you will always act in a way to bring honor to your name and to God.

A POWER NOTE

Did your parents name you after a relative? Does your name have any special meanings? Ask your parents or grandparents what your name means and why they chose it for you. Then think about this: How will you live so that your name will be considered good?

"LET ME HELP"

Find It in the Bible

Praise be to the Lord, to God our Savior, who daily bears our burdens.

PSALM 68:19

Imagine as you carry your backpack, people add little stones to it as you go through the day. Your teachers each give you a small stone. Your friends hand you many different kinds of rocks. Nothing seems really heavy on its own, but added together in your backpack, they create a heavy weight. At the end of the day, your shoulders and your back would hurt as you walked home from school.

But what if your dad walked up behind you and offered to carry your backpack for you? Think how wonderful you would feel to give the backpack over to someone bigger and stronger!

Throughout your day, you may be hurt by some friends, you might worry about school and family, or you might be scared by a bully. Those hurts and worries that you hold onto act like stones that weigh you down. You feel as though you can barely walk.

But then God walks up and says, "Here, let me help. Give me those burdens. I'll bear them for you." You give Him everything—the weight is gone—you are free!

A POWER NOTE

Take an old bag or backpack and fill it with rocks. Walk around your house for five minutes. See how heavy it is? Then take the backpack off and walk around your house again. Notice a difference? Remind yourself that God wants to carry your burdens for you.

AT A CROSSROADS

Find It in the Bible

Stand at the crossroads and look; ask for the ancient paths,
ask where the good way is, and walk in it, and
you will find rest for your souls.

JEREMIAH 6:16

Times Square in New York City may be the most well-known crossroads in the world. In fact, this intersection—Broadway and Seventh Avenue—is called the Crossroads of the World.

The phrase *at a crossroads* is also a way of saying that a person needs to make a decision. The people of Judah were at a crossroads, a decision point. God gave the prophet Jeremiah a message for the people. Because of their wrongdoing, they would soon be under siege. A siege is when an enemy nation sends troops to surround a city in order to take it over. The people had to make a choice. They could choose to continue sinning, but they had another choice. God wanted His people to return to "the ancient paths"—to worship only the one true God as their forefathers had. If they did, God promised that they would find rest.

Centuries later, Jesus used the same phrase, *rest for your souls*, to tell His listeners that He was the way to forgiveness. Those who trusted Him would find rest for their souls. Walk His way and find rest!

A POWER NOTE

At a crossroads? On a piece of paper, write your choices. Pray about your decision and wait until you feel God's peace to move forward.

LOSING AND GAINING

Find It in the Bible

For whoever wants to save their life will lose it,
but whoever loses their life for me will find it.

MATTHEW 16:25

Many people focus on themselves and what they want. Their attitude is, "I have only one life, and I'm going to live it the way I want." They decide that they want to be happy and comfortable—and they don't care who might get hurt in the process. Because that's what often happens when people live only for themselves—other people get hurt.

Jesus says not to live that way. Instead of "saving your own life" (living life the way you want no matter what), He challenges you to "lose your life" (live the way He wants no matter what). God says that when you lose your life that way, you actually *find* it. Why? Because in both good times and bad, God knows what is best for you. He will guide you into the life He had planned for you all along. It's the life where you make a difference for Him and His kingdom in this world.

Which do you choose? Do you want to find life? Then live for God!

A POWER NOTE

Try to unscramble this sentence. Then decide if you want it to be true for you.

I ocohes ot loes ym feli rof rhCsti.

(I choose to lose my life for Christ.)

GOD'S GENTLE WHISPER

Find It in the Bible

After the earthquake came a fire, but the LORD was not in the fire.
And after the fire came a gentle whisper.

1 KINGS 19:12

The prophet Elijah was threatened with death by Queen Jezebel, who was angry that Elijah had defeated the prophets of Baal (see 1 Kings 18). A depressed Elijah ran for his life.

God spoke to Elijah when he hid from Jezebel. How would you expect a powerful God to sound? God could have used something as strong as an earthquake to communicate. Why not? Earthquakes get our attention. The most powerful earthquake ever recorded was in Chile on May 22, 1960. It registered 9.5 on the Richter scale and killed over four thousand people.

But God chose not to speak to Elijah through a powerful earthquake. Instead, God spoke to Elijah in an unusual way: a whisper. You have to be close to whisper to someone, and God was close to His brokenhearted prophet. God knew what His depressed prophet needed—not a show of force, but a show of love.

God speaks through His Word, the Bible, and through the wise words of people in your life. Are you listening? Draw close to God and He will draw close to you.

A POWER NOTE

Write down these promises from God: Psalm 10:17; Psalm 32:8; Psalm 34:15; Psalm 37:28. The next time you feel worried or are afraid, think about God whispering these promises to you.

YOUR POWER SOURCE

Find It in the Bible

Suddenly a chariot of fire and horses of fire appeared and separated the two of them, and Elijah went up to heaven in a whirlwind.

2 KINGS 2:11

God sent Elisha to help Elijah and to someday take his place as prophet. Instead of Elijah retiring and living someplace restful, however, God took him home to heaven. He is one of two people mentioned in the Bible who didn't die. (The first was Enoch in Genesis 5:24.)

Imagine that! A chariot and horses of fire separated Elisha from Elijah. Then Elijah went to heaven in a whirlwind! How surprised do you think Elisha was?

As Elijah went to heaven, he dropped his mantle, or cloak. Elisha picked up that cloak, which was a symbol that the Holy Spirit was now on Elisha in a new way. He walked to the Jordan River, hit the water with Elijah's mantle, and the water parted. Now it was Elisha's turn to do amazing things for God.

Did you know that it's also your turn to do amazing things for God? Ask Jesus to baptize you in the Holy Spirit so you, too, can do great things for God.

A POWER NOTE

Do you have a flashlight in your house? If not, ask your parents if you can get one. Put the batteries inside the flashlight and turn it on to see the light. Now, take out the batteries and try to turn it on. Nothing happens. The batteries provide power for the flashlight, and the Holy Spirit provides power to God's people.

Jesus > Me

Find It in the Bible

He must become greater; I must become less.

JOHN 3:30

The math symbols "greater than" (>) and "less than" (<) are important for math equations. For instance $2 > 1$ (two is greater than one) and $1 < 2$ (one is less than two). So if the story of John the Baptist were a math equation, it would look like this: John < Jesus. And that would suit John the Baptist just fine.

The Old Testament prophets said that a messenger would come before Jesus and get people ready for His arrival. John was this messenger. He knew that his job was to point people to Jesus. He was completely selfless.

In our world today, it can be difficult to be selfless. So many people want attention, or they want to be popular. Many people spend so much time thinking about themselves and what they want that they don't think (or care) about anyone else.

How much better to be a person who lives for Jesus, someone who, like John the Baptist, always wants Jesus to get the glory. When you let Jesus be in control, you'll be the kind of person who pleases God.

A POWER NOTE

Draw the following equation on a piece of paper and color the letters in bright colors with crayons or paints or markers. Put it where you can see it every morning.

JESUS > ME

DOOR TO YOUR HEART

Find It in the Bible

Here I am! I stand at the door and knock. If anyone hears
my voice and opens the door, I will come in and eat
with that person, and they with me.

REVELATION 3:20

When you go to a friend's house, the first thing you do is knock on the person's door. If your friend is home, he or she will answer the door and let you inside. You and your friend can have lots of fun together, but first they must open the door for you.

Jesus is also knocking. He is at the door to each person's heart. He is patiently waiting for that person to open the door and let Him come in. When they decide to open the door, He is excited to see them. Not only will He come inside. He will also spend time with them. He does this because He wants to be with them.

If you have already accepted Jesus as your Savior, He has come in and is living in your heart by His Holy Spirit. But He's still knocking on the doors of the hearts of everyone who hasn't let Him in yet. What can you do to help them hear Jesus knocking? Can you help them understand how great it is when Jesus comes in?

A POWER NOTE

Draw a picture of a door on a piece of paper. Cut open the top, bottom, and one side of the door so you can open it. On the inside of the door write "Come in, Lord Jesus." Now thank Him for His love.

see you soon!

Find It in the Bible

"Men of Galilee," they said, "why do you stand here looking into the sky? This same Jesus, who has been taken from you into heaven, will come back in the same way you have seen him go into heaven."

ACTS 1:11

Saying good-bye to people you love can be difficult. Maybe you have to say good-bye to your grandparents or your cousins after a visit. Maybe a friend is moving away to a new town, and you know you'll miss him terribly. Usually you say something like, "I'll see you again soon!" You don't know when that will be, but you hope that you'll have another fun visit before too long.

Jesus returned to heaven after His time on earth. After speaking with His friends, He went up and up into the sky until a cloud hid Him. Jesus' friends stood staring up where He had gone, and two angels came to speak to them. The angels basically said, "He'll be back! You'll see Him again!"

When Jesus returns to earth, He will take people who believe in Him as their Savior to be with Him in heaven. We don't know when this will happen, so we want to be ready always. Like Jesus' followers back then, we can say to Jesus, "See You soon!"

A POWER NOTE

Draw a picture of what you think will happen when Jesus comes back. Use markers, crayons, yarn, ribbon . . . whatever you like! Hang the picture in your room and write this verse on the bottom or the back. Keep yourself ready for Jesus' return at any time.

LOST AND FOUND

Find It in the Bible

But we had to celebrate and be glad, because this brother of yours
was dead and is alive again; he was lost and is found.

LUKE 15:32

Have you ever thought about running away from home? It's not a good idea. Sadly, however, a lot of kids around your age or just a little older *do* run away from home. In fact, between 1.6 and 2.8 million youths run away every year. Sometimes they get into such trouble that they can't go home again. They must be terribly frightened—and their parents terribly worried.

Jesus told the story of a young man who left his home. He decided to take his money and go out on his own and have a great time. The great time and new friends only lasted until his money ran out. Then he got really hungry. So he decided to go home. He was worried that his dad would be mad, but instead his dad celebrated!

Jesus used this story as an example of how God responds when we come to Him. No matter what we have done, He always welcomes us back. He is waiting with open arms.

A POWER NOTE

Play a game of lost and found with some friends. Have everyone close their eyes while one person hides a ball or other small object. Then see who can be the first to find the hidden object. While you are having silly fun with your friends, remember that God is serious about finding lost souls.

"LIAR, LIAR, PANTS ON FIRE"

Find It in the Bible

For the LORD your God detests anyone who does these
things [cheats and lies], anyone who deals dishonestly.

DEUTERONOMY 25:16

So where did that saying, "Liar, liar, pants on fire," come from?
No one really knows, although some people think it started
from a poem by William Blake published in 1810 that begins,
"Deceiver, dissembler, your trousers are alight" . . . which isn't
quite as catchy.

But let's be honest. Every person has lied. This includes telling
your parents that you didn't eat any cookies or snacks before
dinner, that you didn't sneak the dog pieces of food from the
table, or that you blamed someone else for something you did—
everyone lies.

No one likes being called a liar (or having our pants on fire!) even
if it's true. And we hate it worse when it *is* true and we get caught
in our lie. But you know who hates it worst of all? God.

The word *detest* means "dislike intensely." The Bible says that God
detests anyone who deals dishonestly, and being dishonest means
lying. Telling the truth, even if it gets you in trouble, shows how
much of a big kid you are, and how much you love God. It's best
to tell the truth.

A POWER NOTE

If you've told a lie within the last few days and haven't gotten
caught, go and confess the truth to whoever you lied to. They may
be mad at first, but in the end, it'll be worth it.

PROMISE MADE, PROMISE KEPT

Find It in the Bible

Asa's heart was fully committed to the LORD all his life.

2 CHRONICLES 15:17

A commitment is a promise. If you commit yourself to wrestling or gymnastics, that means you promise to come to all the practices, try your hardest, and work together with the rest of your teammates. But sometimes staying committed can be difficult. Your muscles ache, and the practices are long. Yet fully committed people, no matter how young they are, keep on doing what they promised to do.

King Asa stayed fully committed to the Lord all his life. To be committed to the Lord means that you promise yourself to God, that you promise to live your life showing the world how much you love God and how much God loves you.

What an example Asa is to us! Did he get tired sometimes? Probably. Did he get tempted? Certainly. Did he mess up once in a while? Most likely. But he stayed committed.

How can you follow Asa's example? A life is made up of days, hours, and minutes. Walk with God today, this hour, this minute. Seek to please Him right now. All of those "right nows" will lead up to a fully committed life.

A POWER NOTE

Print "Right *now*, follow Jesus" on a card and put it in a place where you'll see it several times a day—like in your school locker or in your pocket or on your mirror. Use it as a reminder that you just need to decide to follow Jesus in this moment.

LIGHT IN THE DARK

Find It in the Bible

In the same way, let your light shine before others,
that they may see your good deeds and
glorify your Father in heaven.

MATTHEW 5:16

When was the last time you used a flashlight? Were you camping? Did the electricity go out at night? The flashlight beam was probably comforting and inviting in the dark. The first flashlight was invented in 1899 by British inventor David Misell. The invention depended on dry cell batteries that also had just been invented. The flashlight idea depended on these specific kinds of batteries to make it work.

Jesus describes the world as a dark house. In the same way that a flashlight shows you the way through a dark room and comforts you with its light, God wants you to be a light in the dark world. If you act like Jesus, loving and forgiving others, you will be a bright light that attracts people and shows them the way to Jesus.

How can you do that? Think again about your flashlight. How does it work? The batteries power the light. Without them, the flashlight is useless. The Holy Spirit gives you the power to keep acting like Jesus.

A POWER NOTE

Get your friends together and play flashlight tag! You need a dark place for this (like your back yard at night with a parent's permission, or even a dark basement). Each player needs a flashlight. Try to tag each other without turning the flashlights on for more than three seconds at a time.

THe PeRFeCT SPoT

Find It in the Bible

Ah, Sovereign LORD, you have made the heavens and
the earth by your great power and outstretched arm.
Nothing is too hard for you.

JEREMIAH 32:17

Ever find yourself in just the right place? Maybe you had the best seat at a ball game or stood in the perfect spot at a parade and saw everything clearly. Something else is in the perfect spot: planet earth. Though 93 million miles from the sun, if it were any closer, the planet would be too hot and no one would survive. Any farther away, and the planet would be too cold. Again, nothing could survive. Also, the moon's orbit helps keep the earth in perfect balance.

God had all of that in mind when He created the universe. He had a plan that He carried out to make sure life continued on earth.

Though hard times come, do you believe that God can do the impossible in your life? If He is powerful enough to create our amazing world, do you think He is powerful enough to care for you?

A POWER NOTE

Ask your parents if they will help you find a map of the state where you live. Next, find the city where you live on the map and draw a red dot there. Write your name beside it. That is where you live—the perfect spot God has placed you to do great things for Him. Ask Him what He wants you to do for Him.

JUNE

BURIED TREASURE

Find It in the Bible

For where your treasure is,
there your heart will be also.

LUKE 12:34

In June of 2011, the most spectacular "buried" treasure ever found was located inside six underground chambers in the Sree Padmanabhaswamy Temple in southern India. The temple was built in the sixteenth century and, until recently, no one knew of the secret chambers containing gold necklaces and bracelets. It also held one ton of gold in the shape of trinkets, sacks of diamonds, jewelry studded with diamonds and emeralds, other precious stones wrapped in silk bundles, and thirty-seven pounds of gold and other coins.

Jesus tells us that we care most about what is important to us—our "treasure." The verses before this describe how Jesus' followers should not worry about having food or clothing because God will take care of them. He says to take care of others and share. Don't try to keep treasure here on earth, but instead, keep it in heaven. That means we don't worry about how much we have on this earth, but we focus on one day being in heaven, where the ultimate treasure is waiting!

A POWER NOTE

Look around your room. What "treasures" do you have there? Could you share some of that with someone else who could use it? Ask your parents to help you give away some of your treasures.

JUST HOW SMALL?

Find It in the Bible

"Truly I tell you, if you have faith as small as a mustard seed, you can say to this mountain, 'Move from here to there,' and it will move. Nothing will be impossible for you."

MATTHEW 17:20

A mustard seed is just one or two millimeters in diameter. If you drew a line down the center on a penny, you could fit between ten and twenty seeds across in a straight line. You would need about three hundred mustard seeds to cover the surface of a penny!

Clearly the mustard seed is super small, and that was the point Jesus wanted to make to His disciples. God is very powerful, so if you only trust and believe in Him a tiny bit, it's enough. You don't have to worry if you have enough faith because *He* is powerful enough—no matter what.

Remember, just a little faith can make big things happen. If you only have faith as small as a mustard seed, God can still do amazing things for you and through you. Have faith in Him!

A POWER NOTE

Do you like hot dogs and hamburgers? The next time you slather mustard on a hot dog or hamburger, think how many thousands of seeds it took to make that mustard. Remind yourself that even a speck of faith the size of one mustard seed is enough to do great things for God.

WeLL-WATeReD

Find It in the Bible

The LORD will guide you always; he will satisfy your needs
in a sun-scorched land and will strengthen your frame.
You will be like a well-watered garden, like a spring
whose waters never fail.

ISAIAH 58:11

Maybe your parents have planted a flower garden or a vegetable garden. If so, you know that a garden needs to be watered often during the summer to keep the plants healthy. Your garden is probably pretty small compared to the biggest flower garden in the world located in the Netherlands. Called the Keukenhof, this garden covers almost eighty acres and has over 7 million flower bulbs. Imagine watering *all those flowers*!

If you forget to water the garden in your yard, the plants will dry up and die. The people of Israel knew what living in a "sun-scorched" land was like. Israel is a land with very little rain. In fact, for three months every year it doesn't rain at all. Water is very precious in a land like that.

The Bible often uses water as a word picture for God or for a person empowered by God. Through the Holy Spirit, God promises to guide you and satisfy your needs. Like a well-watered garden, you will grow and produce fruit—the fruit of the Spirit (Galatians 5:22–23).

A POWER NOTE

You can become "well-watered" by reading God's Word. Take a "drink" by reading these verses: Psalm 1:1–3; John 3:5; 4:7–14.

PRIMING THE PUMP

Find It in the Bible

"Bring the whole tithe into the storehouse, that there may
be food in my house. Test me in this," says the
Lord Almighty, "and see if I will not throw open the
floodgates of heaven and pour out so much blessing
that there will not be room enough to store it."

MALACHI 3:10

A weary traveler crossed a hot and dry land. He was tired,
thirsty, and dirty. To his great joy, he suddenly came upon a
water pump. But the water came with a challenge. A cup of water
was set on the pump with a note that read, "If you drink this cup
of water, it will refresh you for an hour. If you pour this water
into the pump and push the handle up and down, it will give you
an endless stream of water."

The traveler was super thirsty, and the cup of water was tempting.
He had to decide whether to drink the water he could see or
believe what the note said. He decided to trust the message of the
note. So he poured the water into the pump, pushed the handle
up and down, and, sure enough, within two minutes a steady
stream of water came gushing forth.

God asks us to decide whether we will hold tightly to the things
He has given us or be willing to give them away and trust Him to
meet our needs.

A POWER NOTE

God tells us it's okay to test His generosity. Give your time to work
in vacation Bible school or read Bible stories to youngsters. Pay
attention to how God lavishes His "return on investment."

SKY HIGH

Find It in the Bible

The heavens declare the glory of God;
the skies proclaim the work of his hands.

PSALM 19:1

When you look up at the sky, you're literally looking into a vast universe—you just can't see it because it stretches on forever. The solar system is the group of planets, moon, and space debris that orbits around the sun. It is held together by the gravitational pull of the sun, which is almost one thousand times more massive than all the planets put together.

You can't look at the sun because it's too bright, but you can see how it lights up and warms the earth. And you can see the clouds that go across the sky. Scientists have given them names. The big fluffy ones are called cumulus clouds. Cirrus clouds look curly, and stratus clouds look layered.

God could have just made the daytime sky blue—like your childhood drawings. Instead, He created great beauty in the clouds that can bring rain to water the earth. The heavens do indeed declare the glory of God and the skies proclaim the work of His hands.

A POWER NOTE

Lay on the grass on a summer day and stare up at the clouds. Try to figure out what they look like according to their shapes. See if you can name the type of clouds. Thank God for the beautiful work of His hands.

CHANGE OF PLANS

Find It in the Bible
In their hearts humans plan their course,
but the LORD establishes their steps.

PROVERBS 16:9

You have to prepare to go on a family vacation. Your parents probably spend a lot of time looking at maps, planning a budget, getting reservations at attractions and hotels, and figuring out costs for gas, food, and souvenirs. That's a lot of decisions! But all the planning helps to make sure everyone has a good trip and that you don't run out of money along the way!

Even with all the preparations and attention to details, the trip doesn't always go as planned. Maybe the car gets a flat tire or it rains on the day you wanted to go hiking or someone gets sick.

The author of Proverbs knew humans like to make plans, but God ultimately controls what happens. So planning is important, but we should hold our plans loosely. If God chooses to change your plans, don't worry—relax. His plans are always better than you could imagine. He knows what is best for you, and His plans will guide you to your best place.

A POWER NOTE

Design a calendar with all of your plans for the month. You can include class field trips, visits with friends and family, instrument lessons, sports practices, or anything else you may be looking forward to. Around the edge, write out Proverbs 16:9 as a reminder that God plans your future.

TOO YOUNG?

Find It in the Bible

But the LORD said to me, "Do not say, 'I am too young.'
You must go to everyone I send you to and say whatever
I command you. Do not be afraid of them, for I am
with you and will rescue you," declares the LORD.

JEREMIAH 1:7–8

How old does the boss of a company need to be? In England, Joseph Hayat started his own airplane chartering business at the age of seventeen. Mark Zuckerberg and Dustin Moskovitz, the guys who developed Facebook, came up with the idea for Facebook while students at Harvard. Neither had reached the age of twenty!

Jeremiah was a young man when God called him to be a prophet. That was a tough job—so tough that Jeremiah thought he was too young to take it. But God reminded him that no one is too young to do God's will. The God of the universe was big enough and strong enough to take on anyone who would stand against Jeremiah.

Do you think you're too young to live for God? Do you ever feel as though you are not strong enough to stand up for Him? As God said to Jeremiah, so He says to you. "Do not say, 'I am too young.'" You're never too young to help build God's kingdom.

A POWER NOTE

Practice telling someone about God. Ask a brother or sister or a friend to help you practice. First, tell them how God loves you and has helped you. Then you might invite that person to come to church with you or offer to pray with him or her.

BULLIES AND BADDIES

Find It in the Bible

If your enemy is hungry, give him food to eat; if he is thirsty, give him water to drink. In doing this, you will heap burning coals on his head, and the LORD will reward you.

Proverbs 25:21–22

Did you know that trees have "enemies"? These include fungi that can grow through the bark and clog the flow of sap. The honey fungus spreads its spores through thick brown strands called "bootlaces." These grow between the bark and the interior of the tree and cut off the supply of nutrients from the sap.

When Solomon wrote about an "enemy" in this verse, he was talking about people who treat you mean. Or people who, for one reason or another, have decided that they don't like you. The world (and your school) is full of bullies and baddies.

If someone is really bullying you, you need to tell an adult. But with the people who don't treat you very well, this verse comes in handy. It tells you to act completely opposite to how you feel. Instead of getting back at an "enemy," be nice to that person.

A POWER NOTE

Draw a big tree with lots of branches and leaves and roots going deep into the soil. Put your name on the trunk. Now beneath the roots write "God's Word" and "God's Power." Let this remind you that as you feed your heart from God's Word and as you depend on the power of the Holy Spirit, He will help you respond with love and kindness to unkind people.

Love Your Enemies

Find It in the Bible

But to you who are listening I say: Love your enemies,
do good to those who hate you, bless those who curse you,
pray for those who mistreat you.

LUKE 6:27–28

The Bible tells us to do kind things for our enemies—those who hurt or mistreat us (as you read in yesterday's devotional). Jesus is saying the same thing here—and He adds something else: "Pray for those who mistreat you."

The people who are bugging you may make you really mad—so mad you just want to scream! Well, bring that frustration to God. You can talk about those people with Him. After all, there might be a reason why they act mean. Maybe their lives at home are really difficult. Maybe they have parents who are mean to them or are ill. Perhaps they're hurting from something that is going on in their lives that you don't know about.

But God knows. So pray for them. Pray that their problems will get better. Pray that they will have strength to overcome difficulties. And, yes, pray that they'll be nicer people! Remember, God can work miracles!

A POWER NOTE

Who is bugging you the most right now? Write the names of those people on a sticky tab and stick it in your Bible right beside these verses. Pray for those who mistreat you.

LEARN FROM THE BEST

Find It in the Bible

All Scripture is God-breathed and is useful for teaching,
rebuking, correcting and training in righteousness.

2 TIMOTHY 3:16

What do you want to be when you grow up? Do you want to be a dancer, a teacher, an athlete, an artist, or a detective? You have many options to choose from depending on what you like to do, but they all have one thing in common: You have to learn how to be what you want to be.

To be a dancer, you have to learn the technique of dancing. To be a detective, you have to learn to look for clues and investigate carefully. Everything involves learning.

No matter what job you have, you will want to be a follower of Jesus. How do you do that? Well, you need to learn what God says in His Word, the Bible. God gave us the Bible so we can learn about Jesus and what it means to follow Him.

The Bible isn't like every other book. It's not something you read once and then say, "I read it." It's a book you need to read over and over every day of your life. Why? Because it will teach you, rebuke you (meaning show you if you're doing wrong), correct you, and train you to live for God. Make a promise to yourself that you will read the Bible every day.

A POWER NOTE

Take out a piece of paper and write down three things you want to learn about in the Bible. Do you want to learn about joy, love, and miracles? Write it down and work with an adult to find the answers.

STICKING TOGETHER

Find It in the Bible

Listen to your father, who gave you life, and do not
despise your mother when she is old.

Proverbs 23:22

Some animals stick together. Howler monkeys swing through the rain forest trees as a group. Zebras munch on grass together on the African plains. Bats hang around together in empty barns and caves. Often, as young animals grow up, they stay with the group and, because they're stronger than their parents and other aging adults, they help out. For example, elephants stay in herds all their lives, where they protect and find food for one another.

Your parents are raising you to be on your own one day. That's why they are teaching you how to work hard and save your money and be responsible. You will need all of those skills when you grow up. One day, you will leave home and go into the life God has planned for you.

That's all natural. And even though you're supposed to leave home one day, you should always remember where you came from. You should always listen to the advice of your parents and other trusted adults. You honor God when you honor and care for them.

A POWER NOTE

Ask a grandparent or older trusted adult about life when they were kids. Maybe they can tell you what things have changed the most for them. Ask them what advice they would like to give you.

INSIDE OUT

Find It in the Bible

I know, my God, that you test the heart and are
pleased with integrity. All these things I have
given willingly and with honest intent.

1 CHRONICLES 29:17

What does the word *integrity* mean? It's a word that combines all kinds of personal traits such as being honest, trustworthy, moral, decent, and upright. But it goes even deeper. A person can appear to be all of those things but still have evil thoughts. A person could pretend to be all of those things on the outside but really not be on the inside.

Integrity means that what's going on inside of you and outside of you match up. When God looks at your words and actions, He sees integrity. And when He tests your heart (meaning when He looks at your thoughts, attitudes, motives, and intentions), He sees the exact same thing.

God tests your heart. He knows if you have sinned, even if no one else notices. And He honors your integrity—even if no one else notices.

A POWER NOTE

Ask your mom or dad for an old T-shirt that you can write on. Also get a marker. On the outside of the shirt, write "I have integrity." Then, turn the shirt inside-out and write the same thing on the inside of the shirt. Hang the shirt near your closet to remind you that you want to have integrity inside and outside.

TRUE FRIENDSHIP

Find It in the Bible

And Jonathan had David reaffirm his oath out of love for him,
because he loved him as he loved himself.

1 SAMUEL 20:17

Do you have a best friend, a friend who is always there for you
no matter what you do? How long have you been friends?
How about 102 years? That's how long Edith Ritchie and Evie
Middleton have been best friends! They were twins born in 1910
in Scotland. In 2012, they held the record as the oldest living
twins and, according to them, the oldest living best friends as
well.

David and Jonathan were also best friends. It was a little
complicated because David was chosen to replace Saul as king of
Israel, and Jonathan was Saul's son—who would technically be
in line to be the next king. But Jonathan loved his friend David
and trusted God to do what was best.

What does loving someone that way mean? It means *being* the
kind of friend you would want to have! It means taking time,
even when you're busy, to talk to your friend. It means helping
out even when it's not convenient. It means standing by your
friend through hard times and good times.

A POWER NOTE

Make a list of what you want in a best friend. Describe how you
would want that person to act toward you. Then go back through
the list and decide if you are that kind of friend to others. Write
down things you could do to be a better friend.

CHOOSE WISELY

Find It in the Bible

But if serving the LORD seems undesirable to you, then choose
for yourselves this day whom you will serve, whether the gods
your ancestors served beyond the Euphrates, or the
gods of the Amorites, in whose land you are living.
But as for me and my household, we will serve the LORD.

JOSHUA 24:15

Every day you make choices. You decide what to wear for the day and what to eat for breakfast. Some choices don't seem to matter a whole lot (whether you wear the green shirt or the red one), but other choices can make a bigger difference (choosing to wear boots in the summer, for example, would result in really hot feet!). Every choice you make matters in small or big ways.

One choice, however, matters for your life and for your eternity. That's the choice that Joshua was giving to the people of Israel. The people were settling into the land God had promised them. The people of the land had worshiped idols and even the sun and moon. Now Israel was tempted to worship the same false gods.

Joshua told the Israelites they had a choice. They could choose to serve the idols, or they could choose to serve the Lord. But Joshua made it clear that he and his family would choose the Lord.

A POWER NOTE

Today, think about every time you make a choice and why you make it. Why do you get up with your alarm? Why do you choose to wear what you do? Why do you choose what you eat for breakfast or lunch? What would happen if you made different choices?

A SQUEAKY-CLEAN HEART

Find It in the Bible

I baptize you with water for repentance. But after me comes one who is more powerful than I, whose sandals I am not worthy to carry. He will baptize you with the Holy Spirit and fire.

MATTHEW 3:11

Even when Jesus was here on earth, people were being baptized in water. John baptized people who had repented of their sins in the water of a river. Their baptism symbolized removing, or washing away, their sins. John's baptism didn't make anyone clean on the inside.

Do you know how to make yourself clean on the inside? Of course not! Nobody can wash their insides on their own. When you ask Jesus to forgive your sins, His Holy Spirit comes to live in your heart.

But John also taught about baptism in the Holy Spirit. When you are baptized in the Holy Spirit, the Holy Spirit fills you with His presence. Your life overflows with His power to tell others about God's love. You are not only clean on the inside, but you are filled with power to live for God.

A POWER NOTE

Fill an empty pitcher with water. That is what your life looks like when you are saved and the Holy Spirit lives in your heart. Now set the container in the sink or bathtub and fill it with more water so it overflows. That is what your life looks like when you are baptized in the Holy Spirit. God wants to baptize you with His Holy Spirit so you overflow with His presence and power.

THE CATCH OF THE DAY

Find It in the Bible

"Come, follow me," Jesus said, "and I will send
you out to fish for people."

MATTHEW 4:19

Have you ever tried to jump rope with spaghetti? Have you tried to color with toothpicks? Or measure your height with a quarter? Probably not. That's because we don't do those activities that way. Using those materials wouldn't make sense.

Jesus' disciples probably thought the same thing when He told them to fish for people. "Um, Jesus," they might have replied, "don't we usually fish for . . . fish?"

But Jesus wasn't talking about putting a hook in other people's mouths and dragging them home or throwing a net over them. He meant that when His disciples told people about Jesus, those people would want to come into God's kingdom. They would want to hear more about Jesus.

Just as with fishing, telling people about Jesus can be hard and often takes patience. In the end, fishing for people is not just about your hard work because the Holy Spirit helps the people you talk to understand more about God. That's more exciting than fishing for fish!

A POWER NOTE

Draw a whole school of fish on a piece of paper. You might want to color each fish in a unique way. But save room to write the name of someone you know who doesn't believe in Jesus on each fish. Then think how you can tell these people about Jesus the next time you see one of them.

THE GREATEST MANSION

Find It in the Bible

And if I go and prepare a place for you, I will come back and take you to be with me that you also may be where I am.

JOHN 14:3

Connecticut has a mansion worth $190 million. Why so expensive? Well, it might be the huge pool and tennis court. Or the stone walls and towers that make it look like a castle. Or maybe even the small private island that comes with the house. Whatever the reason, this is not the average home.

And you know what? The home that Jesus is preparing for us in heaven isn't average either! Before you start picturing ice cream machines and bowling alleys, remember that the best part of our heavenly home is that Jesus will be there with us.

At first, that might not sound as cool as having your own hot tub. But think about it. What if you lived in the biggest mansion in the world . . . all alone? Living that way wouldn't mean very much, would it?

Jesus doesn't give us many details about the place He is preparing for us. But just knowing He'll be there should be enough to get you excited. You'll get to ask Him all of your questions and just enjoy spending time with the Father who loves you. Now that's something to look forward to!

A POWER NOTE

Write down three questions you'd most like to ask Jesus when you meet Him. (If you want, you can write questions for your favorite Bible heroes, too!)

NOTHING IS TOO HARD FOR GOD

Find It in the Bible

Is anything too hard for the LORD? I will return to you at
the appointed time next year, and Sarah will have a son.

GENESIS 18:14

The oldest woman to give birth within the last few hundred
years was seventy years old. That's probably older than your
grandmother! Grandmothers don't usually try to have babies.
Often they can't have babies because their bodies are too old. But
in this verse in Genesis, God promised Sarah that even though
she was ninety years old, she would have a baby!

Sarah had wanted to be a mother for many, many years, but it
never happened. She had given up hoping for a baby. So when she
heard the visitor say she would have a child, Sarah laughed! (See
Genesis 18:10–12.) It seemed impossible! Then the visitor asked
this question: "Is anything too hard for the LORD?" (Answer:
no!) What looks impossible from our point of view is never
impossible for God.

When Sarah had her son, God proved to her that He was more
powerful than the weakness of the human body. God has powers
that you can't imagine. Whenever something seems too big for
you to handle, trust in God. Nothing is too hard for Him.

A POWER NOTE

Ask a parent or other adult in your life about a time when he or
she thought something was impossible but then God answered a
prayer. Write it down to remind you that no problem is too tough
for God to handle.

QUICKSAND

Find It in the Bible

I waited patiently for the LORD; he turned to me and heard my cry.
He lifted me out of the slimy pit, out of the mud and mire; he set
my feet on a rock and gave me a firm place to stand. He put a
new song in my mouth, a hymn of praise to our God.

PSALM 40:1–3

You're a brave explorer, cutting a path through the thick underbrush of the jungle. You've been separated from your exploring friends, but you think you can hear them in the distance. As you push through the leafy greens, you feel your foot move from solid ground to . . . sand? In a flash, you fall forward, up to your waist. You've been caught in a pit of quicksand! You're sinking in the wet sand and the more you struggle to pull yourself free, the deeper you go. "Help! Somebody! Anybody!" you cry.

Finally, after two minutes of slow sinking, your expedition leader comes crashing through the bushes. He reaches down, grabs your arm, and with a great heave, pulls you free from the quicksand.

Without God, all of us are stuck in the quicksand of sin. Any time we try and escape on our own, we end up stuck even more. Quicksand doesn't like to let go—and neither does sin.

Only through God are we able to escape the sticky clutches of sin. He reaches down into the muck and pulls us up out of the quicksand. He cleans us, good as new.

A POWER NOTE

If you struggle with sin, God wants to help you. Read these verses in the Bible about that and choose one to memorize: John 8:34–36; 2 Corinthians 5:21; Hebrews 4:16; Hebrews 12:1–2.

A BOLD PLAN

Find It in the Bible

Jonathan said to his young armor-bearer, "... Perhaps the LORD
will act in our behalf. Nothing can hinder the LORD
from saving, whether by many or by few."

1 SAMUEL 14:6

What's the scariest thing you've ever had to do? What did you believe would happen? Jonathan, the son of King Saul, faced a scary situation. But what he believed about God made all the difference.

The people of Israel had enemies. When Saul was king, Israel's worst enemies were the Philistines. The two nations were constantly at war.

Jonathan and the armor-bearer were totally outnumbered. And they only had one sword between the two of them! Yet Jonathan also knew they had a secret weapon: God. Only God could bring about a victory in the face of impossible odds. So Jonathan wasn't afraid to act boldly for God.

Do you have this kind of faith in God? If you believe He is a mighty God, you will be willing to do mighty things through His power.

A POWER NOTE

Read what happened to Jonathan and his armor-bearer in 1 Samuel 14:1–15. It's a super-exciting story. Here's a hint: They had a huge victory!

TOUGH LOVE

Find It in the Bible

Know then in your heart that as a man disciplines his son,
so the LORD your God disciplines you.

DEUTERONOMY 8:5

Did you ever wonder whether animal parents discipline their young? Well, the answer is they do. In a wolf pack, if the young pups wander away from the pack or don't follow the pack leader, the older wolf will stand in front of the pup and show his teeth. This warns the young pup to follow the leader and obey. This discipline protects the pup from danger and helps it grow up to become a good member of the pack.

Your parents have the same goals in mind when they correct you. They want you to grow up to be a responsible, happy adult who loves God. So, they correct you. How do you respond when that happens? Do you get angry and yell? Or, do you listen and learn to do better? If you believe your parents have your best interests at heart, the wise thing to do is to obey.

If you have asked Jesus to live in your heart and life, you are one of God's children. He will guide you to do things He wants, and if you do something wrong, God will discipline you because He loves you. If you let Him, He will help you become the type of person He is proud of.

A POWER NOTE

Look up the words *disciple* and *discipline* in a dictionary. Write down the definitions and think how God might discipline you to be His disciple.

PAY ATTENTION!

Find It in the Bible

Then the LORD opened the donkey's mouth, and it said
to Balaam, "What have I done to you to make you
beat me these three times?"

NUMBERS 22:28

There are many kinds of donkeys in the world. The Poitou donkey, which originated in France, has an extremely shaggy coat. The shortest donkey—a Miniature Mediterranean donkey—averages around thirty inches tall. But one donkey in history beats all of these: Balaam's donkey. You see, this donkey could talk.

Balaam was a false prophet hired by the king of Moab to curse the people of Israel. This king—Balak—watched as the people of Israel passed through his land. He also heard about their powerful God who defeated their enemies. So Balak hoped that having them cursed would help his army defeat the people of Israel.

God didn't want Balaam to curse the Israelites. So God made Balaam's donkey talk to gain Balaam's attention. If Balaam had refused to listen to the donkey, an angel with a sharp sword would have helped him get the point.

God will use any means to get your attention. He doesn't have to make your dog or cat talk to you. He has given you His Word, the Bible.

A POWER NOTE

The word *bless* is the opposite of *curse*. To "bless" means to speak God's truth to someone. Share a word of blessing with someone today.

THE RULER WHO DIDN'T MEASURE UP

Find It in the Bible

But now your kingdom will not endure; the LORD has sought
out a man after his own heart and appointed him
ruler of his people, because you have not
kept the LORD's command.

1 SAMUEL 13:14

The people of Israel decided they needed a king like other nations. God chose Saul to be the first king of Israel. He was tall, handsome, and strong—everything a king should look like—but it turned out that he had a disobedient heart. He decided to do things his own way instead of following the rules God had given him.

Because Saul disobeyed God, God said, "Your kingdom will not endure." This meant that Saul's son would not become king after Saul. God had decided to give the throne to someone else. Saul's disobedience cost his family the privilege of being royalty. Instead, God passed the throne to "a man after his own heart"—a shepherd named David. He became a great king of Israel because he tried to follow God at all times.

A POWER NOTE

Create a mobile. Get a hangar and paste a red heart in the center. Then cut some string of various lengths. Next, write on pieces of paper all of the ways you want to live to show that you are "after God's heart." Take each little paper, glue it to the end of one piece of string, and then tie the string on the hangar. Hang this up to remind you how you want to always be a person after God's own heart.

FIRE IN THE DARK

Find It in the Bible

On the day the tabernacle, the tent of the covenant law,
was set up, the cloud covered it. From evening till morning
the cloud above the tabernacle looked like fire.

NUMBERS 9:15

Maybe your family has a barbeque or campfire in the summer to roast hot dogs. Well, on June 24 the residents of Alesund, Norway, light a bonfire, too: one that's more than 130 feet high! It's the biggest bonfire in the world!

Fire gets our attention, even small ones. It's powerful and lights up the darkness. When God wanted to let the Israelites know He was with them, He chose to appear to them at night like a fire in a cloud, lighting their way.

Later on, the book of Acts reports that when the Holy Spirit filled believers for the first time, they saw flames over each of their heads. Instead of one big fire, there were dozens of little fires. This was God's way of saying, "Things are different now! I'm coming to live inside each of you personally."

Having the Holy Spirit inside you means you don't ever have to be afraid of darkness—in fact, you will bring light to others!

A POWER NOTE

Using red, orange, and yellow construction paper (or markers on white paper), create (or draw) a big bonfire full of beautiful colors. Put the picture on your wall to remind you that God is present with you just as He was with the Israelites in the wilderness.

A DEPENDABLE GUIDE

Find It in the Bible

[Build] yourselves up in your most holy faith
and [pray] in the Holy Spirit.

JUDE 20

Many years ago, a certain Arabic guide would take groups of European tourists far into the deserts of the Arabian Peninsula. The visitors wanted to see the beauty of the desert, but there was always a danger of getting lost in the vast, dry land. This guide was well-known as the most dependable man in the region. He never got lost. Visitors always felt safe with him.

What was his secret? He carried a homing pigeon with him that had a small cord attached to one of its legs. If the guide ever felt uncertain about the direction of his home, he simply let the bird fly into the air while he held the cord. The pigeon always flew in the direction of its home, and the guide followed where the bird flew.

We also have a guide who wants to help us travel in the right direction to reach our heavenly home. Our guide is the Holy Spirit. He speaks to us through God's Word, and He speaks to our hearts. When we are not sure how to pray about something, we can ask Him to help us.

A POWER NOTE

Find a compass and notice how the needle changes direction when you do. If you went on a hike in the wilderness, you would probably use a compass to help you find your way. In a similar way, you can rely on the Holy Spirit to help you find your way through life.

LOOK AND LIVE

Find It in the Bible

So Moses made a bronze snake and put it up on a pole.
Then when anyone was bitten by a snake and looked
at the bronze snake, they lived.

NUMBERS 21:9

What's the largest snake you've ever seen? The green anaconda that lives in the Amazon jungles is the world's largest snake. Some can weigh over 500 pounds and grow up to twenty-two feet long. At least they're not poisonous.

But many snakes are poisonous, as the people of Israel found out. After they complained against God and Moses, God allowed them to suffer the bites of poisonous snakes. Since God cared about them, He gave Moses the unusual cure that today's verse mentions. Who would have thought that something that brought death could lead to healing and life?

Centuries later, Jesus used the image of the bronze snake as a word picture for Himself. His death on the cross would be the cure for the problem of sin. Anyone who looked to Jesus—who had faith in Him—would live forever someday with God.

You may not live in a place where you have to worry about poisonous snakes, but sin can be much worse. When you do something wrong, ask Jesus to forgive you and believe that He has.

A POWER NOTE

Tell someone how you look to Jesus for the promise of life forever with God. If you aren't sure you believe that Jesus died for you, now is your chance to learn more. Turn to John 3:1–21 and read Jesus' conversation with Nicodemus.

THAT'S NOT FAIR!

Find It in the Bible

While Joseph was there in the prison, the LORD was with him;
he showed him kindness and granted him favor in
the eyes of the prison warden.

GENESIS 39:20–21

Has someone ever accused you of doing something wrong that you didn't do? While working in the home of Potiphar, Joseph was accused of a crime. He was completely innocent, yet he was thrown in prison for years. He was the victim of powerful people.

Sounds unfair, right? But God hadn't deserted Joseph, just as He hadn't deserted Him when his brothers first sold him as a slave in Egypt. God proved that by giving Joseph a friend—the warden of the prison, the man who ran the place. He also gave Joseph the ability to interpret people's dreams. This ability would one day be his ticket out of prison and into the most powerful position in the land of Egypt.

Are you ready to cry, "Unfair!" because life seems that way? Even in the middle of unfair situations, you have a friend—God Himself. He will take care of you. Trust Him to bring good out of even very unfair situations.

A POWER NOTE

Look for information on the Internet or in books at the library about places in the world where being a Christian is illegal. Pray for the people in those countries that God will help them in a powerful way in their difficult times.

THE FLOATING ZOO

Find It in the Bible

Pairs of clean and unclean animals . . . male and female,
came to Noah and entered the ark, as God had commanded Noah.

GENESIS 7:8–9

What's the biggest zoo you've ever visited? With 17,000 animals and 130 acres of land, the Henry Doorly Zoo and Aquarium in Omaha, Nebraska, is the world's largest zoo. Over 25 million people have visited since it opened back in 1894. The zoo has a cat complex, a bear canyon, a butterfly and insect pavilion, and even a chrysalis hatching room (butterflies).

In Noah's day, the biggest zoo in the world just happened to be the ark he built. Only eight people saw this zoo—but imagine that maybe it had a room for the bears, another for the big cats, and an aviary for the birds! (Would you want to go into the spider room?)

When God promised to send a flood because nearly everyone on earth was evil, He had a plan. He would save Noah, Noah's wife, their three sons, and their wives because Noah loved and worshiped God. Also, God promised to save every kind of animal species. But Noah didn't have to round them up. God sent pairs of animals to Noah to load onto the ark.

Think of it: Every animal you see today exists because God saved two of every kind in Noah's day.

A POWER NOTE

What can you do to help an animal today? If you don't have a pet, ask a family member or a friend who has a pet if you can do something to help care for that animal.

GOD LIFTS YOUR WEIGHTS

Find It in the Bible
I can do all this through him who gives me strength.

PHILIPPIANS 4:13

A dead-lift in weightlifting is when someone stands and picks up a heavy weight from the ground without using a weight bench for support. The strongest man in the world can dead-lift over 1,100 pounds! The strongest woman in the world can dead-lift over 600 pounds.

In the verse above, however, the apostle Paul wasn't talking about that kind of strength. He was talking about the kind you need to get through hard times.

The Holy Spirit provides strength to lift the weights you carry—a difficult school assignment, a new school, or any challenge. He provides strength to help you carry fear, sorrow, and sadness, too. The Holy Spirit can help you with anything that is too heavy for you to lift by yourself. With God's help you can do whatever you need to do. Best of all, God goes with you to help you use the strength only He can provide. That makes God the ultimate weightlifter!

A POWER NOTE

How much weight can you lift? Maybe you can pick up your little brother or sister, or carry a small bag of soil for your dad. Pick up something around the house that's heavy, but not too heavy, and consider how God gives you the strength to face the hardest challenge or the heaviest disappointment.

A SONG OF PRAISE

Find It in the Bible

The LORD is my strength and my defense; he has
become my salvation. He is my God, and I will
praise him, my father's God, and I will exalt him.

EXODUS 15:2

The children of Israel started the day on one side of the Red
Sea, terrified, because Pharaoh and his army were bearing
down on them to attack them and drag them back to Egypt and
slavery.

But then God told Moses to raise his staff and stretch his hands
out over the sea. When he did, the sea separated, revealing a path
of escape. The people and all their animals walked through the
sea, between walls of water. When they came out on the other
side, God sent the waters back together again, drowning the
Egyptian army that had followed them.

So there, safe and sound on the other side of the sea, Moses sang a
song of praise to God. He started out by thanking God for sending
Pharaoh's horses and riders into the sea. Then he thanked God
for being the people's strength, defense, and salvation.

God took care of the children of Israel, and He takes care of you.

A POWER NOTE

Gather some friends and put on a play about crossing the Red
Sea. Have someone be Moses, some kids be the people, and some
be soldiers in Pharaoh's army. After Moses and the people cross
the Red Sea, have them sing and dance to show their praise to
God. You will find the song in Exodus 15:20–21.

JULY

HOW DEEP AND HOW HIGH

Find It in the Bible

Your love, LORD, reaches to the heavens, your faithfulness to the skies. Your righteousness is like the highest mountains, your justice like the great deep. You, LORD, preserve both people and animals.

PSALM 36:5–6

Go outside and look up at the sky. How far away do you think the sky is? Now think of the deepest place you've ever swum. Was it the middle of a lake? Or the deep end of a pool?

Imagine climbing a mountain. Mount Everest in Nepal is 29,029 feet high, making it the tallest mountain in the world. How about the deepest ocean? The Mariana Trench in the Pacific Ocean is 36,069 feet deep, making it the deepest place in the world.

Everything about God's love is high and deep and big. His love is higher than the sky, deeper than the deepest sea, and no matter how high you climb or how deep you swim, you will never reach the end of it.

God's love is so big that He will always love you. We can never reach the end of His love. People start and stop love, but God doesn't.

A POWER NOTE

Make a collage! Ask for permission to cut out pictures from magazines. Find some to represent that God's love is deep, high, and big. Maybe you can find pictures of the ocean, or mountains, or the stars. Glue the pictures onto a background and write this verse over all the pictures to remind you how big God's love is.

GOOD WORKERS

Find It in the Bible

Do your best to present yourself to God as one approved, a worker who does not need to be ashamed and who correctly handles the word of truth.

2 TIMOTHY 2:15

Ants are super hard workers. There are many different jobs in an ant colony. Some ants take care of the queen and her young. Others forage for food or act as guards. Soldier ants guard the colony and weaver ants build the ant nest. One ant with a most peculiar job is the honeypot ant. These ants are full of stored plant nectar, sort of like balloons filled with sugar water. They hang from the ceiling of the nest and when another ant is hungry, the honeypots drop sugar water from their supply into the mouths of the other ants. There is no such thing as a lazy ant!

God wants you to be a hard worker when it comes to knowing His Word. He wants you to learn it, study it, and memorize it so you can know what it says and know how to talk about it with others.

When people ask you about salvation through Jesus, you want to be able to share that good news with them. When you are tempted to do wrong, you want to be able to remind yourself to stay true to Jesus. This happens when you work hard to fill your mind with God's Word.

A POWER NOTE

Make a decision to use this devotional every day this year. You'll find verses from every book in the Bible, and you'll learn a lot about how God wants you to live. Make it your job this year to learn more about God's precious Word.

THE WISDOM OF OBEDIENCE

Find It in the Bible

To obey is better than sacrifice, and to heed
is better than the fat of rams.

1 SAMUEL 15:22

Have you ever seen a straight river? Probably not! Rivers twist and turn as they wind their way toward the sea. Why are rivers crooked? They follow the downward pull of gravity and always flow downhill. That means the water will follow the path of least resistance. When the flowing water comes to something in its path—a hill for instance—it flows around it.

People are sort of like crooked streams and rivers. Our human nature pulls us to do "crooked" things we shouldn't do. Such as lying or being disobedient or dishonest. Even if we don't want to do these things, our sinful nature pulls us in that direction. That's why God gave us rules to follow and obey. The rules He gave us in the Bible help us stay on a straight path rather than a crooked path.

Sometimes we don't always understand the rules and restrictions God gives us in the Bible. But if we remember that He is a Father who loves us, we should obey His commands out of respect and gratitude. We can be assured He only wants what is best for us.

A POWER NOTE

Get your Bible and discover how people in biblical days disobeyed God and lived to regret it. Look at Moses striking the rock (Numbers 20:1–12); and read about Jonah refusing to go to Nineveh (Jonah 1–2).

GOD IS ON YOUR SIDE

Find It in the Bible

For the LORD your God is the one who goes with you to fight
for you against your enemies to give you victory.

DEUTERONOMY 20:4

When the American colonies started to fight for independence from England, they didn't have much of a chance. England had a huge army with plenty of weapons and training, along with ships and loads of money. The colonies didn't have these. Even though they were fighting for what they believed was right, they weren't powerful enough to win on their own. They needed a strong friend. France was that friend. France helped by providing gunpowder and other important supplies to the colonies, and with its help, America won its freedom.

You're probably not going to march into battle against armies anytime soon. But you will have plenty of other battles to fight, such as fear of being alone or feeling hurt by an unkind remark. Or you can fight against bullying—not with your fists, but with your kind words and prayers. You can fight against your own bad thoughts and sins. When you face these struggles, you don't have to face them alone. If you're fighting for what is right, you can know that God is on your side. He is your strong friend. His Holy Spirit lives in your heart to give you courage and to guide you.

A POWER NOTE

Ask your mom or dad to help you draw a sword on a piece of cardboard. Cut it out. On the blade, write some of the things you struggle with. Then pray that God will help you defeat them.

LISTEN AND DO

Find It in the Bible

Do not merely listen to the word, and so deceive yourselves.
Do what it says.

JAMES 1:22

If you visit Yellowstone National Park, you will have to follow certain rules. One of those rules is how to deal with the local wildlife. Yellowstone managers want people to understand that the park is home to wildlife, and people are the visitors and spectators. Yellowstone rules tell people to stay a safe distance from wildlife. For instance, it is prohibited to get within one hundred yards (that's the size of a football field) of wolves or bears.

Unfortunately, every year people are injured (and sometimes killed) in Yellowstone. They deceive themselves into thinking that they can get a little closer to the wild animals. They don't understand that these animals aren't in a zoo and will act to protect themselves if they feel threatened.

Too often people hear and know rules, but they don't follow them because they think they know better. James tells us that we should not just *hear* what the Bible says, but we need to actually *do* it. If you only listen to God's commands or read them in the Bible, but do nothing to obey them, you are deceiving yourself. Obedience is the way to show others that you are listening to God.

A POWER NOTE

Ask your parents to help you locate the Bible on CDs at a book store or library. Take time to sit and listen to a passage of Scripture such as Matthew 5 or 6. As you listen, ask yourself: "Now that I've heard what God's Word says, what do I need to *do*?"

MUNCHIES MULTIPLIED

Find It in the Bible

Here is a boy with five small barley loaves and two small fish,
but how far will they go among so many?

JOHN 6:9

Picture this: You're out with your family at a big festival. You've been listening to a really interesting teacher all day. Your stomach starts to growl, so you pull your paper bag out and start munching. Suddenly everyone is looking at you because no one else thought to pack food . . . and they want you to share.

How could you possibly share with so many people? The food in your bag is barely enough for you. How far could it possibly go to feed five thousand dads *and* their families?

The boy featured in today's verse was willing to share, but Jesus' disciples wondered how far those two loaves and five fish would go. If you read John 6:1–14, you'll get the whole story. Jesus provided a miracle of compassion for thousands of hungry stomachs that day. He broke the bread, blessed it, and it multiplied. The people were filled, and there was even food left over.

Are you willing to share so that others in need will be filled? Whatever you give to Jesus, He can multiply and use!

A POWER NOTE

You can be a blessing to others locally or around the world when you give to your church and other charities. Can you give something today? Remember, a little goes a long way.

ASK, SEEK, KNOCK

Find It in the Bible

Ask and it will be given to you; seek and you will find; knock and the door will be opened to you. For everyone who asks receives; the one who seeks finds; and to the one who knocks, the door will be opened.

MATTHEW 7:7–8

Have you ever lost something really important to you? Sometimes you find it; other times, it's still missing. What if you found it seventy years later? That's what happened to Jesse Mattos. In 1938, he accidentally flushed his high school class ring down the toilet. In 2010, a worker in the sewers came across the ring and, with some research, was able to find the owner. Jesse had been certain the ring was gone forever. But now, at age ninety, he is wearing his 1938 class ring again!

What if you could know that every time you looked for something, you *would* find it? God promises that about Himself. He says that anyone who calls to Him, seeks Him, or knocks at His door will find Him. He *wants* people to come to Him. He *wants* people to find Him.

God doesn't force anyone to believe in Him, but when people look for Him, God promises that they will find Him.

A POWER NOTE

Gather your friends and play a game of "Hot and Cold." Have one person be It and hide an object in your room or your house. Then try to find the object. Have the person who is It say "hotter" as you get closer to where the object is hidden and "colder" as you move away from the hidden object. Whoever finds the object gets to hide it next!

CONSIDER THE RAVENS

Find It in the Bible

Consider the ravens: They do not sow or reap, they have no storeroom or barn; yet God feeds them. And how much more valuable you are than birds! Who of you by worrying can add a single hour to your life?

LUKE 12:24–25

Ravens are big black birds—sometimes even kind of scary looking. Ornithologists (people who study birds) know that these birds are very smart. They've given ravens problems and watched the birds solve them! Ravens also enjoy flying—some have been seen flying upside-down for long distances.

Ravens never go hungry. God provides their food. They don't need to plant and harvest crops. They don't need to build barns to store food for winter. God takes care of them.

The point is that the ravens don't worry. They just live, and God cares for them—and they don't even know about God! We certainly need to be responsible with our money and plan for the future. But God says we should not *worry* about those things because worry doesn't help anything. We are more valuable than the birds, so we can trust that God will take care of us! So don't worry. Trust God!

A POWER NOTE

Draw or cut out some black birds. Now use chalk to write on each black bird one thing that you're worrying about right now. Next, tape all of your birds to another piece of paper and write "Consider the ravens" on the paper. Let your picture remind you that God will take care of your worries if you let Him.

Refreshed by the Spirit

Find It in the Bible

For John baptized with water, but in a few days you
will be baptized with the Holy Spirit.

ACTS 1:5

Remember the last time you took a swim on a hot summer day? You were sweating under the sun, and your feet were hot from the pavement surrounding the pool. You plunged right in, and all of a sudden a comforting coolness surrounded you. Everywhere around you, was the calming, refreshing feeling of water.

Before Jesus returned to heaven, He told His followers that He had something far better to baptize them with than water. He promised to baptize them with the Holy Spirit. This first happened on the Day of Pentecost. The Holy Spirit came into the room with the sound of rushing wind and flames of fire that sat over each head. Each of the people there began to speak in new languages that the Holy Spirit gave them. They were filled with the Holy Spirit.

When you are baptized in water, your body is covered with water. When you are baptized in the Holy Spirit, your mind and heart are completely covered with the Holy Spirit. You are filled with His presence and His power

A POWER NOTE

If you have not received the baptism in the Holy Spirit but you would like to, ask an adult to pray with you about this. God wants to give you this special gift.

GOD REFRESHES MY SOUL

Find It in the Bible

He refreshes my soul. He guides me along the
right paths for his name's sake.

PSALM 23:3

On a hot summer's day what do you like to have most? A glass of cold water, a glass of cold soda, or an ice cream bar? No matter what your choice, you choose for one reason—to get relief from the hot weather. Imagine that you live in Death Valley, California. On July 10, 1913, the area recorded the highest temperature ever—134 degrees!

Psalm 23:3 says that God is refreshing to the soul. Your soul is the part of you that thinks, feels, and makes choices. When the going gets tough, when you feel sad or angry, if you go to God, He'll refresh your soul like a cool drink refreshes you on a hot summer's day.

At the same time, God makes sure you're going on the "right paths," in the right direction. A parent will give you a cold glass of water on that hot summer's day, but will also make sure you don't spend too much time in the hot sun and get a sunburn. God gives you refreshment and guidance. And that's important *every* day!

A POWER NOTE

Experiment. What tastes better? A cold glass of water or a warm glass of water? Try this with different drinks, and remember how God wants to refresh your soul.

THE ANTIDOTE FOR REVENGE

Find It in the Bible

Do not seek revenge or bear a grudge against anyone among your people, but love your neighbor as yourself. I am the LORD.

LEVITICUS 19:18

When someone says something mean to you, what do you do? Many people try to get back at the people who hurt them. But revenge can have deadly consequences. History tells us of a case of revenge between two political rivals: Alexander Hamilton and Aaron Burr. After they worked against each other for years, Vice President Aaron Burr finally challenged Hamilton, the Secretary of the Treasury, to a duel with pistols. On July 11, 1804, Burr shot Hamilton. Hamilton later died of his injuries. Not really a very good way to handle a disagreement!

The news is full of stories of people who hurt others as they seek to get even. Revenge often starts with anger. The one who is angry thinks about the thing that made them angry over and over, which leads to bitterness. Knowing that revenge often leads to someone getting hurt, God wanted His people to avoid it. He gave them a rule to remember and also an antidote to revenge: love others as yourself.

A POWER NOTE

The Holy Spirit can help you to not only forgive someone but also to show love to that person. Ask Him how you can do that. You might start by praying for the person who has been mean to you.

GOD'S PATH

Find It in the Bible

I have no greater joy than to hear that my children
are walking in the truth.

3 JOHN 4

Have you ever gone hiking through the woods or on a rocky trail? Hiking is fun but you have to be careful where you go. Some paths are longer than others, so you have to decide which one is the best based on how much time you have. Some paths are harder than others, so you have to choose which one is safe enough. When you pick the right path, you have to follow it. If you walk off the path, you could get lost; and that could be worse than picking a bad path.

Finding the best path on your own can be difficult, but thankfully a parent or adult with you makes the choice. Your job is to stick with the group and not wander off on your own. To have the most fun and be safe at the same time, you must obey the rules.

Like hiking, God delights when we follow His path in our walk with Him. When we walk in the truth of His Word, we don't stumble because He directs our way. He will guide us to the end. But He is sad when we ignore Him and try to find our own way. God knows what's best for us. He hates to watch us stumble and fall when we don't obey His guidance.

A POWER NOTE

Write down everything you've been doing and thinking about today. Then circle the top three good things you want to be better at. Try to do them well in the next few days as you continue on God's path.

WHAT ARE YOU AFRAID OF?

Find It in the Bible

When you lie down, you will not be afraid;
when you lie down, your sleep will be sweet.

PROVERBS 3:24

Nearly everyone is afraid of something. Researchers have even come up with fancy words to describe fears. Do you have a problem with *ophidiophobia*? That's a fear of snakes. How about *coulrophobia*, which is the fear of clowns? Maybe you even have *hippopotomonstrosesquipedaliophobia* . . . that's the fear of long words!

Sometimes, especially at night, we think about our fears. Maybe we're afraid of the test tomorrow at school or the tryouts for a sports team. God knows that these events can be scary, but He also knows that worrying about them doesn't help us at all! I mean, have you ever gotten a better grade because you stayed up late worrying about a math or spelling quiz?

Remember that God is bigger than all of your fears and problems. Then decide not to worry any more but to trust God to handle the things that worry you. You can rest easy knowing that He has everything under control.

A POWER NOTE

When you are afraid, make a list in your mind of everything you're thankful for. Don't just count the "big" things like family and a house to live in—list the little things like the sound of rain on the roof or the smell of your favorite cookies. When you think of God's good gifts, you won't have room for scary thoughts!

HAPPILY EVER AFTER

Find It in the Bible

The wolf will live with the lamb, the leopard will lie down with the goat,
the calf and the lion and the yearling together;
and a little child will lead them.

ISAIAH 11:6

Little Red Riding Hood knocked on the door of her grandmother's cottage. To her surprise, a wolf opened the door . . . and smiled. "Your grandmother and I were just having tea," he said. "Why don't you come in and join us?" So Little Red Riding Hood, the Wolf, and the Grandmother talked all afternoon and ate cookies together. And everyone lived happily ever after.

"That's not how the story goes!" you're probably saying. And you're right. But wouldn't it be nice if it was? If all the evil people in fairy tales became kind and the dragons decided to use their ability to breathe fire in order to make s'mores, the world would be a happy place.

The truth is, God didn't create the world with bad things like fear and death. He never wanted us to fight each other or lie or cheat. Those things happen when we sin and do things our own way. But the wonderful news is that someday, God will make everything right again. This verse from Isaiah talks about that new time when the lamb will be safe with the wolf. God will make everything right. Talk about happily ever after!

A POWER NOTE

Pick one of your favorite fiction books or fairy tales. Now tell the story as it would happen if the characters were in God's perfect world.

NO QUITTERS ALLOWED

Find It in the Bible

Let us not become weary in doing good, for at the
proper time we will reap a harvest if we do not give up.

GALATIANS 6:9

Think back to the last movie or TV show you saw that was about superheroes. They're always ready to save the day when people call on them. They rescue people from death, ruin evil plots, and even stop aliens from destroying the planet!

But imagine what would happen if your favorite superhero yawned and said, "I'm only halfway done getting people out of this burning building, but I'm going to stop. I'm getting really dirty and sweaty. Besides, the fire department should be here soon. They can deal with it."

Some hero, right? We expect our superheroes to finish what they start, no matter how hard it gets.

Guess what? God wants us to do the same thing—to finish well. We shouldn't get "weary," or tired, of doing good.

Sometimes, doing what is right can be really difficult. God knows that, and He'll give you all the strength you need. What you need to do is stick with it and never give up.

A POWER NOTE

Think of something good you could do to help someone today. Maybe you could play with a younger sibling or do a chore without being told or tell your parents "thank you" for dinner. Then go do it!

HIDE AND SEEK

Find It in the Bible

You are my hiding place; you will protect me from trouble
and surround me with songs of deliverance.

PSALM 32:7

When you play Hide and Seek, where are your favorite places to hide? Do you have a spot that nobody knows about? Just sitting in that spot can be fun, knowing everyone will have a tough time finding you. And you never have to be "It" because you're never the first person found! You're safe there.

That's just what God wants to be for us—He wants to be our hiding place, our safe place. When life seems overwhelming or confusing, He wants you to run to Him, crawl into the safe spot, and sit quietly with Him. Whatever is going on outside, God is watching over you.

And God knows everything about us. We can't hide anything from Him, and He doesn't want us to. God promises to forgive us, and He loves us more than we could ever imagine. Even when we try to hide from God, He sits with us in our hiding space, waiting for us to acknowledge that He has already found us.

A POWER NOTE

Find a quiet place in your house that you can designate as your "hiding place." Maybe it's inside your closet or in a quiet corner of the basement. When you've picked a spot, sit there for a few minutes. Think about how God knows exactly where you are, and thank Him for His constant presence.

COUNTING THE SAND

Find It in the Bible

How precious to me are your thoughts, God! How vast is the
sum of them! Were I to count them, they would
outnumber the grains of sand.

PSALM 139:17–18

Think about the beach—or if you haven't been to the beach, think about the nearest sandbox. Now imagine that someone asks you to count every single grain in a handful of sand. Pretty soon you realize that you could never count every grain. Just one handful of sand contains millions of grains! So just imagine how many grains of sand are in that whole sandbox or on that whole beach or in all the beaches in the world!

The Bible says that the number of times God thinks about you is greater than the number of grains of sand in the whole world! In other words, you're never away from God's thoughts. He is always thinking about you. Incredible!

Sometimes you may feel as though no one knows when you are sad or lonely or hurting. But God does. He knows what's going on in your heart and mind every single moment. You're never alone and never forgotten. That's how much God loves you.

A POWER NOTE

Ask your parents to help you get a cup of sand. You can buy small bags of sand at home improvement stores. Put the sand into a clear container that you can keep on your desk. Every time you look at it, the sand will remind you of all the times God thinks about you.

TEAM UP

Find It in the Bible

Again, truly I tell you that if two of you on earth agree about
anything they ask for, it will be done for them by
my Father in heaven.

MATTHEW 18:19

The Sequoia trees in California can grow as tall as 300 feet
above the ground. These trees are super tall, but they have
very shallow root systems that reach out in all directions to
capture moisture from the ground. It's rare to see a redwood
tree standing alone, because it would topple over in a high
wind. That's why they grow in clusters. Their intertwining roots
provide support for one another against the storms.

God has placed His children in one big family so they can support
one another. God hears your prayers, and He enjoys it when
you talk to Him. But He also wants you to team up with others
in prayer. The Bible says that God loves it when His children
gather and pray together. It means that you have agreed together
about asking God for something—and it gives that much more
encouragement when you see God's answers.

Life is hard, and we need one another. Let's share together in
prayer.

A POWER NOTE

The next time you want to ask God for something, talk to your
friends and family. Write down your request and beside it, write
the names of the people who are praying with you about it. When
God answers your prayer, be sure to let these people know so they
can rejoice with you.

CREATED WITH A PLAN

Find It in the Bible

Through him all things were made; without him
nothing was made that has been made.

JOHN 1:3

Think of your house or the building you live in. Your house or apartment building didn't just appear. It was built. Some workers poured cement and laid the foundation. Carpenters framed up the walls, and others put up drywall. Different people made sure the electricity worked right and the plumbing provided water. But these people didn't just show up and start working—they all worked from a plan drawn up by an architect. Without that plan, the workers wouldn't know what to do, and the house would look like a mixed-up mess.

Think of God as the Architect *and* the Builder. He had a plan and made everything—in fact, nothing would exist at all without Him. He made the sun and moon and the air and water. Then, after those were in place, He created plants and animals that need the sun, air, and water.

God's perfect plan created a perfect world for all of us. And if He had such a plan for creation, He surely has a great plan in place for you!

A POWER NOTE

Find several pieces of white paper and fold them in half to make a booklet. On the front write the title "God Is the Builder." Then find some old magazines and cut out pictures of nature that you can paste in your booklet. You will be amazed at the wonderful world God has built for you.

A CONSTANT REFUGE

Find It in the Bible

The LORD is good, a refuge in times of trouble.
He cares for those who trust in him.

NAHUM 1:7

If you live in certain parts of the United States, you know about the threat of tornadoes. Did you know that in an average year, about 1,000 tornadoes are reported? Not all of them do horrible damage—that's why scientists have categorized them according to their wind speeds. On what they call the Fujita Scale, an F0 tornado has winds from 40–72 miles per hour, while an F5 has wind speeds over 261 miles per hour. That's the most dangerous tornado. It can actually pick up semi-trucks and houses and hurl them through the air!

If you live in an area that has tornadoes, you probably have a place to go for safety—such as a basement or a storm cellar. An underground location provides a safe refuge from the wind and debris of a passing tornado.

A safe refuge is valuable in times of trouble. God has promised to be your refuge when you face difficult or dangerous situations. He cares for His children and is ready to take care of you. You only need to run to Him and seek His protection. Why? Because He cares for those who trust in Him.

A POWER NOTE

Read stories of how God protected His people in times of trouble. Start with Joshua's battle against Jericho (Joshua 6). Also look at the way God protected young David against the giant Goliath (1 Samuel 17).

Gentle Answers

Find It in the Bible

A gentle answer turns away wrath, but a harsh word stirs up anger.

PROVERBS 15:1

You've seen it happen—someone gets mad at someone else. That person reacts and yells back. Then the first person yells even louder. The words continue to get louder and meaner. Usually someone storms away in anger. Other times, a fight breaks out. That kind of situation is always bad. Like the Bible says, harsh words just stir up the anger and make it worse.

What if, instead, the second person responded gently? That doesn't mean the person has to give in or give up, but it does mean they speak the truth in a gentle and kind manner. Even though they may still disagree, they choose not to have a big, loud argument or a boxing match.

The Lord says He wants our words to be gentle and kind—especially when we're faced with someone who is angry. When we keep calm and respond gently, we can diffuse many tense situations.

God can even use your words to tell another person just how much Jesus loves them. When you obey the Lord with your words, you show that you love Him, too.

A POWER NOTE

The next time you feel like saying something mean or ugly because you are angry or upset, stop and count to ten. Then think about what the Lord wants you to say and how He wants you to say it. Put the brakes on your mouth!

PLEASING WORDS AND THOUGHTS

Find It in the Bible

May these words of my mouth and this meditation of my
heart be pleasing in your sight, LORD,
my Rock and my Redeemer.

PSALM 19:14

David, the king of Israel, prayed that his words *and* his thoughts would please God. David loved God dearly, and God loved him. David was a great king and a great warrior for his people. He wrote lots of songs about how much he loved God. He even wrote songs when he was worried or afraid.

David wasn't perfect; he committed some terrible sins. But he always asked God to forgive him, and he tried to live better. He wanted his words and his thoughts to be pleasing to God.

How about you? Do the words of your mouth please God, or do you sometimes say mean things or use bad words? What about the things you think in your mind? God sees all of that, too. Do your thoughts please Him?

Being careful what you say and what you think isn't easy; but when you ask the Holy Spirit for help, He'll teach you how to watch your words *and* your thoughts.

A POWER NOTE

The next time you enjoy a scoop of ice cream, stop to think how quickly it would melt if you put it in a pan on a hot stove. In a similar way, mean and angry words can melt people's hearts. Next time you are tempted to say something mean or angry, think about melting ice cream and find something nice to say instead.

SAYING "I'M SORRY" TO GOD

Find It in the Bible

You are to lay your hand on the head of the burnt offering, and it will be accepted on your behalf to make atonement for you.

LEVITICUS 1:4

One of the most expensive items in the world is an iPhone 3GS Supreme, designed by Stuart Hughes. Why is it so expensive? Because the casing has 136 diamonds and is made of twenty-two-carat gold. The price is $2.97 million.

There is something that has an even higher price than that phone: sin. Anything you do to break one of God's rules has the same high price: death. This includes physical death and eternal separation from God. But God loved people so much that He wanted to forgive their sins. Yet the price for sin still had to be paid. So God chose to give His Son, Jesus, to pay the price for sin.

Long before Jesus was born, God gave the people of Israel a symbol of the payment they had to make for their sins. That symbol was the sacrifice of animals. To "make atonement" means to offer something to pay a debt. When the people saw an animal die, they understood how serious their sins were.

After Jesus died on the cross, we don't have to sacrifice animals to say "We're sorry" to God. Jesus' death on the cross paid for every wrong that was ever done. All we need to do is tell Him we're sorry for our sins and accept His sacrifice as payment for our sins.

A POWER NOTE

Write the word *atonement* vertically. Beside each letter write a phrase that tells of God's great love. The phrase for the letter "A" might be "amazing gift of salvation."

GOD ALWAYS SEES YOU

Find It in the Bible

My frame was not hidden from you when I was made in the secret place,
when I was woven together in the depths of the earth.
Your eyes saw my unformed body; all the days
ordained for me were written in your book
before one of them came to be.

PSALM 139:15–16

What color are your eyes? Your hair? Did you know that the average human has between 90,000 and 150,000 hairs on his head? Also, the rarest combination of hair and eye color is red hair and brown eyes.

David, the king of Israel and the writer of this psalm, celebrated the fact that God knew all about him. God knew how many hairs were on David's head. He also knew everything David felt and how long David would live.

God knew what you would look like before you were born. He knows everything about you—including what you think no one else knows. Since He knows so much about you—even things your best friend doesn't know—you can trust Him to take care of you.

A POWER NOTE

Take a minute to look at yourself in a mirror. Remember that God knew you even before you were born. To Him, nothing about you is hidden. You don't have to pretend with Him. If you feel lonely or afraid, don't forget that God is with you to help you.

GROW IN GENEROSITY

Find It in the Bible

A generous person will prosper;
whoever refreshes others will be refreshed.

PROVERBS 11:25

A re you generous? Check this out: the fifty most generous donors in recent years gave to charity a combined total of over $7 billion. How many is a billion? Well, a billion seconds ago, the year was 1959. That's a lot of seconds. And $7 billion is a lot of generosity!

When Solomon and other writers wrote the book of Proverbs, they included advice about being generous. Many people in Israel didn't have the means to provide for themselves. Those who had much were expected to provide for those who had nothing. That's why throughout the Bible, you'll find rules about helping people in need.

Stingy is the opposite of *generous*. Sometimes people are stingy because they're afraid they won't have enough for themselves if they give. But generous people give because they trust God. Giving helps a person grow in trust instead of fear.

A POWER NOTE

Write a list of ways you can be generous. You don't have to spend money. You can spend time helping someone or you can be generous with words of praise.

THINK ABOUT GOOD THINGS

Find It in the Bible

Finally, brothers and sisters, whatever is true, whatever is noble,
whatever is right, whatever is pure, whatever is lovely,
whatever is admirable—if anything is excellent or
praiseworthy—think about such things.

PHILIPPIANS 4:8

If you put a glass of water on the table and bump the table, some water will spill out of the glass. Milk or orange juice won't spill out, but water. Whatever is inside the glass will spill out. That's the way it is with our hearts. What's inside is what will spill out when we get bumped in life. We can fill our hearts with good things or ugly things based on our thoughts.

When Paul wrote the verse above, he was sitting in jail because some people didn't want him to preach about Jesus. Do you think he wanted to say mean things about the people who put him there? Did he think bad things about them? No, he didn't do that. Instead, he wrote a letter that teaches us to think good things even when life is hard and people are mean.

When someone hurts us it's easy to think bad things about that person. We might even want to say ugly things about them. But if we want to please God we will respond in love.

A POWER NOTE

Find a glass that is empty. On six pieces of paper, write these words: *true, noble, right, pure, lovely, admirable*. Put these pieces of paper inside the glass to help you think about what kind of thoughts you are putting in your mind and heart.

DO YOU BELIEVE?

Find It in the Bible

They replied, "Believe in the Lord Jesus, and you will be saved—
you and your household."

ACTS 16:31

If you get lost in the woods on a camping trip, or your parent is late picking you up from practice and it's getting dark, you might feel scared. When you're in a scary situation, do you ever think to pray and sing?

Some people accused Paul and Silas of doing something bad when they had really done something good. They were flogged (which means they were beaten on their backs with whips), and their feet were put in stocks (meaning they couldn't stand up or move). They were in a lot of pain in a dark, smelly prison—and yet they were singing! The next thing they knew, God performed a miracle and sent an earthquake to open the prison doors. They were free!

The jailer realized there was something special about these two prisoners. He asked them, "What must I do to be saved?" Paul and Silas explained that he needed to believe in Jesus.

Do you believe in Jesus as your Savior? Believing in Him means you know that He died for you on the cross, and you want to live to please Him. It's the most important decision you'll ever make.

A POWER NOTE

If you have never told Jesus that you believe in Him and want Him to come into your heart, ask Him today. If you already believe in Jesus, write out Acts 16:31. Then say thank-you to Him for saving you and coming to live in you.

Son of the Living God

Find It in the Bible

Simon Peter answered, "You are the Messiah,
the Son of the living God."

MATTHEW 16:16

Jesus asked Peter, one of His disciples, "Who do you say I am?" Many people thought Jesus was just another prophet or a really cool teacher. But Peter understood something more important—he knew that Jesus was the Messiah, the Son of God.

This meant that Peter knew that Jesus was the fulfillment of Old Testament prophecies about a coming Messiah who would cleanse people from their sins. He knew that Jesus was God's Son—a human being who was also God. He knew that Jesus was the one God's people had been waiting for across the centuries.

Peter had his doubts about Jesus and his moments of difficulty (he did, after all, betray Jesus—you can read that sad story in Matthew 26:69–75). But he also repented and became a great leader in the early church.

When you have Jesus in your life, you have the Son of God watching over you every minute of the day. His Holy Spirit dwells in your heart to guide you faithfully. You can trust Him because He'll never let you down.

A POWER NOTE

On a piece of paper, write down the question Jesus asked, "Who do you say I am?" Write the word *faith* vertically, and come up with one word that begins with each letter to describe who Jesus is to you. (For instance, "F" could be "Friend.")

BASKeT CASe

Find It in the Bible

Then his sister asked Pharaoh's daughter, "Shall I go and get
one of the Hebrew women to nurse the baby for you?"

EXODUS 2:7

Moses was born into a Hebrew family just as Pharaoh made a
law that all Hebrew boy babies should be killed. In order to
save little Moses' life, his mother put him in a basket among the
reeds on the edge of the Nile River. God provided for his safety
by delivering that little basket right into the hands of Pharaoh's
daughter, who came to the river to bathe! She wanted to take care
of the baby but needed a woman to help her nurse him. Miriam,
Moses' sister, had been hiding in the reeds nearby, keeping
watch. She came out and volunteered their mother! Pharaoh's
daughter agreed, Moses' family was reunited, and Moses was safe
from Pharaoh!

Just as God protected Moses, God provides us with people in our
lives who help and protect us. God had a plan for Moses, a plan
that was laid out for him even before he was born. And God has a
plan for your life, too.

A POWER NOTE

Fold a paper bag in half and draw the shape of a simple boat. Cut
it out through all layers so you have two paper boats. Now glue
the two together around three edges, leaving the top unglued.
Next, gather some tiny sticks and glue them onto the sides of
your boat. Does it look like a little basket? As God took care of
baby Moses, He will take care of you.

THE "TIRED SWIMMER CARRY"

Find It in the Bible

Cast all your anxiety on him because he cares for you.

1 PETER 5:7

L ifeguards are trained to save lives in the water. One method they use is called the "tired swimmer carry." Often a swimmer may get exhausted. When that happens, panic can set in and the swimmer may start thrashing his arms and legs to try to stay above water.

But a lifeguard is trained for situations like these. The lifeguard will swim out and speak to calm down the swimmer. Once the swimmer has stopped thrashing, the lifeguard will get close and support the tired swimmer to tow him back to shore. The swimmer can rest on the strength of the lifeguard who will swim through the waves.

When was the last time you felt overwhelmed by something? Maybe you are worried about a test at school, problems with a friend, or a family crisis. Whatever it is, God wants you to rest in Him. He is your ultimate Lifeguard for the storms in life.

A POWER NOTE

On separate small pieces of paper, write down whatever is making you anxious today. Then fold them into tiny pieces, put them all together, and toss them into your wastebasket, telling God that you are casting all of your worries on Him.

GOD'S FOREVER WORD

Find It in the Bible

The grass withers and the flowers fall,
but the word of our God endures forever.

ISAIAH 40:8

Did you know there are more than 9,000 different kinds of grass? Depending on the season and the amount of moisture, grass can be a beautiful green, but in the fall and winter, it turns yellow. And did you know that we eat grass? Wheat, rice, corn, barley, oats, and rye are some of the grasses that people eat. We don't eat the leaves of the grass like cows do, we eat the seeds.

Throughout chapter 40 in Isaiah, the prophet used *grass* as a word picture for someone or something that only lasts a short while. Grass in Bible times was often used to feed fires. If you burn grass, it is gone in an instant. It can't stand up to fire.

God's Word is different from grass. Grass lasts a season, but God's Word lasts forever. It never changes. The apostle Peter, who was one of Jesus' disciples, believed this. He quoted this verse in one of his letters (1 Peter 1:25).

A POWER NOTE

Ask your parent or some other adult if you can plant some grass seeds. You can find the seeds at home improvement stores. Just put a little soil in the bottom of a disposable cup, place a few grass seeds on top, and sprinkle with water. Put it in a sunny window, keep it lightly watered, and watch for the grass to sprout. Your grass may not last very long, but God's Word will last forever.

A WORLD OF DIVERSITY

Find It in the Bible

The earth is the LORD's, and everything in it,
the world, and all who live in it.

PSALM 24:1

A young boy's grandmother gave him three dollars for his birthday. The next Saturday, his mother decided to go to several garage sales and the young boy went with her. At each stop, he looked at the toys. At one place, he bought some toy soldiers. At another place, he bought some little robots. At other places, he bought little figures of action heroes, clowns, and barnyard animals. When he got home, he put all of his collections together in one big pretend city. His older sister asked, "Do all those different characters belong together in one city?"

The little boy responded, "I like it when things are not all the same."

In a similar way, God has created a world in which polar bears, giraffes, kangaroos, squids, and eagles live where He says they will live. Likewise, He has created all the people of the world, with various skin colors, facial features, and languages. The amazing diversity of God's creativity is mind-boggling. God's world is a display of His marvelous handiwork!

A POWER NOTE

Choose just one variety of animal and use your computer or library to look at the vast range of God's creativity. Birds alone include everything from an ostrich to a pigeon. See what you can learn about God's wonderful, creative imagination!

Love Your Enemies

Find It in the Bible

Love your enemies and pray for those who persecute you,
that you may be children of your Father in heaven.

MATTHEW 5:44–45

Think about a time when someone talked bad about you behind your back or told a lie about you. How did you feel? Were you angry or upset? How did you react? God tells us to love our enemies, but at times, that can be hard.

People beat Jesus and spat at Him and nailed Him to a cross. Through it all, Jesus never tried to hurt His killers. As He was dying, instead of being angry at the people, He asked God to forgive them because they didn't know what they were doing.

Jesus knows that sometimes it can be difficult to love others, but He loves everyone and He wants us to do the same. He set an example of how we are to treat people. He said that when we love our enemies and pray for those who persecute us, we act like God's children.

No, it isn't easy, but God promises that we can do it by the power of the Holy Spirit, who lives in our hearts.

A POWER NOTE

The next time someone gets angry with you or does something mean to you, pray for that person. Then, when you see the person, smile and say nice things to him or her. Show that you are God's child.

TO LIVE IS CHRIST

Find It in the Bible
For to me, to live is Christ and to die is gain.

PHILIPPIANS 1:21

You do something 18 times a minute, 1,080 times an hour, 25,920 times a day, yet you hardly think about it. What do you do? You breathe. If you live to be 70 years old, you will breathe for 25,567 days. Each breath is a gift from God that gives you life.

What do you like most in life? Do you love to play sports or play a musical instrument? Perhaps your favorite thing in the world is your pet.

The apostle Paul's favorite thing in all the world was simply to live for Jesus. He landed in prison because he preached about Jesus and salvation, and some people didn't like it. But that didn't stop him. Even when he was in prison, he kept writing letters to teach people about Jesus. That was the most important thing in the whole world to him. If people put him to death for preaching, then he was glad to die for Jesus' sake.

It's okay to enjoy your sports or your music or your pets, but remember that the most important thing is to live to please Jesus. He gives you life each day so you can live for Him!

A POWER NOTE

Can you tell people about Jesus, like Paul did? Think of someone you want to talk to about salvation in Christ and write their name on a piece of paper. Put it where it will remind you to share the love of Jesus with them.

WILDFIRE

Find It in the Bible

Likewise, the tongue is a small part of the body,
but it makes great boasts. Consider what a great
forest is set on fire by a small spark.

JAMES 3:5

Fire can be useful. You might keep warm around a fire, cook over it, or use it for light. Fire was especially important before electric lighting and heating were invented.

But fire can also be dangerous. When a fire gets out of control, it's called a *wildfire*. Every year, the United States has about 80,000 wildfires. In the year 2012, over 9 million acres of land were burned by forest fires.

How does a wildfire start? It begins with a small flame—maybe even just one match. Up to 90 percent of wildfires in the United States are started by people being careless.

Just like a fire, your tongue can help others or hurt others. Your kind words can make people feel warm inside. But your tongue can also do great damage. If you say something mean or tell a lie, you hurt other people and yourself. You can't take words back after you say them, and just a few words can cause a lot of damage. God wants you to be careful with your words and use them to help people, not hurt them.

A POWER NOTE

Draw a picture of a match and flame. Inside the flame, write three or four examples of kind words that can start a warm fire instead of a dangerous wildfire.

Jesus is the Light

Find It in the Bible

When Jesus spoke again to the people, he said, "I am the
light of the world. Whoever follows me will never
walk in darkness, but will have the light of life."

JOHN 8:12

Imagine spending over two months deep below the ground in a dark tunnel. On August 5, 2010, a mine in Chile collapsed, trapping thirty-three miners. A rescue operation began to bring the men to safety from 2,400 feet below the ground (that's over half a mile!). When they were brought to the surface, the men had been underground for sixty-nine days. One thing they received right away? Sunglasses, to protect their eyes from the light. They were surely happy when their eyes adjusted, and they could see the light again!

We don't live in dark tunnels—in fact, the sun shines every day—yet Jesus calls the world a dark place. He means that the world is full of the darkness of sin and evil. But no one has to be stuck there. Jesus brings light! He promises that if we follow Him, He shines light so we can see sin and avoid it. He gives guidance and comfort, even when we feel surrounded by darkness.

A POWER NOTE

Do this experiment. Go into an extremely dark room (like a closet with the door closed) and sit for about ten minutes. Then, switch on the light or walk outside into the sun. What happens? Your eyes need a few minutes to adjust. With Jesus, a much better way is to stay in the light always!

GOD IS YOUR REFUGE

Find It in the Bible

But let all who take refuge in you be glad; let them ever
sing for joy. Spread your protection over them,
that those who love your name may rejoice in you.

PSALM 5:11

What scares you most? Maybe it's the loud rumble of a thunderstorm. Perhaps spiders give you the creepy-crawlies, or maybe monsters in a movie make you shudder. What do you do when you're frightened? Do you hide under the covers of your bed, hum a happy song, or run to your parents?

Everybody gets scared once in a while, but we can trust in God because He promises to be a refuge for us. You probably don't use the word *refuge* much. It's from an old French word that means "hiding place." The word is so old that it was first used in AD 12, when kings still lived in big stone castles.

God wants you to hide in Him when you are frightened. He promises to be a safe place and to protect you from whatever might hurt you. Like the strong castle walls that protected ancient kings, God wants to be a strong refuge for you.

A POWER NOTE

Try building a castle puzzle! Make a copy of a picture of a castle from a book at your school or the library. Paste it onto a piece of card paper and draw wiggly lines on top of it to create a puzzle. Cut out the pieces and put the puzzle together. Remember that God is your refuge. Thank Him for protecting you.

Love of Money

Find It in the Bible

Whoever loves money never has enough; whoever loves wealth is never satisfied with their income. This too is meaningless.

ECCLESIASTES 5:10

In our society, people who have a lot of money are often fascinating to those who have less money. On the Web you can find lists of the richest people in America or the richest people in the world. One person is actually at the top of both lists: Bill Gates, co-founder of Microsoft.

Perhaps you know someone who longs to be rich. Perhaps that person is you. The Bible has more to say about money than many other subjects. After all, many people love money, and they believe it solves problems. Yet it often creates many more problems and conflicts.

God gave Solomon great wealth and wisdom (see 1 Kings 3:3–14). But Solomon didn't always act wisely. Toward the end of his life, he shared some of the lessons he learned in the book of Ecclesiastes. One of the lessons was that money doesn't bring anyone satisfaction. People who have money want more of it. People without money want it. Yet Solomon knew that there is only one way to feel satisfied: depend on God.

A POWER NOTE

The Bible never says that money is wrong. Yet people can have wrong attitudes about money. You can know what's true about it. Read other passages in the Bible that talk about money. For example: Matthew 6:24; 2 Corinthians 9:8–11; 1 Timothy 6:9–10.

GOD'S NAME IS SPECIAL

Find It in the Bible

You shall not misuse the name of the LORD your God, for the LORD will not hold anyone guiltless who misuses his name.

EXODUS 20:7

Names in nature often tell us something about a plant or creature. The zebra longwing butterfly is black with white stripes like a zebra. The arian small blue butterfly is the smallest butterfly in the world. It is the size of a grain of rice. The hotlips plant has red "lipstick" markings on its leaves. Names have meanings.

God's name is super special, and it tells us what He is like. He is kind and loving. He is holy and pure and powerful. This means He never does anything wrong. He is our loving heavenly Father, and we worship Him.

We show our love for God by how we speak about Him. Since God's name is part of who He is, we treat it in a special way. We don't make jokes or use bad words with any part of God's name. Sadly, many people say God's name when they are excited or even when they are mad, but this doesn't show respect and honor for Him.

A POWER NOTE

One way of treating God's name special is to praise Him and tell others about Him. Make a plan to say one loving thing about God to another person each day for one week.

A FALSE IMAGE

Find It in the Bible

You shall not make for yourself an image in the form of
anything in heaven above or on the earth beneath
or in the waters below.

EXODUS 20:4

What animal is longer than three dump trucks and has a heart the size of a small car? The answer is a blue whale. How much food does it eat? Try four tons of tiny fish each day—that's three million calories! Even a baby blue whale drinks 100 gallons of milk every twenty-four hours!

God not only created the blue whale, but He provides all the food for this amazing creature. Back in Bible times, the people of Egypt made objects and statues of gold, silver, stone, and wood and called these things "gods." They worshipped these statues and said the images had power. Do you think an idol of stone could create the blue whale? No way!

When God gave the people of Israel rules to obey, He told them to worship only Him. He didn't want His people to make an object of wood or stone and say that the object was Him. God doesn't have a body, but He is present everywhere in the universe and is all-powerful.

A POWER NOTE

God wants you to know the truth about Him. If you want a clear picture of God, look in the Bible. Read verses like Exodus 34:6–7 that describe what He is like. Use these verses to write a description of God.

THE HIGH COST OF DOING WRONG

Find It in the Bible
For the wages of sin is death, but the gift of God is
eternal life in Christ Jesus our Lord.

ROMANS 6:23

God has given us rules to follow and when we break His rules we sin. The price (or the wage) we have to pay is death. This includes being separated from God forever. The good news is that Jesus died for every wrong thing we have ever done. Our bodies will all die at some time, but our souls will live forever. You can live with God forever if you believe in Jesus and ask Him to forgive your sins. This is the gift of eternal life.

A young girl gave her teacher a Christmas gift of a beautiful seashell. "Where did you get this?" the teacher asked. The girl told her that such shells were found only on a certain faraway beach. The teacher was deeply touched that the girl had walked so far to find the shell. "You shouldn't have walked so far just to find a gift for me," she said. The girl smiled and replied, "The long walk is part of the gift."

God has given us the gift of eternal life through salvation, and His Son, Jesus, came a long, long way to bring this gift to us.

A POWER NOTE

God loves you, and He sent His Son to die for your sins. This is good news. Write the verse above on a piece of paper or on a card. Give it to someone and tell them the good news.

Deep Water

Find It in the Bible

When you pass through the waters, I will be with you; and when you pass
through the rivers, they will not sweep over you. When you walk through
the fire, you will not be burned; the flames will not set you ablaze.

Isaiah 43:2

Imagine swimming in the Congo River. At over 750 feet, the
Congo River is the deepest river in the world. When you're in
deep water, you might feel safest if you use a life vest or a boat is
nearby, especially if you're not a strong swimmer.

In this verse of Isaiah 43, water and fire are word pictures for
hard times. Consider the devastation of a flood. It destroys and
sweeps away everything in its path. A fire also burns buildings
and forests to the ground.

But passing through water is something God's people recalled in
their history. God miraculously brought them through the Red
Sea and the Jordan River (Exodus 14; Joshua 4). Though hard
times came their way, God helped them.

When hard times come, you don't have to feel as if you're in over
your head—like you would be in a deep pool or lake. God is with
you. He's better than the best life vest or life preserver. He'll never
fail you.

A POWER NOTE

Find an old magazine and cut out a picture of water—perhaps
a river or a lake—then glue matching colors of tissue paper on
top of it. Hang your tissue "painting" in your room to remind
you that God will help you through deep waters when they come:
things like a hard test, losing a friend, or an illness.

DON'T WORRY

Find It in the Bible

Therefore do not worry about tomorrow, for tomorrow will worry about itself. Each day has enough trouble of its own.

MATTHEW 6:34

Have you ever carried a lantern or a flashlight on a dark road at night? If you have, you know that you can't see more than one step ahead of you. As you take one step, the light of the lantern moves forward and lets you see the next step. You can reach your destination safely through the darkness step by step. That lantern is with you all the way, but it gives light only for one step at a time.

Many times we tend to look way down the road of life and worry about what is ahead. We wonder what will happen tomorrow or next week. When Jesus gave the Sermon on the Mount (recorded here in Matthew), He told His listeners that they didn't have to worry. God takes care of the grass, the birds, and everything in the world. So we can count on Him to take care of His people, too. We don't have to worry about what might or might not happen tomorrow because we can trust God.

A POWER NOTE

The next time you feel worried about something, use a concordance in the back of a Bible (Mom or Dad can help) and look up the words *worry* and *fear.* Then, make a list of some of the verses that tell you not to be anxious or afraid. Keep that list of verses where you can find it for the next time you start to worry.

HOLDING GOD'S HAND

Find It in the Bible

Yet I am always with you; you hold
me by my right hand.

PSALM 73:23

Little children hold their parent's hand when they walk in a parking lot and in a store. They do this to be safe. Otherwise a child might get hurt or lost. That is the parents' way of making sure their children stay close to them, even if the kids don't think they need it.

In your faith, God does the same thing. He is always close to you, caring for you and loving you. In this psalm, Asaph wrote about God's presence in his life. He declared that God held him by his "right hand." When you feel alone or afraid, God will come beside you and keep you safe from your fear. He has given you the Holy Spirit to comfort you and to guide you.

Be careful that you don't resist holding God's hand. Sometimes you may feel as though you can do something by yourself, but inviting God to help you is best. He will make sure that you never get lost, just like your mom or dad do when they walk you through a crowd of people or across a busy street.

A POWER NOTE

Trace the outline of your hand on a piece of paper. Cut it out and write Psalm 73:23 (the verse above) on the hand. Use it as a bookmark or put it up on your bulletin board to remind you that God holds you close.

PROMISES

Find It in the Bible

For no word from God will ever fail.

LUKE 1:37

H as anyone ever made a promise to you and then broken it? Sometimes people make promises and, though they intend to keep them, something happens and they decide to break their promises. Maybe something better came along. Or they realized that keeping the promise would be painful and they needed to protect themselves. In any case, when promises are broken, people get hurt. We trust people who make promises to us, so we feel betrayed when they break their promises.

Thousands of years ago, God promised the prophets of Israel that He would send a Savior to pay the penalty for sin. Then, He chose Mary to be the Savior's mother. When the angel Gabriel came to tell Mary that she would be the mother of Jesus, he said that God keeps His promises. His word never fails.

God is the only one who is able to keep *all* His promises *all* the time. The next time someone disappoints you by breaking a promise, you will be upset—and that's okay. But don't forget the promises that God has made and will fulfill. He will never let you down.

A POWER NOTE

Look up these promises from God in the Bible. Let them remind you of God's promise to keep His promises, *always*: Deuteronomy 31:6; John 16:33; Psalm 103:12; 1 Corinthians 10:13; James 1:5; Philippians 1:6; John 3:16.

OUR CREATIVE GOD

Find It in the Bible

So the man gave names to all the livestock, the birds
in the sky and all the wild animals.

GENESIS 2:20

Scientists estimate that the world could have as many as 10 million species of animals—and many of them haven't even been seen yet! Every year, more and more animals are discovered. In 2013, scientists added several new animals to the rolls—such as the olinguito (pronounced *oh-lin-GHEE-toe*), a mammal that lives high in the trees in South American cloud forests. Two others were the cocoa frog (a frog with chocolate-colored skin, also found in South America) and the glue-spitting velvet worm (a two-and-a-half inch worm, found in Vietnam, that shoots a sticky substance at its prey).

In the beginning when God made the world, He created all the birds, fish, cattle, bugs, and other animals in the world. Then, He created a man and called him Adam. Adam had the privilege of giving names to each animal God created.

Imagine the creativity of a God who made so many creatures—fuzzy, furry, slippery, beautiful, ugly, scary. So many animals exist that we haven't even seen them all yet! What an amazing and creative God we serve!

A POWER NOTE

Go through the whole alphabet and try to name one animal for every letter. After you do it once, try it again. See how many times you can keep naming animals for each letter of the alphabet.

POUR OUT THE SPIRIT

Find It in the Bible

I will no longer hide my face from them, for I will pour out my Spirit on the people of Israel, declares the Sovereign LORD.

EZEKIEL 39:29

It's a hot summer day. You just want to cool off, so you get the hose and the sprinkler and turn on the cold water. With your swimsuit on and the sprinkler running, you get refreshed by the cold, spraying water.

Some day in the future, the people of Israel will greatly need to feel refreshed. They will have just gone through the worst battle ever—the battle of Armageddon. With Jesus' help, they will have won, but they will still need to feel the refreshing presence of God's Spirit as they recover from the battle.

Our verse is God's promise to give the battle-weary people of Israel the refreshing they need. He will pour out His Spirit on them. He will give them the refreshment they will desperately need.

Just as God will someday pour out His Spirit on the people of Israel, He wants to pour out His Spirit on you right now. He wants to baptize you in the Holy Spirit. When the Holy Spirit fills our lives, He refreshes us. It's even more refreshing than jumping into cool water on a hot day. It feels great!

A POWER NOTE

On the next hot day, play in the sprinkler! Think about how great it feels to have God the Holy Spirit in your life.

TOO HOT TO HANDLE?

Find It in the Bible

If we are thrown into the blazing furnace, the God we
serve is able to deliver us from it, and he will deliver us
from Your Majesty's hand. But even if he does not,
we want you to know, Your Majesty, that we will not serve
your gods or worship the image of gold you have set up.

DANIEL 3:17-18

The furnace in this story wasn't like the one in your basement
that heats your house, or the fireplace in your living room. It
was probably a gigantic furnace used to bake clay into bricks or
to heat metals to purify them. That would mean the temperature
of the roaring flames inside was way hotter than any person
could survive.

Daniel's three friends had two choices: (1) disobey God by bowing
down to the idol, or (2) refuse to bow down and be thrown into
the furnace. They chose number two. They refused to bow to
the idol and told the king that God could protect them from the
dangerous fire. Even if He didn't, however, they still refused to
disappoint God.

That is amazing faith! Not only were they willing to be persecuted
in a way that would frighten most people to death, but they knew
they could count on God to be with them in the middle of this
difficult experience.

A POWER NOTE

Read the rest of this story in Daniel 3:19–30. Think about how
God helped His friends with a fire that was too hot to handle.

HEALING WORDS

Find It in the Bible

The words of the reckless pierce like swords,
but the tongue of the wise brings healing.

PROVERBS 12:18

In ancient times, before guns and cannons and bombs had been invented, wars were usually fought in hand-to-hand combat. The soldiers had armor and battled with swords. The long-sword (the largest sword used by soldiers in the Middle Ages) could be up to five feet long. That may be even taller than you! Imagine the damage such a big sword could do!

Your words can be just as sharp as swords. Even though your words don't cause physical harm, they can still hurt people. Calling people names and teasing are easy ways to hurt people's feelings, but God doesn't want us to hurt people with our words. He wants us to heal people with our words.

Think about the words you say before you say them. Don't be reckless and says things that will hurt people. Instead, be wise. Ask God to help you speak words that bring healing.

A POWER NOTE

Think of two people whom you would like to compliment. Determine that tomorrow you'll say kind and sincere words to those people. And if the Spirit guides you to say a kind word to someone else, follow Him!

WALK THE LINE

Find It in the Bible

Do not turn to the right or the left; keep your foot from evil.

PROVERBS 4:27

Did you know that scientists are studying why people can't walk in a straight line when they're blindfolded? They have done numerous experiments by blindfolding people and asking them to walk straight, and then they tracked their walk. When people have a focal point in the distance and walk toward it, they can stay pretty straight. But when blindfolded, they can't sense what is straight and have a tendency to walk in circles.

This proverb was written long before scientists studied this, but we know that when we don't have something to walk toward, when we look down at the ground, or when we close our eyes, we can easily get off course. That's why we should not go through life "blindfolded." In other words, if you want to walk along God's path for you and stay straight, you need to keep your eyes open and focused on Jesus. You do this by reading His Word and learning His ways.

A POWER NOTE

Do the straight-walking experiment with a friend. In a safe space, choose a spot to walk toward in a straight line. Do it without a blindfold, then try to do it blindfolded. See how far you can walk a straight line with a blindfold on. Think about walking straight on God's path.

PRIORITIES

Find It in the Bible

"You expected much, but see, it turned out to be little. What you brought home, I blew away. Why?" declares the LORD Almighty. "Because of my house, which remains a ruin, while each of you is busy with your own house."

HAGGAI 1:9

There are many different kinds of houses in the world. In Masuleh, Iran, the houses are stacked on top of each other up the hillsides. The houses on each level share a wide, flat roof made of clay. If you lived there, your neighbors above you could play dodge ball on your roof, and you could jump rope on the roof of your neighbors below.

When the people of Israel returned to Jerusalem, God wanted them to rebuild the temple. Instead, they rebuilt their own houses! Doing what God wanted wasn't a high priority. So God told the prophet Haggai to remind them to make rebuilding God's house a priority.

After all, if they didn't have God at the center of their lives, they didn't have anything. What about you? What are your priorities? Does God come first in your life?

A POWER NOTE

It would be fun to see photos of houses from around the world and of churches from around the world. Perhaps you can see these on the Internet at your house or in books at the library. If you had to choose to build your house or God's house, which would you choose? Why?

PERFECT TIMING

Find It in the Bible

But do not forget this one thing, dear friends: With the Lord a day
is like a thousand years, and a thousand years are like a day.
The Lord is not slow in keeping his promise,
as some understand slowness.

2 PETER 3:8–9

The ancient Aztec people believed that the sun was weak and needed help. They thought that if they did all the right things and pleased their false gods, then their gods would help the sun rise each day. If their false gods were not pleased, the sun might not rise.

We know that the Creator God of the Bible controls the sun, which has a diameter of about 865,000 miles. It is ten times larger than the largest planet, Jupiter, which is big enough to contain all the other planets put together.

Each day comes for twenty-four hours—but because God is eternal, the days may be like a thousand years to us, and a thousand years to us might be like a day to Him. Sometimes when you pray, you may wonder why God takes so long to answer. But you have to wait. God is not affected by seconds, hours, days, week, months, and years—He sees the beginning to the end. And everything He does will be in His perfect timing.

A POWER NOTE

Is the sun shining today? If so, grab something to do outside. Enjoy God's sunshine today! While you are outside, thank the Lord for His marvelous creation and promises.

A LIVING SACRIFICE

Find It in the Bible

Therefore I urge you, brothers and sisters, in view of God's mercy,
to offer your bodies as a living sacrifice, holy and pleasing to God—
this is your true and proper worship.

ROMANS 12:1

The Bible teaches us to offer our bodies as living sacrifices. That sounds a little scary, but really, it means that all we are, including our talents and abilities, should be used to glorify God and point others toward Him. This is how we worship Him.

Do you think you're too young to do anything for God? Well, guess who named the planet Pluto? An eleven-year-old schoolgirl in England suggested the name, and it stuck. Did you know that two children helped to invent the first telescope? Their father made eyeglasses and they were playing in his shop one day when they held up two eyeglass lenses in a straight line and noticed that the weather vane on the building next door was magnified. Their father put the two lenses in a tube and this became the first telescope.

Even when you're young, your life counts! You are never too young to bring glory and honor to God. When you do this, your life becomes an act of worship.

A POWER NOTE

On a piece of paper, list your talents and abilities. Then, next to each item, write ways you can use each one to show God's love to others. Perhaps you love animals. Maybe you could offer to help a neighbor give her dog a bath. This act of kindness would bring glory to God.

TWENTY-FOUR CARAT GOLD

Find It in the Bible

But he knows the way that I take; when he has tested me,
I will come forth as gold.

JOB 23:10

Gold is rare and valuable. People have been mining gold for thousands of years. After the rocks or nuggets are pulled from the ground, a process called smelting purifies the gold. By adding heat or acids to the gold, smelting removes impurities. The purest gold is called twenty-four carat.

Job was going through a super difficult time. He had lost his wealth, his children, and his health. People thought Job should blame God and just give up and die. But he didn't. He recognized that God knew what he was going through. He also knew that no matter how tough his situation, he would be better at the end of it. He knew that he could be "twenty-four-carat gold" after passing the difficult tests. He would be pure and still pliable to God's will.

God sees the difficulty you are going through right now. He is working in your life to clear out any impurities. You are so valuable and rare—He also wants you pure. Trust God. He's making twenty-four-carat gold out of your life!

A POWER NOTE

Find some jewelry catalogs on the Internet. Look at rings and other pieces of gold jewelry. How do the prices change as the carats increase? Would you rather be ten carat or twenty-four carat?

FRee TO . . .

Find It in the Bible

In those days Israel had no king;
everyone did as they saw fit.

JUDGES 17:6

Bo was a really good dog; that is, except when his master, Mike, was gone from the house. Bo knew the rules when Mike was at home; but when Mike left for work and was gone all day, Bo got into the kitchen garbage and spread it all over the floor. When no one was around, Bo did what he wanted.

At this time in the Bible story, the people of Israel didn't have a leader. They had no king, and they didn't obey God. Everyone did whatever they wanted to do. The book of Judges has lots of stories of people doing bad things, which led to them getting conquered by foreign armies. Then God would send a judge (a strong, godly leader) to help get the people back on the right track. But as soon as the judge died, the people managed to get themselves into trouble again. Without laws and leadership, the people went their own ways and disaster resulted.

Like Bo, the people of Israel got into trouble when they thought no one was watching. We can be like that, too. At first, doing whatever we want feels like fun. But God puts laws and leaders in place to keep us safe. And even when we think no one is around, we should to do what is right. After all, God always knows!

A POWER NOTE

Think about the laws for your home, school, and city. Think about what might happen if everyone disobeyed those laws and did just as they pleased.

In Step With God

Find It in the Bible

Do two walk together unless they have agreed to do so?

AMOS 3:3

For the church picnic, the organizers planned a three-legged race. Partners had to stand next to each other and have one leg each tied to the partner's leg. At the end of the race, the winning team, by far, was an elderly grandfather and his ten-year-old grandson who crossed the finish line far ahead of everyone else. Many of the other twosomes had fallen or bumped into each other or tripped over each other's feet. The grandfather, however, had been in the military, so he told his grandson to follow the cadence (beat) he would set. So the grandfather rhythmically called out, "Step . . . step . . . step," and the grandson obeyed. They moved forward in unison at a steady clip and won the race.

When walking through your Christian life, imagine that you are connected to God in the same way as the boy and his grandfather—walking in step with Him, to His cadence. How can you walk with God? Read the Bible and other books that teach about the Bible, then make a point to live in obedience to God's Word. Try to go to church regularly, and talk to your heavenly Father every day.

A POWER NOTE

Try a three-legged walk with a friend or someone in your family. First walk anyway you like, then try to walk together in step to a beat. Which helps you walk farther? In a similar way, you need to walk in step with your heavenly Father every day.

SOMETHING TO BRAG ABOUT

Find It in the Bible

But let the one who boasts boast about this: that they have
the understanding to know me, that I am the LORD,
who exercises kindness, justice and righteousness on the earth,
for in these I delight, declares the LORD.

JEREMIAH 9:24

Did you know that a butterfly wing is scaly? If you could look at the wing with a magnifying glass, you would see thousands of tiny scales, each arranged in a special pattern for a special purpose. These scales form the colors, patterns, and shapes of the wing. Sometimes the pattern attracts a mate or helps the butterfly hide from predators. In cool climates, the scales absorb heat from the sun to warm the butterfly's muscles. Without this warmth, the butterfly wouldn't be able to fly.

The butterfly can't brag about its beautiful wings; only God can brag because He made those beautiful wings.

God created the butterfly and God created you. You weren't a mistake or an accident—God had a purpose in mind when He made you, and He has a plan for your life. He gave you unique gifts and talents. But that's exactly the point: *He* gave them to you!

That's why the Bible says we have no room to boast. You are who you are because of God's incredible imagination.

A POWER NOTE

Draw three boxes on a piece of paper and make them look like presents wrapped with unique paper and bows. On each box, write down something that makes you special. Remember that each of these is a gift from God.

SHAKEN BUT NOT AFRAID

Find It in the Bible

God is our refuge and strength, an ever-present help in trouble.
Therefore we will not fear, though the earth give way
and the mountains fall into the heart of the sea.

PSALM 46:1–2

On August 27, 1883, a mountain gave way and fell into the sea. That was the day that a volcano on the island of Krakatoa (near Indonesia) erupted. Two-thirds of the island collapsed into the surrounding ocean, which then caused tsunamis (big ocean waves) that crashed into shorelines thousands of miles away. That eruption is considered to have been the worst in recorded history with over 36,000 people killed.

Where could you go if the mountains fell into the sea? There wouldn't be many places to run. Hopefully, you won't have to face such a disaster, but sometimes you may feel like your world is being shaken just as badly. Something comes along and destroys your plans. A situation happens that hurts you. These things shake up your world.

Where can you go? God says you can go to Him. He promises to be your refuge, your strength, your ever-present help in times of trouble.

A POWER NOTE

See if you can unscramble this sentence. It will help you to be brave and to have faith in God.

odG si ym efgreu dan httgsner dna
reev-ntreeps phel.

(God is my refuge and strength and ever-present help.)

ReBUILDING

Find It in the Bible

Then I prayed to the God of heaven, and I answered the king,
"If it pleases the king and if your servant has found favor
in his sight, let him send me to the city in Judah where
my ancestors are buried so that I can rebuild it."

NEHEMIAH 2:4–5

Once the water receded from New Orleans after Hurricane Katrina had devastated the city in late August, 2005, some people returned and started to rebuild homes, offices, and schools. It was a massive effort to get rid of mud, mold, and mildew, to tear down destroyed buildings, and to rebuild the city.

The Israelites had returned to their land after being in exile for seventy years. Their homes and the temple had been destroyed. But Nehemiah knew that the people could rebuild. He offered to go to Jerusalem and lead the rebuilding effort from the ground up.

At times our lives—our souls—are similar to damaged cities. We feel so disappointed or upset that we need to rebuild our attitudes and feelings. We start from the ground up. We build on our solid foundation, our faith in the Rock, Jesus. We get rid of old, bad feelings and attitudes and replace them with new attitudes and actions.

A POWER NOTE

Draw a figure of yourself and then draw a "wall" around it. Label some "gates" (good attitudes you want to have), and ask God to help you as you build your life.

RULE BREAKERS

Find It in the Bible

If my people, who are called by my name, will humble
themselves and pray and seek my face and turn
from their wicked ways, then I will hear from heaven,
and I will forgive their sin and will heal their land.

2 CHRONICLES 7:14

At the beginning of every school year the teachers and principal go over the school rules and the consequences for breaking them. "Why even bother?" you might wonder. "Everyone already knows all the rules!" Even though everyone knows the rules, they get broken pretty quickly. Someone cheats or gets into a fight or breaks some school property. Although people know better, they still do what is wrong.

God knew His people would break the rules He had given them, too. That's why He told them what to do when that happened. They needed to humble themselves (feel sorry for what they've done and tell God they were wrong). They needed to seek God's face in prayer, and (most importantly) stop doing what is wicked and do good.

God makes the same promise to you. No matter how many times you mess up (even when you know better), you can humble yourself, talk to God in prayer, and decide to not do that wrong thing again. And what does God promise? That He will forgive and restore!

A POWER NOTE

Make a list of five rules that are difficult for you to follow, either at home or at school. What could you do to obey the next time you're tempted to disobey?

CAST YOUR CARES

Find It in the Bible

Cast your cares on the LORD and he will sustain you;
he will never let the righteous be shaken.

PSALM 55:22

C amels are sometimes called "ships of the desert." That's because people who ride long distances on their swaying backs often feel seasick. But they might also be called that because of the heavy loads they can carry. Camels have super strong muscles in the upper parts of their legs that let them carry heavy loads for a long distance. A camel can carry 992 pounds of weight while walking twenty-four miles in a day. That would be like carrying twenty kids at one time. What a heavy load!

Sometimes we feel like we are carrying a heavy load in life. Things happen that make us angry, or afraid, or frustrated. It's no fun to carry a load of disappointment and sadness. The good news is we don't have to. Someone is near who wants to hear how you're feeling and who understands your hurt, fear, and pain.

That someone is God. He cares about everything that makes you angry or worried. When you truly rely on Him, He will give you strength to get through all the problems and issues that just seem too heavy.

A POWER NOTE

The next time you pray about your fears and worries, do this. Put your hands out flat in front of you, palms up. Pretend like you're holding all of your worries in your hands. Then say that you want to put that load on Jesus, and when you say it, turn your hands over and "drop" all of your worries and cares on Him.

SHOWING LOVE

Find It in the Bible

Love the LORD your God with all your heart and with
all your soul and with all your strength.

DEUTERONOMY 6:5

How do you show your love to others? If you were a swan, you would bob your head in the water and then put it close to the loved one. If you were a monkey, you might groom the monkey you love by picking bugs off of your loved one's coat. And if you were a cat, you'd be licking your friend! Eww!

But to show love to other people, you probably spend a lot of time with them. You have conversations to get to know them better. You say good things about them. You think about them a lot, value their ideas and advice, and even give them gifts. Love includes a lot more than just saying, "I love you!"

So how do you show God that you love Him? You can spend time with Him, listening to Him and talking with Him. When you pray and read the Bible, you talk to God, and God talks to you. You can also do the things He wants you to do, and you can tell others about Him.

A POWER NOTE

Show God you love Him by planning a time to hang out together! Pick a specific time and place to be alone with God. Then have a conversation with Him—read your Bible, pray, and enjoy getting to know Him more.

SEPTEMBER

IT'S A-*MAZE*-ING!

Find It in the Bible

Trust in the LORD with all your heart and lean not on
your own understanding; in all your ways submit to him,
and he will make your paths straight.

PROVERBS 3:5–6

Sometimes in the summer or fall, a farmer will create a maze in his cornfield when the corn is so tall you can't see over it. He takes out some of the stalks to create a pattern that is full of wrong turns and dead ends. You start at one end and try to find your way out the other side. You go forward, back up, try again, make wrong turns, and finally you find your way out. That's all part of the fun! The world's largest corn maze is in Spring Grove, Illinois. It covers thirty-three acres! That's the size of twenty-five football fields!

Sometimes life can seem like a big maze. Some days you feel as though you're just wandering, running into dead ends, making wrong turns, and getting nowhere. Fortunately, God doesn't leave you to lose your way in the maze of life. He's right there at every turn, offering to point you in the right direction. His Holy Spirit guides you, promising to take you along the path God has planned for you. Now that's a-*maze*-ing!

A POWER NOTE

Find something around the house to use as a blindfold. Put on the blindfold and ask a parent, sibling, or friend to direct you around the house. Listen closely and practice following instructions. See how long you can go without uncovering your eyes!

unseen Deeds

Find It in the Bible

But when you pray, go into your room, close the door and
pray to your Father, who is unseen. Then your Father,
who sees what is done in secret, will reward you.

MATTHEW 6:6

John Chapman lived in Massachusetts back in the 1800's. He had heard that people living in the Midwest didn't have many apple trees so he decided to help them. He traveled all over Ohio, Indiana, and Illinois with a bag of apple seeds that he used to plant small orchards of apple trees. He came quietly into a town, planted the seeds, and left quietly. He didn't want people to praise him for his work. Today he is known as "Johnny Appleseed."

Everyone enjoys praise and appreciation. Hearing positive words makes us feel good. Nothing is wrong with that—except when we refuse to do nice things for others unless someone is watching. That was the problem Jesus was talking about in this verse. Some religious leaders were praying loudly in public, not because they wanted to talk to God but because they wanted people to see them pray and be impressed.

Jesus explained that a much better way is to go into a quiet place and pray in secret.

A POWER NOTE

Make an apple bird feeder. Spread peanut butter all over an apple. Roll the apple around in a bowl filled with birdseed. Next, tie a string around the apple stem and hang it on a low tree branch. Think of something helpful you could do without anyone finding out about it.

WAKING UP

Find It in the Bible

I lie down and sleep; I wake again, because the LORD sustains me.

PSALM 3:5

What wakes you up each morning? Maybe you have an alarm clock that rings or buzzes. People have been using alarm clocks for a long time. The philosopher Plato (428–348 BC) had a water clock that made some kind of sound to awaken him for his early morning lectures. A Buddhist monk and inventor, Yi Xing (727–683 BC), created a clock that would strike a sound. Evidently people have always needed help getting up early!

That's why you need to get to bed on time and get enough sleep. Sleep lets your body rest, but it's also important to wake up so that you can enjoy life each day. Can you imagine how difficult it would be to play with your friends or learn about science at school if you were still sleeping? It would be impossible!

The Bible says we get up each day because God gives us energy and keeps us alive. Each new day is a gift that allows us to wake up and play with friends, go to school, and spend time with our families.

A POWER NOTE

Do you wake up to an alarm clock in the morning? If not, ask your mom or dad if you can use one for a morning or two. When the alarm rings, thank God out loud for waking you up and giving you energy.

Send Me!

Find It in the Bible

Then I heard the voice of the LORD saying, "Whom shall I send? And who will go for us?" And I said, "Here am I. Send me!"

ISAIAH 6:8

Volunteering to do fun or simple tasks is easy. When you help the teacher with a bulletin board or you get out of class early to run an errand for her, that's fun. But doing the yucky jobs—like cleaning up after painting class or picking up litter on the playground (especially if it's cold outside!)—is not so fun. When we volunteer to do something, we generally want to do something fun.

But Isaiah the prophet didn't think that way. He knew that being a prophet was difficult work. Lots of times people didn't listen to the prophets that God sent to them—and often they just laughed and made fun of them. Sometimes prophets were even killed by the king if the king didn't like what they said.

Being a prophet could be quite difficult and dangerous, but when Isaiah heard that God needed someone to do that task, Isaiah didn't hesitate. He said, "Send me!" Isaiah showed the kind of attitude we should have. We should do our best to step out and help where we are needed, even if the job doesn't seem fun.

A POWER NOTE

Volunteer to do a job that doesn't look like it will be fun for you—like cleaning your room or helping the teacher with a messy task. The next time someone needs volunteers—be willing to say "Send me!"

"I'VE HAD ENOUGH!"

Find It in the Bible

Even youths grow tired and weary, and young men stumble and fall;
but those who hope in the LORD will renew their strength.
They will soar on wings like eagles; they will run and not
grow weary, they will walk and not be faint.

ISAIAH 40:30–31

Everyone's least favorite day in gym class is here: the mile run. The whistle blows, and you take off. You run so many laps that you almost lose count. When you finally finish, you're sweaty, thirsty, and exhausted.

Now imagine your gym teacher says, "Hey, we have five minutes left. Anyone want to play some basketball?" Maybe a few really energetic kids say yes. But you probably lay back on the grass and say, "I've had enough! I just want to rest."

God understands that humans get tired. And it's more than just being physically tired. Sometimes we get tired of doing good, tired of praying for someone who never seems to change, tired of doing the right thing when you wonder if it's really worth it.

Well, if you're just doing good things to check them off a list, the effort probably isn't worth much. But God wants you to obey Him because you love Him. And in this verse, He promises to give you the strength you need to keep going.

A POWER NOTE

Read the story of Elijah in 1 Kings 19:1–12. What are some ways God made Elijah stronger when he said, "I've had enough"?

A GREAT PLAN

Find It in the Bible

Salvation is found in no one else, for there is no other
name under heaven given to mankind
by which we must be saved.

ACTS 4:12

What would it be like to live in a different time? What if you lived in ancient Egypt with the pharaohs? Or maybe you'd like to live in a castle as a king or a queen during the Middle Ages? What would you wear and eat?

Living in those times would be very different from now, but one thing is still the same—God. He existed before all of those times, during those times, and still is with us today. Even before Adam and Eve, or Noah, or Joseph, and before Jesus was born on earth, God was thinking about what you are doing right now. Way back when Egyptians were building pyramids, God knew who you were going to be, and He had a plan for you.

God's plan is for you to know Him, to believe in Jesus as your Savior, and to live by the guidance of the Holy Spirit. He wanted that for you before the world was even made. That's how awesome God is!

A POWER NOTE

Choose a time in history that you'd like to learn more about. Research information on that historical time at the library or on the Internet. Write down five ways that your life would be different if you lived at that time. Then write down how you might have lived as a Christian at that time.

TALK TO GOD

Find It in the Bible

For God knows that when you eat from it your eyes
will be opened, and you will be like God,
knowing good and evil.

GENESIS 3:5

Satan knew just what to say to tempt Eve, "You will be like God." That doesn't sound like such a bad thing, does it? Aren't we all trying to live like Jesus and follow His example?

But that's not what was happening. Satan knew that God had told Adam and Eve not to eat from that one tree. Eve knew it was wrong, so when she listened to Satan and ate the fruit, she was disobeying God. Before Adam and Eve ate the fruit, they walked and talked with God each day. They were completely happy and never hungry or scared.

God knew that if they ate the fruit, they would be changed. They would indeed have their eyes opened and would know good from evil—instead of just knowing good. They would feel sadness, pain, and hunger. Worst of all, they wouldn't be able to talk face-to-face with God anymore!

Because of Adam and Eve's sin, we still feel sadness and pain until we go to heaven. But thankfully, God sent Jesus to die on the cross for our sins so that we can talk to Him and know Him again.

A POWER NOTE

Read the story of Adam and Eve in Genesis 3. Underline the places where you see they disobeyed God. Then look at Genesis 3:15 where God already had a plan in place to undo what they did. What was that plan?

SPEAK UP!

Find It in the Bible

She said to her mistress, "If only my master would
see the prophet who is in Samaria! He would
cure him of his leprosy."

2 KINGS 5:3

Leprosy is a skin disease. In Bible times, it was highly contagious and often led to other diseases. Leprosy was also bad because a cure hadn't been found for it yet. Naaman had leprosy. We don't know if he was born with it or if he got it partway through his life, but we know he had it as an adult.

One day, a little girl from Israel was brought into Naaman's house to work for him and his wife. She saw that Naaman had leprosy and wanted to help him, so she spoke up with a suggestion. She told Naaman to go see the prophet Elisha in Samaria because he could heal Naaman. Can you guess what happened? Naaman listened! He followed the little girl's advice and found Elisha. He was miraculously healed because a little servant girl spoke up!

Think about a time you saw someone who needed help. Maybe you had an idea of how to help the person but were too afraid to say anything. The little Israelite girl was probably nervous, too. She was a young girl in a strange city, but she spoke up anyway because she wanted to show God's love to Naaman.

A POWER NOTE

Next time you see someone who needs help with something, help them without being asked. In doing this, you will show God's love.

263

DO THE RIGHT THING

Find It in the Bible

Do not let your heart envy sinners, but always be
zealous for the fear of the LORD. There is surely a future
hope for you, and your hope will not be cut off.

PROVERBS 23:17–18

Did you know that even when you are standing still, you are moving? Scientific measurements show us that continental land masses sit on enormous slabs of rock that slide very slowly at the rate of one to eight inches per year. America is gradually moving westward, away from Europe, at the rate of three inches per year.

Every day we face decisions about whether to move toward what is right or toward what is wrong. Sometimes doing what is right can be difficult, especially when your friends do something you know is wrong. You can feel all alone if you don't go along with them.

Although living God's way can be hard, He wants you to do the right thing no matter what. When this verse says "the fear of the LORD," it means you should respect Him and recognize how great He is. The word "zealous" comes from an old Latin word that means "tolerating no unfaithfulness." God wants you to be faithful to respect Him and His rules.

A POWER NOTE

Practice standing up to pressure by playing a game with your friends. All but one person must close their eyes, and the one with eyes open may say anything to persuade everyone else to open their eyes. The last one with his eyes closed wins!

THE FALL

Find It in the Bible

Pride goes before destruction, a haughty spirit before a fall.

PROVERBS 16:18

"I can bounce higher than you!" Sam yelled, climbing up onto the trampoline with Edmund.

"No, you can't! I can go higher than anyone," Edmund boasted.

"Prove it," Sam said, crossing his arms.

Edmund bounced higher . . . and higher . . . until something went wrong. Instead of bouncing back up again, he collapsed on the trampoline. "I think I hurt my ankle!" he cried.

Edmund just learned that pride comes before a fall. Trusting in your own abilities or thinking you can get through life without needing help is dangerous. Even if you don't end up hurting your ankle, you could forget to give thanks to God for the gifts He has given you. You might even start to think that you earned them for yourself, and that they make you better than other people!

Remember that God is the one who gives you talents and abilities. Without Him, you couldn't do anything!

A POWER NOTE

What are some of your talents? What abilities make you special? Make a list of things you can do to improve your talents. Thank God for giving them to you, and pray that instead of being prideful, you will use your talents to help people in the way God wants you to.

FACING FEAR

Find It in the Bible

You will keep in perfect peace those whose minds
are steadfast, because they trust in you.

ISAIAH 26:3

A mother sea otter and her baby live in a forest of seaweed along the ocean shore. She cuddles her pup to keep him warm and grooms his fur to keep it clean and waterproof. She feeds him her healthy, sweet milk and holds him close against the soft fur of her stomach. When the mother needs to dive into the ocean to find food, she wraps strands of seaweed around her baby to create a cradle. This kelp cradle keeps him from drifting away, and the air bubbles in the kelp help to keep him warm until she returns.

The baby sea otter knows his mother will care for him and keep him safe. He trusts his mother to teach him about life in the sea. Much like that mother otter, we have a heavenly Father who cares for us. He has shown us in the Bible that He is trustworthy. We can read how He has cared for His people for thousands of years. We know for sure that His promises are trustworthy and true.

When you face struggles in life, how can you have peace in your heart? By keeping your thoughts fixed on Jesus and His love for you.

A POWER NOTE

Find a dictionary (perhaps in a library, at school, or on the Internet) and look up these three words: *peace, steadfast, trust.* Write out the definition of each word and think how you can keep your thoughts fixed on Jesus.

Inside the Chrysalis

Find It in the Bible

The LORD is good to those whose hope is in him,
to the one who seeks him; it is good to wait quietly
for the salvation of the LORD.

LAMENTATIONS 3:25–26

Picture yourself as a caterpillar. No, not one happily munching on a leaf: one stuck in a chrysalis (the hardened case around the caterpillar that is attached to a leaf). It's dark. You can hardly move. And there you are just . . . stuck there. Waiting patiently.

Of course, we all know that a caterpillar in a chrysalis *is* doing something. It's growing and changing into a butterfly. But it probably doesn't seem like it to the caterpillar, at least not at the time.

In the same way, sometimes we don't like what is happening around us. Maybe we think God is taking too long to answer a prayer request. Or something bad happened to us and we wonder why.

But guess what? God's timing is always best. He's using everything that happens to you to help you grow. We know that He always keeps His promises, and He loves us, no matter what. Sometimes, the best thing we can do is trust God and wait patiently.

A POWER NOTE

Read the verse for this devotion out loud. Then read it as fast as you can. Now very, very slowly. Remember that God has a purpose in the way He plans our lives. Even when the timing is different from what we'd like, He knows best!

Second Thoughts

Find It in the Bible

Those who guard their lips preserve their lives,
but those who speak rashly will come to ruin.

Proverbs 13:3

"Blurt" is a fun game to play with friends. Here's how it works: You think of a word. Then tell the others to blurt out the first word that comes to mind when they hear the word you say. No second thoughts. Just "blurt" it out!

What others say can be funny to hear. Most people blurt out totally different things. If you say "dragon," one friend might say "awesome," another "scary," and another "fire." If you say "flower," you might get the answers "rose" or "bread" (if someone thought you were saying "flour").

In a game like this, blurting out the first thing that pops into your head can be harmless fun. In real life, though, sometimes speaking before you think can get you into a lot of trouble. You might hurt someone's feelings or accidentally share a friend's secret.

God warns us about the power of our words. He knows that once we say them, we can't get them back. We need to be careful not to blurt!

A POWER NOTE

Think about what you might blurt out in the following situations: A friend doesn't invite you to his party. Your teacher blames you for something you didn't do. Your mom asks you to do something when you're busy. Now stop and think how you could react in a better way.

THE ROCK

Find It in the Bible

For who is God besides the LORD? And who is the
Rock except our God? It is God who arms me with
strength and keeps my way secure.

PSALM 18:31–32

A *monolith* is the word geologists use to describe a huge, individual rock. They cannot determine the largest monolith in the world because so much of the rock is under the ground or under water. But some of the most famous monoliths include the Rock of Gibraltar (1,396 feet high) on the southern coast of Spain, El Capitan (3,000 feet high) in Yosemite Valley National Park, and Devils Tower (1,267 feet high) in Wyoming.

In this psalm, David calls God his "Rock." God is as solid and immovable as the biggest monolith in the world. Nothing can defeat Him and nothing can break Him. He can withstand anything.

God is always with you. He is mighty and powerful. He is stronger than stone, and He stands firm forever. Could you have anyone better on your side? Remember to thank God for His constant care and protection. He's the strongest rock there is—thank Him for keeping you safe today!

A POWER NOTE

At your library or on your computer, look up pictures of the famous monoliths mentioned above. Remember that God is even bigger and stronger.

STAR LIGHT, STAR BRIGHT

Find It in the Bible

When I consider your heavens, the work of your fingers,
the moon and the stars, which you have set in place,
what is mankind that you are mindful of them,
human beings that you care for them?

PSALM 8:3–4

Have you ever tried to count the stars? Counting all of them is impossible, though scientists estimate that the universe has more than 300 sextillion. That's a 3 with twenty-three zeros after it! Some of the stars are so far away, you'll never see them. Others are far away, but you're just now seeing the light from them after that light has traveled for many years to reach you (which is why some stars are "light years" away).

Astronomers have located and named millions of stars and groupings of stars called constellations. For example, the Big Dipper is a group of seven stars that looks like a soup ladle.

God put every one of those stars in its place on purpose. He knows each and every one of them by name. If God takes such good care of the stars, then He will take much better care of you, a being created in His own image.

Always remember that God, who put all the stars in the sky, also made you.

A POWER NOTE

Check out a book on stars and constellations at your local library. Then, on a clear night, go outside and try to find the pictures in the sky that you see in the book.

Better Than Rubies

Find It in the Bible

For wisdom is more precious than rubies,
and nothing you desire can compare with her.

PROVERBS 8:11

People have been interested in precious gems for thousands and thousands of years, since before the Bible was written! Gems are found in jewelry, crowns, and even dog collars! One of the rarest gems is the ruby. This precious stone comes in varying shades of red. The world's biggest cut ruby weighs 302 carats (that's about 300 times bigger than the diamonds in engagement rings). If you want to buy that ruby, you need to pay about $500,000.

But God says that being wise is more precious than owning rubies. Rubies might get lost or stolen, and rubies won't help you make good decisions.

But since wisdom is in your thoughts and attitudes, no one can ever take it from you. Being wise makes God happy, and it is a skill you can use your whole life. You can use wisdom at home, at school, at soccer practice . . . everywhere! It helps you make good choices.

A POWER NOTE

Mix up a package of red gelatin following the instructions. Spray an empty ice cube tray with oil and fill it with the warm liquid. Let it set in the refrigerator for a couple of hours, then remove the red gelatin cubes. Cut them into the shape of gems and enjoy them with whipped cream. When you enjoy the good flavor of the gelatin, remember that wisdom is also a good treat.

RULES, RULES, RULES!

Find It in the Bible

Then he went down to Nazareth with them and was
obedient to them. But his mother treasured all these
things in her heart. And Jesus grew in wisdom and stature,
and in favor with God and man.

LUKE 2:51–52

Does your family have a lot of rules, like not staying up too late or only playing for so much time on the computer? Being told what to do and what not to do is not a lot of fun.

But look at it this way: rules protect you. If your parents didn't care, then they wouldn't make rules. If they didn't care what happened to you, then they wouldn't ask you to let them know where you are going. If they didn't care about your health, then they would let you stay up as late as you wanted.

Rules can be frustrating, but usually people who make rules just want you to be safe and happy. Jesus had rules to follow, too. He was twelve years old in this verse. When Jesus obeyed, He got smarter and stronger, both physically and mentally. That can also happen for you! Obeying the rules might be hard now, but it will bring good things later in life.

A POWER NOTE

Have a family talk about rules. Then ask your mom or dad to write them on a piece of paper. Have everyone in your family sign the paper. Then hang it in your family room to remind everyone that obeying the rules is good.

A MIGHTY FORTRESS

Find It in the Bible

The LORD is my rock, my fortress and my deliverer;
my God is my rock, in whom I take refuge,
my shield and the horn of my salvation.

2 SAMUEL 22:2–3

Europe has all kinds of ancient castles. On one section of the Rhine River in Germany stand over twenty castles. Most of them are crumbling ruins now, but at one time they were fortresses protecting the inhabitants of the castle and the townspeople below. From their high vantage points, the people could see enemies coming on land or on the river. The walls of these fortresses were most often made of wood or stone and were very thick, making them hard to break or climb over. The people inside the fort had an advantage because they could fire arrows and spears down at their enemies and duck behind the walls when their enemies fired back.

God is your fortress. He will protect you from whatever attacks Satan may try to use against you, no matter what.

When life gets hard, all you have to do is run to God and ask Him for help. He is a fortress. Run in, close the gate, and sit quietly for a while. God will give you the rest, armor, and weapons you need before you head back out to battle.

A POWER NOTE

Build a pretend fortress out of craft sticks and glue. Twist together strips of paper to make arrows. Throw the "arrows" at your fortress from a short distance away. The paper "arrows" are the lies Satan tells us, and the craft stick fortress is God protecting us.

WISDOM

Find It in the Bible

For the LORD gives wisdom; from his mouth
comes knowledge and understanding.

PROVERBS 2:6

What is wisdom, exactly? Some people confuse wisdom with knowledge. Having *knowledge* is learning facts, like knowing and being able to recite all the times tables without help. Knowing how to swim is knowledge. Understanding, however, is knowing what to do with the facts.

Wisdom is knowledge and understanding combined. That's why understanding is mentioned in the same sentence as wisdom and knowledge in the verse above. You know how to swim, but it takes wisdom to be safe and to understand why you don't go swimming outside in the middle of winter.

Wisdom combines facts with common sense, knowing what to do and what not to do and why. God promises to give you wisdom. All you have to do is ask.

A POWER NOTE

Make a "wisdom" mobile. Ask an adult for a clothes hanger, some string, and five pieces of paper. On each piece of paper write these words: *wisdom, knowledge, facts, understanding, common sense.* Decorate the pieces of paper if you'd like. Then put a hole  at the top of each paper, push a piece of string through it, and tie it to the hanger. Hang your wisdom mobile in your room to remind you how wisdom works.

A WISDOM SCAVENGER HUNT

Find It in the Bible

So give your servant a discerning heart to govern your
people and to distinguish between right and wrong.

1 KINGS 3:9

Look around you right now for a quick scavenger hunt. Find three things that are soft and three that are hard. Now find three that are expensive and three that are cheap. Three that are old and three that are new.

Once you know what being "soft" means, spotting those items is pretty easy, right? You learned your opposites when you were in preschool.

One pair of opposites can be tricky: right and wrong. In some situations, we can easily spot what's wrong: murder, for example. Other actions are clearly right: helping someone in need, for example. But what about the choices that are not quite so obvious? What do you do when you're not sure if something is right or wrong?

That's when you ask God for help, just like Solomon did. A "discerning" heart is one that is wise enough to know what's right and what's wrong. This is not something you have to do on your own. The Holy Spirit will help you make choices in those tricky situations if you just stop and ask.

A POWER NOTE

The next time you read a story, practice deciding what's right and what's wrong. Give a thumbs-up when characters make a good choice and a thumbs-down when they make a wrong one.

BLOOPERS

Find It in the Bible

After that whole generation had been gathered to their ancestors,
another generation grew up who knew neither the LORD
nor what he had done for Israel. Then the Israelites
did evil in the eyes of the LORD.

JUDGES 2:10–11

Have you ever watched video bloopers and thought, *That's a really bad idea*? Maybe it was a guy diving off his roof into a pool. Or a woman balancing a stack of presents and a birthday cake.

You probably know what will happen next. The guy is going to do a belly-flop. The woman is going to trip and send the cake flying through the air. Sure enough, when all that happens you're not surprised.

The book of Judges reports a similar situation. Every time the Israelites disobeyed God, terrible things happened. When they decided to obey God once again, good things happened.

Often, what is obvious to us looking back isn't so clear when the temptation to disobey is right in front of us. Like the Israelites, we sometimes experience the same bloopers over and over again. Let's obey God the first time and every time!

A POWER NOTE

Think of something you did today that was wrong. How would you do things differently if you could replay the scene? What can you do to "blooper-proof" your life?

1,000

Find It in the Bible

Know therefore that the LORD your God is God;
he is the faithful God, keeping his covenant of love
to a thousand generations of those who love him and
keep his commandments.

DEUTERONOMY 7:9

In this verse, 1,000 is the number of generations that God promises to bless if they obey Him. A "generation" is about twenty years. So, what about generation 1,001? Does God stop keeping His promises for them? No. The Bible is just using a really big number to remind us that God's love and mercy are really big. They stretch on forever . . . way longer than it takes to count to 1,000!

Thinking of 1,000 generations can be cool. If you remember your grandparents, well, they're just two generations (about forty years) before you. Going back 1,000 generations would make a pretty big family tree! Yet God loves you just as much as He loved the people many generations before you, and He will love the ones many generations yet to come. His love never changes.

A POWER NOTE

Have a parent help you draw a tree. On the trunk put your name along with the names of your brothers and sisters. Then draw two branches—one for your mom and one for your dad. Then, draw branches off from them and put the names of their parents, and so on. See how many branches you can add to your tree. Thank God for loving each of those people on your tree.

TIME-OUT!

Find It in the Bible

Then God blessed the seventh day and made it holy,
because on it he rested from all the work of
creating that he had done.

GENESIS 2:3

When you hear the word *time-out*, what do you think of? Maybe what first comes to mind is a corner or chair where your parents sent you when you disobeyed. There, you were forced to sit in silence until the time was up. Or maybe you think of a break in the middle of a sports game. It's a chance for you to hear instructions from your coach, get a drink of water, and take a quick rest.

In Genesis, God took a time-out after He created the world. So why did God need to rest? After all, God doesn't get tired or worn out or sweaty like we do. The Bible later says that He rested to set an example for us. We take one day of the week to rest because He did.

God's time-out isn't a punishment, like the first meaning of the word we talked about. Instead, it's like a time-out in sports. It lets us spend time getting advice from our "Coach" (God) by going to church or reading our Bible. Sometimes life can be busy. But if you're too busy to take time-out with Jesus, you're too busy!

A POWER NOTE

Write down everything that you do on a normal day. Think about Sunday, your day of rest. What can you do differently to rest and spend more time with God on that day?

BREATH OF LIFE

Find It in the Bible

In his hand is the life of every creature and
the breath of all mankind.

JOB 12:10

How long can you hold your breath? The world record for the longest time someone has held their breath is twenty-two minutes! The average person, though, can only hold his breath for thirty seconds to a minute. This is because we need to breathe to live. Each breath of air brings oxygen into the lungs. The oxygen is then carried by the blood throughout the body and is used to make the energy we use each day. Think about how many breaths you take in order to make all that energy. You probably breathe around 26,000 times per day. That's a lot of breaths!

The Bible says that God holds your breath and your life in His hands. He cares about you so much that He knows every time you breathe in and every time you breathe out. He gives you each breath so that you can keep living each day.

A POWER NOTE

Go outside and blow bubbles. If you don't have a bottle of bubble mix, make your own! (Make sure you ask your parents for permission first!) Simply mix 4 cups of warm water with a ½ cup of sugar until the sugar dissolves. Then stir in a ½ cup of dishwashing liquid. As you blow your bubbles, remember that each bubble contains one of your breaths. Thank God out loud for the way He cares for you and gives you breath.

IMPOSSIBLE LOVE

Find It in the Bible

Jesus looked at them and said, "With man this is impossible,
but with God all things are possible."

MATTHEW 19:26

"I can't do it!" Riley told his dad after school.

"Can't do what?" Dad asked.

Riley crossed his arms. "I can't like Johnny. He is so rude to everyone. Johnny took the soccer ball at recess yesterday and wouldn't share. And today, he spilled glue all over the floor and blamed it on me."

Dad shook his head. "Riley, you know that God tells us to be kind to others, even people who aren't kind to us."

"I would be, Dad, but really, Johnny makes it impossible," said Riley.

"Impossible?" Dad asked. "Don't you think God can help you with the impossible?"

Riley frowned. "Well, yes. I know that God can do the impossible."

Dad was quiet and started pulling out an after-school snack. Riley thought some more and sighed. "Okay, tomorrow at school I'll invite Johnny to eat lunch with me and my friends."

A POWER NOTE

Write down something that seems impossible to you. Next, ask God for strength to deal with it. Remember: nothing is impossible for God.

TRUSTING THE GUIDEBOOK

Find It in the Bible

I will instruct you and teach you in the way you should go;
I will council you with my loving eye on you.

PSALM 32:8

When you need advice, you have several places to get help. If you don't understand your math homework, you can ask the teacher to meet with you after class or get a friend who understands it to help you. If you want to know how to fix a broken toy, you might ask one of your parents. If you need help with one of your chores, your brother or sister might help you (well, if you ask *very* nicely!).

But what if your questions are deeper than that? What if you need to know what to do when someone hurts your feelings? Or when you're not clear about the right thing to do? Or if you have big questions about God or heaven?

While you can certainly get advice from people, don't forget that God gave you the perfect guidebook to give you all kinds of advice. That guidebook is the Bible, and it contains exactly what God wants you to know about Himself, yourself, and life. The Bible is His way of being there to counsel and guide you. When you read it carefully, you will learn how to walk in God's way.

A POWER NOTE

Create a bookmark for your Bible using some thick paper and colored markers. Write "My Guidebook" on the bookmark and keep it in your Bible to mark where you're reading.

We are one

Find It in the Bible

For we were all baptized by one Spirit so as to form one body—
whether Jews or Gentiles, slave or free—and
we were all given the one Spirit to drink.

1 CORINTHIANS 12:13

There are hundreds of different kinds of trees in the world. There are palm trees, pine trees, and fruit trees. We depend on these trees, but not just for fruit. Rubber is produced from the sap of rubber trees found in South America. And cork is actually the bark of the cork oak. Harvesters cut away huge chunks of the outer bark of the trunk every eight or ten years. Over time this layer of bark grows back and can be harvested again. Do you like the taste of cinnamon? It is made from the bark of young trees that grow in India and Sri Lanka.

There are many different kinds of trees, but they all belong to the general family of "trees." In a similar way, there are people from many countries around the world who believe in Jesus as their Savior. They look different and they speak different languages, but they all belong to the family of God. All these Christian people are called the body of Christ. What a gigantic, amazing family it is!

A POWER NOTE

Make a leaf wreath. Bend a wire hanger into a circle. Now cut leaves in various colors from tissue paper or construction paper and glue them onto the wire. Cover the wire completely with leaves. After the glue dries, hang it where it will remind you of the variety of God's children.

PRAISE OF CHILDREN

Find It in the Bible

Through the praise of children and infants you have
established a stronghold against your enemies,
to silence the foe and the avenger.

PSALM 8:2

You're never too young to do something wonderful. In 1998, six-year-old Ryan Hreljac was shocked to learn that children in Africa had to walk many miles to carry clean water to their homes. He decided to help them by building a well in their village. He did chores for many months to raise the money for one well. The first well was built in Uganda in 1999. Since that time, Ryan's parents have helped him set up a foundation that has built 667 wells in sixteen countries, providing clean water for over 714,000 people.

You may be young, but you never need to wonder whether you can do anything to help God. Samuel was just a little boy when God called him (1 Samuel 3:1–10). A little slave girl helped her master learn about God (2 Kings 5:1–19). A little boy shared his lunch with Jesus—and saw a miracle (John 6:1–15). A young man saved the apostle Paul's life (Acts 23:12–22).

One thing you can do right now? You can sing! You can praise God with your voice. You can talk to God and tell Him how much you love Him.

A POWER NOTE

What are some of your favorite songs from church? What about some songs you learned when you were little? Sing some of your favorite songs to God.

NO MORE FEAR

Find It in the Bible

The LORD himself goes before you and will be with you; he will never leave you nor forsake you. Do not be afraid; do not be discouraged.

DEUTERONOMY 31:8

Have you ever been very afraid? Your hands get sweaty and your heart starts to beat really fast. When you are with a friend or someone older, scary things like storms, walking in the dark, or being lost may not seem so scary anymore.

In this verse, God reminded Israel that He was the One who had brought them out of Egypt. He had led them in the wilderness and would go before them into the land of Canaan. He wanted them to know that no matter what, they should not be afraid or discouraged because He would never leave them or reject them.

This is God's promise to all His people—then and today. He will lead you and stay by your side. When you believe in Jesus as your Savior, the Holy Spirit comes to live in your heart and guides you. So when you are afraid or become discouraged, remember God's promise. He goes before you and will be with you. He will never leave you or forsake you. Don't be afraid and don't be discouraged.

A POWER NOTE

The Lord wants to give you courage and comfort. Write out the verse with your name in the blanks. "The Lord Himself goes before _____ and will be with _____. He will never leave _____ nor forsake _____. _____ should not be afraid; _____ should not be discouraged."

A GIFT OF LOVE

Find It in the Bible

Each of you should give what you have decided in your
heart to give, not reluctantly or under compulsion,
for God loves a cheerful giver.

2 CORINTHIANS 9:7

Can you describe the best gift you've ever received? What did you like most about it? It's fun to receive gifts, especially when it's something you really want. But it can be even more fun to give gifts to others. What was the best gift you ever gave to someone?

When you go to a birthday party are you excited for your friend to open your gift? It sure is fun to give a gift when you know your friend will like it! We like to give gifts to our friends because it shows we like them and we want them to be happy. After all, we've taken the time to pick out something special for them.

In the same way, God wants you to enjoy giving gifts to Him. When you give Him money from your allowance or when you take time to help others, you give Him a gift. What makes the gift amazing is that it comes from a heart of love.

A POWER NOTE

Set aside a little bit of your allowance or money you earn to give to God. Or take time to help someone in your family. When you give these gifts with a big smile, just imagine how happy this makes God.

OCTOBER

Jesus Loves The Little Children

Find It in the Bible

Jesus said, "Let the little children come to me, and do not
hinder them, for the kingdom of heaven belongs to
such as these." When he had placed his hands on them,
he went on from there.

MATTHEW 19:14–15

If you walked into a forest, you would find many different kinds
of leaves. Some are light green or dark green or lime green or
even yellow. Some are purple, some are copper, and some, like the
variegated holly, are both green and yellow.

Some leaves are smooth and some are prickly. Some are so tiny
you can barely see them, while others, like the leaf of the Catalpa
tree, can reach one foot in length. No matter what they look like,
the leaves of a tree are the power stations that provide fuel for
the tree.

God loves variety! Just think of all the different animals, and
plants, and insects, and flowers He created. He also created
human beings to look different from one another. Some have
white skin and blonde hair, some have black skin and black hair,
and some have brown skin and black hair. God made all the
varieties of children in the world and He loves them all. He wants
us to love them, too.

A POWER NOTE

Gather information in the library or on the Internet about
children in other parts of the world. Look at photos of children
in Africa, China, and India. Remember, God loves all the children
in the world.

SING IT OUT LOUD!

Find It in the Bible

Let everything that has breath praise the LORD. Praise the LORD.

PSALM 150:6

One day a missionary decided to visit the villagers in a little church high in the mountains near his home. He walked all morning, higher and higher into the mountains. As he got near to the little village, a thick fog rolled in and covered the path. He couldn't see ahead even one foot. How was he going to reach the safety of the village before dark? Suddenly, he heard a lovely sound floating on the wind. The villagers were singing a song of praise to God. As they sang and sang, he was able to follow the sound of the songs and reach the village safely.

Our words and songs of praise are guides for us as well. They guide our thoughts to be thankful and hopeful. They can guide others to believe in God. When we praise God, we are happy and He is happy.

We have many reasons to praise God! He's all-powerful, all-knowing, righteous, just, wise, and, most of all, loving. Some people don't realize how great God is. But the Bible says that one day everything God has ever created will praise Him.

A POWER NOTE

Write a haiku poem of praise to God. Write the poem in three lines and use no more than seventeen syllables for all the words. Describe how amazing He is, then read it aloud and share it with someone else.

TERRIBLE OR WONDERFUL?

Find It in the Bible

You intended to harm me, but God intended it for good to accomplish what is now being done, the saving of many lives.

GENESIS 50:20

In the book, *Alexander and the Terrible, Horrible, No Good, Very Bad Day*, bad things happen to Alexander all day long. He gets gum in his hair, his teacher doesn't like his homework, and even dinner is terrible (lima beans!).

But as bad as Alexander's day was, it couldn't compare to Joseph's. In less than twenty-four hours, his brothers ripped off his beautiful coat, threw him into a deep pit, sold him into slavery, and told their father he was dead. Talk about a rough day! But it didn't stop there. Joseph was taken far away from his homeland to Egypt and was forced to work in a rich man's house. There, he was falsely accused of a crime and thrown into prison for life!

But God used all of the bad stuff Joseph experienced for good. Through his gift of dream interpretation, he was freed from jail, became Pharaoh's right-hand man, and saved millions of people from a famine. None of these incredible things would have happened if Joseph hadn't experienced his "terrible, horrible, no good, very bad day."

A POWER NOTE

Make a list of the tough stuff happening in your life right now. Pray that God will use these bad things for His good. When you see a good result from an item on your list, write that beside the tough stuff. Remember to thank God for bringing good out of bad.

DON'T FORGET

Find It in the Bible

Then when you eat and are satisfied, be careful
that you do not forget the LORD.

DEUTERONOMY 6:11–12

Think about your morning routine. You wake up, get dressed, brush your teeth, and have some breakfast. You go through your day, learning, playing, and eating, and then the next day you do it all over again. Much of the time, you probably don't even notice these things because they are just a normal part of your day.

God had led the Israelites out of Egypt with great miracles. He had protected them in the desert. He was bringing them to the land He had promised to give them. But God warned that once they arrived in the Promised Land, settled in, and got comfortable, they must never forget all that He had done to get them there. God had provided everything they needed.

God provides everything that you need, too. When you're hungry and dinner time comes, don't forget to thank God for giving you your meal. And when you're really tired and you climb into bed, be sure to remember that God is the One who gave you your bed. Everything you have is because of God. So thank Him.

A POWER NOTE

Every day this week, write down at least one thing that you are thankful for. Grab a notebook and a pen and keep them where you can see them so you will remember. Then at the end of the week, thank God for each item on your list.

Be Still

Find It in the Bible

He says, "Be still, and know that I am God; I will be exalted
among the nations, I will be exalted in the earth."

PSALM 46:10

A substitute teacher arrived at her classroom one morning only to find the students screaming, yelling, banging desks, and throwing books. She immediately went to the light switch and turned off the lights. The room went black, and the students stopped moving and yelling. After a minute of darkness and silence, the teacher turned one set of lights back on and said, "Now that I have your attention, I want you all to find your seats and take out your spelling books." The students did as they were told. Only in order and quiet would they be able to learn anything.

In our noisy world of radios, TVs, tablet computers, and cell phones, moments of solitude and quiet are rare. God knows that we need the quiet. "Be still," He says. "Sit quietly. Remember who you are and who I am." Only in the quiet can you focus on peaceful communication with your heavenly Father. Only then will your soul be refreshed.

A POWER NOTE

Make a list of places where you can find some peace and quiet. It may be sitting on the patio at your home, in the school library, or a place in your church. Next, make a list of things you want to talk about with God. Then, find your place and begin your quiet visit.

292

INVITING GOD

Find It in the Bible

He went out to meet Asa and said to him, "Listen to me,
Asa and all Judah and Benjamin. The LORD is with you
when you are with him. If you seek him, he will be found
by you, but if you forsake him, he will forsake you."

2 CHRONICLES 15:2

The rhinoceros and a small white bird called the egret form a unique friendship. They stay close to each other and help each other. As the rhino walks through the grasslands of Africa, it stirs up insects for the egret to snatch in its beak. The egret helps the rhino protect its baby because a rhino can't see very far away but the egret can spot danger (like a hungry hyena) many miles away. When the egret sees danger it flaps its wings, and the mother rhino knows it's time to move her baby to safety.

If you've ever lost a good friend, you probably felt lonely and longed for a new friend. If you've ever felt ignored by someone, you know how painful that can be.

That's how God feels whenever we ignore Him. When you invite God in, He isn't just close to you, He lives *in* you. But if He feels you want to walk away from Him, He will let you. The amazing thing is that no matter how far away you walk, God always wants you to come back. All you have to do is choose!

A POWER NOTE

Fold a piece of paper in half to form a card. On the front of the card write "You Are Invited." On the inside, write a message to God and tell Him how much you want to stay close to Him.

No Take-Backs

Find It in the Bible

LORD, who may dwell in your sacred tent? Who may live on your holy mountain? . . . [The one] who despises a vile person but honors those who fear the LORD; who keeps an oath even when it hurts, and does not change their mind.

PSALM 15:1, 4

When people make promises, sometimes they seal them in certain ways to show they're serious. A handshake, for example, seals an agreement. Sometimes a legal document is signed by someone called a notary who then puts an embossed seal on that paper. This shows that the agreement is serious with no take-backs.

The question at the beginning of Psalm 15 asks who can dwell with God—and then answers with the types of people God wants with Him. The Bible says that one of the ways to please God is to be a person of your word, someone who keeps promises even when you would rather do something else, someone who doesn't change your mind just because something better comes along.

Promises are important. Don't make them if you're not sure you can keep them—and if you make them, be a person of your word, even when it hurts. That will honor God.

A POWER NOTE

What would life be like if we weren't sure God would keep His promises? But He does! In your Bible, make a mark beside these verses (maybe a P) so you remember that these are God's promises to you. Start with Psalm 33:18, Romans 10:13, and 1 John 1:9.

HOW TO LIVE FOR GOD

Find It in the Bible

He has shown you, O mortal, what is good. And what does
the LORD require of you? To act justly and to love mercy and
to walk humbly with your God.

MICAH 6:8

You might be confused about how to live for God. You might look at the Bible and think, "That book is so big! How can I remember and do everything in it?" You might think God has a lot of rules to follow, and you're afraid to mess up.

While reading and learning from the Bible is very important (so keep it up), much of what God wants from you can be explained in just a few words. The prophet Micah explained here that to live a good life, God asks that you:

- act justly (always be fair and do what is right),
- love mercy (always be kind),
- and walk humbly with Him (remember all He has done for you and try to please Him).

Jesus put it this way: "'Love the Lord your God with all your heart and with all your soul and with all your strength and with all your mind'; and, 'Love your neighbor as yourself'" (Luke 10:27). How to live for God is pretty clear: Love God and love others.

A POWER NOTE

On a sheet of paper, draw two columns. At the top of one, put "Love God." At the top of the other, put "Love My Neighbor." During the week, write down what you did each day that showed your love for God and others.

TENDING THE FLOCKS

Find It in the Bible

You are my sheep, the sheep of my pasture, and I am
your God, declares the Sovereign LORD.

EZEKIEL 34:31

In a most entertaining book, *All Things Bright and Beautiful*, a veterinarian tells the story of a local man who was a master at herding cows, sheep, and horses all by himself. Everyone wondered where this amazing talent came from. Finally, the man revealed the secret of how he was able to herd every kind of animal. He said that he had learned how to imitate the sound of a horsefly, which has a terrible sting. If an animal would start to stray, the man would make the horsefly sound. Because the animal was instantly afraid of being stung, it would quickly return to the safety of the herd. This worked every time.

At times God has to nudge us back to where we belong. No one enjoys being disciplined or reprimanded, but God knows better than we do where potential danger lies. So He brings us back in line if we begin to stray from the straight and narrow path. He does this because He loves us—we are like the precious sheep of His pasture and He is the Good Shepherd.

A POWER NOTE

Draw a picture of a sheep on a piece of paper. Now find something that you can use to glue onto the sheep for "wool." You might find some cotton or pieces of white fabric. Beside the sheep write, "I am the sheep of God's pasture." Thank God for taking such good care of you.

THE TRUST GAME

Find It in the Bible

For it is by grace you have been saved, through faith—
and this is not from yourselves, it is the gift of God.

EPHESIANS 2:8

Have you ever played the trust game? You fall backward and trust your friend to catch you. That can be a little scary. What if your friend decided to play a joke on you and just let you fall? You could land on your back and hurt yourself—and you'd probably be pretty mad at your friend, too.

When you trust God, however, He will never let you down. That's what having faith is all about—trusting God. Just like when you turn backward from your friend and trust him or her to catch you, so you trust God even though you can't see Him.

We believe that Jesus came to earth and died for our sins to give us salvation. This was a gift of grace. We don't deserve His kindness and love, but He gives it to us anyway.

God doesn't ask for anything in return. He gives you the opportunity to have faith and believe in Him for salvation because He loves you. Even though you can't see Him, you can trust Him. He'll never let you fall.

A POWER NOTE

Ask one of your parents to play the trust game with you. Talk to them about God's grace that gives the gift of salvation.

He Knows It All

Find It in the Bible

But God made the earth by his power; he founded the world
by his wisdom and stretched out the heavens by his understanding.

JEREMIAH 10:12

The earth is the only planet in the universe that can support human life. It has just the right combination of air, water, and weather to allow for plant and animal life. More than two-thirds of the earth's surface is covered with water. All the many forms of life on earth are tied to the presence of water. There is more water in the Sahara Desert than there is on the planet Venus!

Our amazing earth was made by God's power. He planned and prepared everything down to the smallest detail. He made the sky and the rest of the universe (see Genesis 1). Jeremiah reminded the people of Judah about God because they worshiped idols. These gods weren't real; they were made by man. But the God of Israel was real and involved in their lives. His power created the universe. His understanding has no limits. God knows everything about everything! Best of all, He knows everything about you.

A POWER NOTE

Draw a picture of a globe. But instead of adding the shapes of continents, draw things that represent your life. For example, if you like to play baseball, draw a baseball. Add names of family members and friends. This is your "world." Who's the boss of your world? Is God? Do you trust Him to handle all the details of your life? Talk to God about what He would have you do.

A STRONG DEFENDER

Find It in the Bible

Surely God is my salvation; I will trust and not be afraid.
The LORD, the LORD himself, is my strength and my defense;
he has become my salvation.

ISAIAH 12:2

Say the word *defense*, and you might picture a lot of different things. Maybe you're imagining the goalie near the soccer net keeping the ball from going into the net. Maybe you're thinking of a big brother stepping between his little sister and a bully. Maybe you're picturing a courtroom and the defense attorney, trying to get the prisoner set free.

When God says that He is our defense, all of these are great pictures. He's like a powerful soccer player who never makes a mistake and is always on our side. He's like a family member who will stand between us and anyone who wants to hurt us. He's like an attorney who explains why we are not guilty—because Jesus already paid our penalty.

No matter how bad things get, we can depend on God. You can have no better defender than God!

A POWER NOTE

Draw a soccer ball on a piece of paper. Decorate it with the colors of your own imaginary team. Now write across the ball: *God is my defense.* Cut out the ball and put it in your backpack as a reminder. The next time you're afraid or worried, remember that God is your defender.

THE WHOLE STORY

Find It in the Bible

I the LORD search the heart and examine the mind,
to reward each person according to their conduct,
according to what their deeds deserve.

JEREMIAH 17:10

Sherlock Holmes is a famous fictional detective created by a Scottish author. For over a hundred years, people have told stories about the way he could pick up on tiny clues to solve a crime. He might be able to prove that you broke your brother's portable media player by observing a grass stain on your knee or a smudge on your T-shirt. Then justice will be done—meaning that the true culprit will be found out.

Most people, though, have a harder time figuring out the truth. We jump to conclusions and make mistakes. If you've ever been punished for something you didn't do, you know that justice isn't always done. But God is different. He sees everything we do . . . and He knows why we do it. He knows the whole story.

Sometimes, life on earth doesn't seem fair. Good people suffer. Bad people get rich and live happily (or at least, they seem to). When you get frustrated with this, remember that God is still in control. In the end, He'll always make sure justice is done.

A POWER NOTE

The next time you say or do something—good or bad—stop. Then ask yourself, "Why am I doing this?" Look for "clues": Do I want something from someone else? Am I trying to look cool? Will I be disappointed if no one notices me?

HeLPFUL SPIeS

Find It in the Bible

But when you give to the needy, do not let your left hand
know what your right hand is doing, so that your giving
may be in secret. Then your Father, who sees
what is done in secret, will reward you.

MATTHEW 6:3–4

Have you ever thought about being a spy? Spies do really cool things like going on secret missions, wearing sunglasses, and fighting the bad guys. They also have awesome new gadgets. But spies can't tell anyone what they're doing or they wouldn't be spies, right?

In a way, we can be spies for God. Maybe we don't have top secret gadgets or classified information, but we can do secret acts of service to help other people. When we do something good for someone, no one else ever has to know about it, and God likes that.

Think of the difference between a spy and a celebrity. Celebrities get all kinds of attention, but spies are never recognized for their work. We can be like spies and do good things for people without all of the attention. God is pleased when we serve people and don't ever need the praise of others to keep us going.

A POWER NOTE

Quick. Pull out a piece of paper, and write "Top Secret" as a title. Underneath, write good things that you can do to help people. Work at doing these helpful things in secret. Remember, God will know!

FRIENDS ALWAYS

Find It in the Bible

A friend loves at all times, and a brother is
born for a time of adversity.

PROVERBS 17:17

You've probably seen birds flying south for the winter. All summer they live in their nests and sing cheerful songs. But when fall arrives, they fly south, traveling at speeds of forty to fifty miles per hour. If you have a bird feeder in your yard, you might even notice specific types of birds that always come by. But as soon as it gets cold, many of them leave!

Sometimes people can be just like birds—they act like friends when things are going well, but as soon as it gets uncomfortable, they leave. The word *migrate* means "to change," and sometimes people we think are our friends migrate just like birds.

Being a good friend can be difficult, but God doesn't want you to be like the birds that fly away as soon as the weather gets too cold. Instead, He wants you to be a real friend and stay loyal and helpful even in hard seasons. Standing up for someone who is being bullied can be scary. And listening to a friend who is having a bad day isn't much fun. A true friend is a friend *all* the time.

A POWER NOTE

Make a bird feeder! You can easily do this with a pinecone, some peanut butter, and some birdseed. Fill all the spaces in the pinecone with peanut butter and sprinkle birdseed over it. Hang it from a tree and watch the birds! When you see them, remember to be a real friend no matter what the season.

THE STAIN REMOVER

Find It in the Bible

I, even I, am he who blots out your transgressions,
for my own sake, and remembers your sins no more.

ISAIAH 43:25

Do you know what a cephalopod is? (That's pronounced *se-fa-luh-pod*.) It's a certain kind of sea creature that can release a dark inky substance into the surrounding water—usually in order to escape from a predator. Two cephalopods you may know are the squid and the octopus. When they sense danger, they release their ink so they have a chance to escape.

In the water, the ink will eventually disappear, but if you spill ink all over your paper, you'll have to use a blotter to try to clean it up. Chances are, however, the stain will stay.

But God has a different way. You don't need to squirt ink to try to hide from God. He sees your sin. In fact, the stain of sin on your life shows up perfectly well to God every time. But He can take every stain He sees and remove it completely.

Because Jesus died on the cross to pay the penalty for sin, the wrongs you've done can be blotted out permanently when you ask Him to forgive you. Jesus is the ultimate stain remover!

A POWER NOTE

Ask a parent to show you how a laundry stain-remover works. Find a small cloth rag and stain it with coffee or tea or berries. Now spray the stain-remover on the stain, let it sit for a few minutes, and wash the rag with soap and water. Did the stain disappear? God can remove the stain of sin from our hearts completely!

MIGHTY WARRIOR

Find It in the Bible

The LORD your God is with you, the Mighty Warrior who saves.
He will take great delight in you; in his love he will no
longer rebuke you, but will rejoice over you with singing.

ZEPHANIAH 3:17

Alexander the Great—a leader who conquered many nations—once stated, "I do not fear a pack of wolves led by a sheep, but I fear a flock of sheep led by a wolf." Alexander knew that the strength and power of a military unit was only as strong and effective as its leader. Even timid men could find inner strength if they believed they were being led by a wise and courageous leader. During World War II, General George Patton would give pep talks to his troops. He would visit them in hospitals, on the front lines, in their tents, and in the chow halls. The men knew he was continually checking on their welfare. As a result, they followed him into battle and were victorious, even against great odds.

The Bible teaches us that God is like a Mighty Warrior. He brings victory to those who serve Him. Even better—He takes great *delight* in you! That means He is thrilled with you, He loves you, and He even rejoices over you with singing.

A POWER NOTE

Use your computer or library resources to study the lives of great military leaders such as Grant, Pershing, MacArthur, Patton, and Schwarzkopf. What can you learn from their campaigns and battles? Now, use your Bible to discover how God is even mightier than the greatest of human generals.

VICTORIOUS

Find It in the Bible

The LORD said to Gideon, "With the three hundred men that lapped I will save you and give the Midianites into your hands. Let all the others go home."

JUDGES 7:7

When you play a game that involves captains picking team members, how are people chosen? The strongest and fastest people get picked first, right? And the slow, weaker people are usually picked last. The team that usually wins is the one that was able to pick the strongest and fastest people.

When Gideon began preparing for battle, his army was already smaller than the bigger and stronger Midianites. Then the Lord asked him to decrease the size of his army even more—from 32,000 to 300. That was a *huge* decrease. Yet, when the battle was over, Gideon and his army were victorious. Why? They trusted God, and God defeated the enemy.

God doesn't need the strongest or fastest people on His team. He wants followers who are faithful and will trust Him. God's idea of winning might not match yours, but if you allow God to lead you through life, you will be victorious.

A POWER NOTE

The next time you play a game, imagine that God is playing with you. Have good sportsmanship and encourage your teammates *and* your opponents. That way, no matter the outcome of the game, you will play in a way that honors God.

GOD IS WITH US

Find It in the Bible

Why, my soul, are you downcast? Why so disturbed within me?
Put your hope in God, for I will yet praise him,
my Savior and my God.

PSALM 42:11

W hat do you do to cheer yourself up? Do you like to listen to music or read a good book? What about riding your bike or playing a game of soccer with friends? We often experience disappointment and discouragement caused by an argument with a friend, a bad grade on a test, or another difficult situation.

Sometimes what discourages us seems small, but at other times it seems so big we can't think of anything else. No matter the size of the problem, we can always find something to be upset about. But thankfully, we don't have to deal with our problems alone.

Another name for Jesus is "Immanuel," which means "God with us." God is with us all the time. You can hope in Him, meaning that whenever you're upset or disappointed, you can turn to God for help. You won't be able to fix the bad grade on the test or go back in time to stop the argument from happening, but you can know that He can help you through your problems.

A POWER NOTE

Try to unscramble this sentence. Make it your motto for life:

I ilwl epsari ym variSo nda ym oGd.

(I will praise my Savior and my God.)

IN CASE OF EMERGENCY

Find It in the Bible

Turn your ear to me, come quickly to my rescue;
be my rock of refuge, a strong fortress to save me.

PSALM 31:2

When people get into emergency situations, they often yell out to anyone around, "Call 9-1-1!" That is the national emergency phone number in the U. S. and Canada. Did you know that every year about 240 million 9-1-1 calls are made? That's a lot of emergencies!

When you have a real physical emergency, you should dial 9-1-1. But anytime there is an emergency, you should also "call" upon God in prayer. Like 9-1-1, God always hears, answers, and willingly sends help. Unlike 9-1-1, God wants you to call Him *whenever* you want. You don't have to wait for a big emergency. God cares about every detail of your life, and He wants you to talk to Him about the little things as well as the big ones.

More than half of all the calls to 9-1-1 are false alarms—not real emergencies. Imagine how much time is wasted on these calls! But calling God is never a false alarm. No matter why you call on Him, He hears and He cares. You can never waste God's time because He always wants to help you!

A POWER NOTE

Draw a picture of a phone. Then, on the screen or in a speech bubble, write out a phone call to God. Remember to thank Him for always listening!

WISE OLD OWLS

Find It in the Bible

Who is wise? Let them realize these things. Who is discerning?
Let them understand. The ways of the LORD are right; the
righteous walk in them, but the rebellious stumble in them.

HOSEA 14:9

You might have heard someone say, "That person is as wise
as an owl." Why do people consider owls to be wise? One
reason might be because they can turn their heads 270 degrees,
which allows them to see much more of their surroundings than
most creatures. In a similar way, a wise person will look at all the
facts of a situation before making a choice.

Another reason an owl might be considered wise is because of
a special rod at the back of each of its large eyes. This rod allows
light to pass through its eyes two times instead of just once. For
an owl, this turns the night into day and helps him be a skillful
hunter. If we are wise, we will look for the light of God's Word
before we make a decision, not just once but over and over.

God promises to give you wisdom and discernment (the ability to
understand what is right to do in a situation). You gain wisdom
by following the ways of the Lord. You can learn His ways by
reading your Bible and listening to godly adults.

A POWER NOTE

Look in some books at the library or visit the Internet and view
photos of owls. Try to draw one of the owls on a piece of paper.
Beside it write: "'I will be wise in the ways of God." Carry the
paper in your backpack to remind you to seek God's wisdom.

BEDTIME PRAYERS

Find It in the Bible

Tremble and do not sin; when you are on your beds,
search your hearts and be silent.

PSALM 4:4

What do you think about before you go to bed? Does your mind drift to what happened earlier in the day? Do you remember all the fun you had? Or maybe you think about how disappointed you were because the day wasn't that much fun. Are you trying to figure out ways to get your parents to let you stay up? Maybe you don't think—because you just want to fall asleep.

Or maybe you can't sleep.

While you are lying in your bed, do you ever pray? God loves to hear from you, and He wants to be the last thing you think about when you go to bed and the first thing you think about when you wake up.

When you get ready for bed, make sure to thank God for giving you another day to live for Him. Then, fall asleep knowing that you are wrapped in a blanket of God's love.

A POWER NOTE

If you have trouble falling asleep when you pray, try kneeling by your bed. That way, you can stay focused on God and not drift off in the middle of talking to Him.

LOST AND FOUND

Find It in the Bible

For the Son of Man came to seek and to save the lost.

LUKE 19:10

Have you ever lost something that was important to you—a favorite toy, a school project, or some money? How did you feel when you discovered it was missing? You probably rushed through the house and searched through everything until you found it again. Maybe you asked other people to help you look. How did you feel when you found it?

People are God's favorite creation. We are more precious to Him than anything in the universe. In the beginning, He planned for us to stay with Him forever. But Adam and Eve disobeyed God in the Garden of Eden, and their sin separated them and us from Him. God felt just like you feel when you lose something important. So He sent His Son, Jesus, to die on the cross to save us from our sin.

Jesus left heaven, lived on earth, and died on the cross—all to bring us back to God. When we accept Jesus as our Savior, God rejoices because He has found His lost treasure—that is you and me! Because of Jesus, we can be friends with God again.

A POWER NOTE

Play a lost coin game with some of your friends. While they close their eyes, hide a coin in the room. Then let them look for it. Give a prize to the person who finds the coin the most times. Jesus searches for people who don't know Him because He wants them to accept His salvation.

GOD KEEPS HIS PROMISES

Find It in the Bible

I will never leave you nor forsake you.

JOSHUA 1:5

If you looked high into the trees of the rainforest of Indonesia, you just might see an orangutan mother swinging from branch to branch in the treetops. Clinging to her fur, close against her side, is her baby. No matter how high she climbs, the baby clings to its mother for milk and safety. For over eight years, she teaches him where to find fruit and how to survive in the forest. Day and night, she never leaves the side of her little one.

That devoted mother orangutan reminds us of God's promise to Joshua that He would never leave or abandon the Israelites. God had brought them out of slavery, through the wilderness, and eventually to the Promised Land of Canaan. God was completely faithful in His promise, even when the Israelites were not. God continued to care for them and love them, and He continues to love and care for us thousands of years later.

If you ever have trouble trusting God, just remember that He always keeps His promises. He will never leave or abandon you, and He will always love you.

A POWER NOTE

Ask an adult if you could use some super glue to glue two things together. It might be two small rocks or any small objects. Once the super glue dries, those two objects are stuck together permanently. Let this glue sculpture remind you about God's promise that He will never leave you or forsake you. He sticks to you like super glue!

LETTERS TO GOD

Find It in the Bible

Now when Daniel learned that the decree had been published,
he went home to his upstairs room where the windows
opened toward Jerusalem. Three times a day he got down
on his knees and prayed, giving thanks to his God,
just as he had done before.

DANIEL 6:10

The United States Postal Service handles about 22 million pieces of mail every hour. That's 363,300 every minute, and 6,050 every single second. Imagine how much work is involved in sorting all those letters and then delivering them to the right addresses!

God gets many more prayers than the post office gets letters, yet He cares about and answers every single one. That's why Daniel wasn't willing to stop sending his prayers to God. Even though Daniel was under threat of death, he continued to pray three times a day, just as he had always done.

God wants to talk to you in the same way that you talk to your friends. That's what prayer is all about. The Bible is like a letter from God to you—and praying is like sending a letter right back to God! So, like Daniel, don't let anything get in the way of your prayer time with God. It's the most important time of the day.

A POWER NOTE

Write a letter to God (on paper or the computer). You could tell Him about your day, ask Him for something you need, or thank Him for all the things He does for you.

LISTENING TO LEARN

Find It in the Bible

Listen, my son, and be wise, and set your heart on the right path.

PROVERBS 23:19

Back in the days of King Solomon, children didn't go to school. In fact, schools didn't even exist! Imagine not having a school or teachers. How would you learn? In Bible times, children learned by listening to their parents' stories and advice. Fathers taught their sons how to be strong, how to protect their sheep or farm, and how to work with their hands. Mothers taught their daughters how to be kind, how to cook for their families, and how to weave new clothes. Parents also taught their children how to worship God and how to tell right from wrong.

Today, you have school and teachers, but your parents are also your teachers. You can learn a lot from them. Your parents have had many experiences, both good and bad. If you are ever unsure of what the right way to go is, they can teach you from their experience.

In addition, your Father in heaven wants to give you wisdom and help you be on the right path for your life. God knows everything there is to know—including the path your life will take! When you need wisdom, get advice from your mom and dad, and trust God to show you the way.

A POWER NOTE

Ask one of your parents to tell you a story about a time when they learned something that helped them do the right thing. Listen carefully, and then try to see how you can apply it to your life.

STRENGTH FROM ABOVE

Find It in the Bible

The Sovereign LORD is my strength; he makes my feet like the feet of a deer, he enables me to tread on the heights.

HABAKKUK 3:19

Certain kinds of deer, such as the mule deer (so named because of its big ears), love to climb high up on the mountains and forage for food until the snows drive them down to lower elevations. Up on the mountains, the footing is rocky and steep, but they are able to balance and walk along those areas as they search for food.

What tasks seem too hard for you to handle? Studying for a class in which you aren't doing well? Patching up a disagreement with a friend? Many times you will think you aren't strong enough to face a difficult situation. And you're right! *You* aren't. But Someone is.

The Bible tells us that God is all-powerful. He can do anything and everything that He wants to do. Most of all, He wants to pass His strength on to you. Some think that strength comes from within. Actually, it comes from above. God gives you His strength because He knows you can't do it on your own.

A POWER NOTE

In a vertical line, write the word *challenge* on your computer or on a piece of paper. Now write nine words or phrases that begin with each letter in that word to describe ways that God helps you with difficult challenges. For example "g" might be "gives me guidance from His Word." He is your strength!

THE OLD TESTAMENT AND JESUS

Find It in the Bible

And beginning with Moses and all the Prophets,
he explained to them what was said in all the Scriptures
concerning himself.

LUKE 24:27

Did you know that the whole Bible is about Jesus? You might think that you only read about Jesus in the Gospels—Matthew, Mark, Luke, and John. But really, the whole Bible is the story of Jesus.

The Bible tells us how sin came into the world and what God did about it. Maybe some parts of the Old Testament are hard to read and understand, but take your time. As you get older, keep learning more and more about what the books of the Old Testament are about. You'll begin to see how God was working in history, getting everyone ready for His Son who would be born to save the whole world.

That's what these disciples learned when they sat at the table with Jesus. Imagine how they must have listened as this teacher (they didn't know it was Jesus right then) told them how their Scriptures (our Old Testament) were all about Him!

A POWER NOTE

Look up these verses in the Old Testament and underline them. Then look up the verse beside it in the New Testament and see how they are about Jesus!

Micah 5:2................... Luke 2:4
Psalm 22:18 .... Matthew 27:35
Zechariah 9:9............. John 12:14–15

THE POWER OF LOVE

Find It in the Bible

Many waters cannot quench love; rivers cannot sweep it away.

SONG OF SONGS 8:7

Rushing rivers are extremely powerful. If you've ever seen the rapids of a river, you know how fast they flow and how strong they are. In fact, did you know that the Grand Canyon was carved out by the water of the Colorado River? Starting in the Rocky Mountains, the Colorado River travels 1,450 miles into the Gulf of California. With systems of dams and levees and lakes and power plants, the river provides the electricity for much of the southwestern United States. That's some power! But before the dams were built to harness it, the river overflowed its banks, creating floods in the plains and sweeping away everything in its path.

Rivers have great power, and rushing rivers can sweep away houses, even whole towns. But rivers, writes Solomon, cannot sweep away love. Why? Because love is more powerful than the strongest river. You know how you feel about the people you love—your family, your close friends. And even that love is only a reflection of God's love for you. His love is so strong and powerful that He was willing to give His Son to die for you.

A POWER NOTE

Create a mini waterfall! Place some waterproof containers in different sizes upside down in the bathtub under the spigot. Turn on the water and watch how the water moves down around the containers. Remember—that's nothing compared to the power of God's love for you!

ROCK CRYSTALS

Find It in the Bible

He has made everything beautiful in its time. He has also
set eternity in the human heart; yet no one can fathom
what God has done from beginning to end.

ECCLESIASTES 3:11

A geode is a hollow rock that's rough and grey on the outside but glittery and colorful on the inside. Most of the time, people don't know a rock is a geode until they crack it open. They could stand in a whole canyon of geodes and not know it. But if they have the right tools and know what to look for, they can crack open the rocks and find beautiful shiny crystals inside.

Life can be that way sometimes. Something bad happens, and you might feel as though your life is nothing more than a rough, grey stone. Whatever is happening may not make sense at the time. But that's where God comes in. He never allows bad things to defeat His people. Whenever something bad happens, God makes those bad things work for your good. In the same way that a geode has beautiful crystals, He may help you grow in faith or patience or kindness.

God is always working to make bad things turn out for your good.

A POWER NOTE

You can crack your own geode! Some stores sell "Crack Your Own Geode" kits. With your parents' help and permission, follow the instructions to crack open the geode. When it's open and you can see the sparkles inside, let them remind you that God will always help you find His beauty even in hard situations.

HIS BATTLE, NOT YOURS

Find It in the Bible

Do not be afraid or discouraged because of this vast army.
For the battle is not yours, but God's.

2 CHRONICLES 20:15

Think about your history classes or movies of classic battles. As the armies faced each other on the battlefield, every soldier was probably frightened. Imagine standing on a grassy hilltop and looking over at thousands of soldiers who are ready to attack you. Wouldn't you be afraid? What if the mighty God of the universe stood by your side? Would you still be afraid?

When the soldiers of Edom attacked Judah, King Jehoshaphat and the people of Judah asked God to help them. The Spirit of the Lord told the king and his people that they did not need to be afraid or discouraged. God promised He would fight for Judah.

While you may never be a soldier in a battle, life is sort of like a battle. Our enemy is Satan and everything evil. The battles take place in our minds, our emotions, and our choices. We can't win this spiritual battle on our own. We need God's strength and the mighty power of the Holy Spirit.

A POWER NOTE

See if you can unscramble this sentence. The next time you feel like you are fighting against Satan, say this sentence out loud to give you courage.

Teh ttabel si ton einm, ti si od'sG.

(The battle is not mine, it is God's.)

318

"Eye" See You

Find It in the Bible

The LORD will watch over your coming and
going both now and forevermore.

PSALM 121:8

You only have two eyes. They're on the front of your face, of course, so you can only see so far up, down, and to the sides without turning your head. What if you had a third eye on top of your head—or lots of eyes that looked all different directions? In New Zealand lives a kind of reptile called a tuatara (pronounced *tu-ah-tar-ah*). It looks like an iguana, even though it isn't a lizard, and it has a fully-functioning eye on top of its head! Many insects have eyes made of hundreds of simple eyes that work together.

Unlike humans with two eyes, tuataras with three, and insects with hundreds, God can see everything, all the time. You cannot hide from Him, nor will He ever lose sight of you. On one hand, this means He sees everything you do—good or bad. It also means that even when you sin, He keeps watching over you. When you're doing something hard and scary and feel all alone, He sees you and is with you. He sees everyone involved and everything that is happening.

A POWER NOTE

Sometimes parents and teachers say that they have "eyes in the back of their heads," meaning that no one can get away with goofing around even when they aren't looking. While your mom or dad's back is turned, ask him or her how many fingers you're holding up. As you can tell, people don't really have eyes in the back of their heads. But remember that God sees you all the time.

TRUE STRENGTH

Find It in the Bible

For the eyes of the LORD range throughout the earth to strengthen those whose hearts are fully committed to him.

2 CHRONICLES 16:9

What do you think is the strongest animal on earth? Surprisingly, it's not a big animal like an elephant or a rhinoceros. Nor is it a powerful predator like a lion or a tiger. If "strong" means how much weight the animal can move compared to its own weight, the strongest animal on earth may be the dung beetle. This insect is not very big—smaller than your thumb—and its life is not very glamorous, considering that it mostly eats dung (which is a nice word for poop). But the dung beetle can move stuff that weighs over one thousand times its own weight! That would be like you pulling several buses full of people!

We like to think we're strong, but when fighting against sin, most of us are pretty weak. We sin even when we don't want to. It's as though we can't even lift our own weight. But when we love God with all of our hearts, we honor Him with our actions, and ask for His help, He gives us strength. When you are committed to God, He promises to strengthen you. He has given you the power of the Holy Spirit to make you strong.

A POWER NOTE

Try doing a few pushups. This is a test of your physical strength. Do you feel pretty strong? Now think of times you have been spiritually weak, like when you told a lie or did something you weren't supposed to. Ask God to help you be spiritually strong so that next time you are tempted, you won't sin.

SCARED STIFF

Find It in the Bible

Then Caleb silenced the people before Moses and said, "We should go up and take possession of the land, for we can certainly do it."

NUMBERS 13:30

Have you ever heard the phrase "playing possum"? When opossums feel threatened, they literally become scared stiff. Fear causes their bodies to enter a comatose state that makes them look dead. But looking dead often keeps them alive.

In Moses' day, a really large crowd of people got scared stiff. The people of Israel had left Egypt to travel to the land God promised to give them. After sending twelve spies to look over the land, they found a big surprise—fierce people lived there. Imagine a land filled with bullies—really *big* bullies! Taking over the Promised Land seemed impossible to the people of Israel, and they were scared stiff. They decided that they didn't want to take the land.

But Caleb wasn't scared! He knew that with God on their side, they would be stronger than the biggest bully. Caleb tried to help the people see that they could take the land if they would just trust in God.

Unfortunately, the people chose their fear over faith, and they never did enter the Promised Land. But God allowed Caleb to enter because Caleb trusted in Him.

A POWER NOTE

Make a list of things that make you afraid. Then write one of these fear-fighter verses below the list: Joshua 1:9; Psalm 27:1; Psalm 56:3. God is bigger than anything you fear.

DECLARE AND BELIEVE

Find It in the Bible

If you declare with your mouth, "Jesus is Lord," and believe in your
heart that God raised him from the dead, you will be saved.

ROMANS 10:9

What two items always go together? How about peanut
butter and jelly? Cake and ice cream? Salt and pepper?
Socks and shoes? Many things come in pairs. Sometimes you can
just have a jelly sandwich or just wear shoes without socks, but
some things always come in pairs, like day and night. We can
never have one without the other. They come hand-in-hand and
are always seen as a pair.

This verse mentions two things that need to go together, too. We
must not only *say* that we believe in Jesus, we must also *really*
believe in Jesus. Our belief has to go deeper than just saying the
words; our belief has to be sincere.

Declare and believe. That is God's connected pair. Keep those two
things together in your heart, and God will save you from your
sins.

A POWER NOTE

Go around your house and find pairs that go together. Look at
the objects you found, and remember what two things God put
together. Then, say out loud, "Jesus is Lord," and say a prayer
thanking God for raising Jesus from the dead.

HAPPY ENDINGS

Find It in the Bible

I am the first and I am the last; apart from me there is no God.

ISAIAH 44:6

Good stories have a beginning, a middle, and an end. People who write fiction books know they need to create good characters and scenes, have a conflict, and then bring the story to a happy ending. But one story didn't have a beginning and will never have an end: God's story. We can't understand or even imagine that God had no beginning, but it's true. And He will exist forever.

The phrase, "I am the first and I am the last" is also used in Isaiah 41:4; 48:12; Revelation 1:8, 17; and 22:13. But in the New Testament, you'll find the phrase written as "I am the Alpha and the Omega." Alpha and Omega are the first and last letters of the Greek alphabet. God wants us to know He has no beginning and no ending.

As one of God's creations, your story has a beginning—your birth. If you believe in Jesus, you already know how your story ends: You'll live forever with Him. And you know what? Your life will have good scenes, characters, and even conflict. But if you ask Jesus to forgive your sins and live in your heart, you can be sure of one thing. You will have the happiest ending of all!

A POWER NOTE

What fiction book have you been reading? Where does the story take place (scene)? Who are the good and bad characters? Aren't you glad that no matter how your life story goes, you will have a happy ending?

A GOOD OUTPOURING

Find It in the Bible

And afterward, I will pour out my Spirit on all people. Your sons
and daughters will prophesy, your old men will dream dreams,
your young men will see visions. Even on my servants, both
men and women, I will pour out my Spirit in those days.

JOEL 2:28–29

In Old Testament times, the Spirit only worked through certain
people whom God called, but He did not remain with them
permanently. The prophet Joel foresaw a great event—the day
when the Holy Spirit would be poured out on God's people to
remain with them forever.

Before Jesus returned to heaven, He promised to send the Holy
Spirit to all who trusted Him as Savior (see Acts 1:8). The Holy
Spirit first came upon Jesus' followers on the Day of Pentecost
(Acts 2:3–4). When Peter preached on that day, he quoted from
this prophecy of Joel to explain that it was coming true right
then! (See Acts 2:16–21.)

Jesus no longer lives here on earth with us, but He has sent the
Holy Spirit to live in us when we are saved and to fill us completely
when we are baptized in Him. Jesus wants to baptize you with
His Holy Spirit. You just need to ask Him.

A POWER NOTE

Ask a parent for a clear glass of water and some fruit drink
powder. Pour the drink mix into the water and stir until it is
completely dissolved. That's what it's like when the Holy Spirit
fills you. He *changes* your life, making you more and more like
Jesus.

SOS!

Find It in the Bible

And everyone who calls on the name of the LORD will be saved.

JOEL 2:32

What do you do first when you're in dangerous trouble? The answer depends on the situation and the place, right? At home, you probably call your mom or dad. At school, you look for a teacher, principal, or some other adult.

Many years ago, ships that were in distress on the high seas sent out an SOS (Save Our Ship) call. This Morse code message—which was three dots, three dashes, and three dots—was developed at a conference in 1906 in Berlin and became the official worldwide message of distress in 1908.

All people are in trouble, but many don't know it. Sin puts everyone in danger of being separated from God forever. That's why God invites people to call out to Him—to send Him an SOS. And you don't have to do dots and dashes; you just need to call out and tell Him you want to be saved.

God will always hear and answer when you call to Him for help. He wants to save you!

A POWER NOTE

Have you asked God to save you? Send out an SOS today through prayer! If you've already done so, pray for other people you know who haven't yet admitted they need Jesus to be their Savior.

Love Like Ice Cream

Find It in the Bible

See what great love the Father has lavished on us, that we
should be called children of God! And that is what we are!
The reason the world does not know us
is that it did not know him.

1 JOHN 3:1

Imagine your mom and dad taking you out for ice cream for no
special occasion. They order your favorite ice cream sundae
with all your favorite toppings poured on top. When you ask
them why they decided to treat you they say, "Just because you're
our child, and we love you."

Your heavenly Father also loves you deeply and calls you His
child. He shows His love in many ways. You can see God's love
in nature or experience His love in the joy you feel from having
fun with friends. You feel it every time someone gives you a hug
or encourages you. And you read about it in the Bible, especially
when you read about Jesus' death on the cross for you.

Because God is your heavenly Father, He loves you with an endless
love that you can't fully understand. Just like you enjoy adding
toppings to an ice cream sundae, God enjoys lavishing His love
on you because you are His child. Thank Him, right now, for His
lavish love.

A POWER NOTE

Make an awesome ice cream sundae! See how many different
kinds of toppings you can put on it—from sprinkles to nuts to
syrup (even maple syrup!) to whipped cream. Make it lavish—
just like God's love!

DON'T GLOAT!

Find It in the Bible

You should not gloat over your brother in the day of
his misfortune, nor rejoice over the people of Judah
in the day of their destruction, nor boast so
much in the day of their trouble.

OBADIAH 12

A fight between two families in two states—the Hatfields
(West Virginia) and the McCoys (Kentucky)—lasted for
over thirty years, starting in 1863 with thefts. These thefts led
to murders and years of courtroom trials. This feud has become
so famous that it is used to describe two people or families who
can't get along, "They're feuding like the Hatfields and McCoys!"

Though Edom and Israel were related (their ancestors were
Esau and Jacob, who were brothers), the two groups feuded for
hundreds of years. The people of Edom had refused to help the
people of Israel while Israel wandered in the wilderness after
leaving Egypt. But now, the prophet Obadiah predicted that the
people of Edom would be defeated. Yet he warned the people of
Israel not to celebrate when trouble found their enemies.

God is merciful and wants His people to be merciful, too. Part
of showing mercy is to avoid being happy when others are
miserable.

A POWER NOTE

Make a list of things that happen when people treat others badly
and a list of things that happen when they treat others kindly.
Which list brings more joy?

one PATH

Find It in the Bible

Jesus answered, "I am the way and the truth and the life.
No one comes to the Father except through me."

JOHN 14:6

Bridges get us where we need to go—often they are the only way across a chasm or canyon or deep river. Most bridges are made of concrete and steel, but if you lived in the jungle, you might cross a deep ravine on a bridge made of bamboo and vines! Sometimes these types of bridges move and swing and you have to hold on and walk very carefully to get across to the other side.

If you had to use that kind of bridge, you might be tempted not to cross at all. But what if the market or the hospital was on the other side of the ravine? If there was only one way to get there, and it was to cross the bridge, you would cross over on that scary swinging bridge.

In the same way, there's only one way for a sinner to be able to get to God. We have to cross the one bridge provided for us—and that one way is Jesus. Fortunately, He's not a scary, shaky bridge. He's solid, secure, and safe. Jesus is the way, the truth, and the life. He is the bridge of life.

A POWER NOTE

How many bridges do you cross in a day? Perhaps you drive across one to get to school. What's the biggest bridge you've ever seen? Bridges make it easier to get where you want to go. Next time you cross a bridge, thank Jesus for providing the way to God.

LISTENING FOR GOD

Find It in the Bible

The LORD came and stood there, calling as at the other times, "Samuel! Samuel!" Then Samuel said, "Speak, for your servant is listening."

1 SAMUEL 3:10

Samuel was a young boy who had lived in the temple for much of his life. One night, God called out to Samuel, but the boy didn't know who was calling him. He thought the priest Eli was calling for help, but Eli hadn't called Samuel. God called to Samuel a second time, but Samuel still didn't recognize the voice. When God called a third time, Eli realized that God was speaking to Samuel. He told Samuel what to do. The fourth time God called his name, Samuel responded to God. "Speak," he said, "for your servant is listening."

Sometimes it can be difficult to know when God is speaking to us. He doesn't usually speak out loud, but He does still speak. He may speak to you through the Bible or your parents or your children's leader at church. He may also speak to you by giving you thoughts. When that happens, the thoughts will always match what God says in the Bible. Your job is simply to listen for God's voice and obey Him.

A POWER NOTE

Find a big open space and play the game Marco Polo with some friends. Blindfold yourself and yell, "Marco!" while everyone else runs around and answers, "Polo!" Listen closely and try to tag the others by following their voices. Use the game to help you remember that God calls out to you, even when you can't see Him.

WHITE AS SNOW

Find It in the Bible

"Come now, let us settle the matter," says the LORD. "Though your
sins are like scarlet, they shall be as white as snow; though
they are red as crimson, they shall be like wool."

ISAIAH 1:18

If you've ever skinned your knee really bad or had a nosebleed,
you know that when blood gets on your clothes, it stains them.
Blood stains are very difficult to remove.

Isaiah says that sin stands out to God like scarlet color on a white
shirt. We can't hide it or wash it out ourselves—it's a deep stain.
Because God is holy, our sin prevents us from being at peace with
Him.

But God made a way! He gave Jesus to die for our sins. When we
believe in Jesus and confess our sins to God, He cleans the bright
crimson color of sin out of our lives. He makes us become pure
white like snow.

Jesus does what we can't do ourselves. He takes away our sins and
makes us pure and holy so we can be at peace with God. Sure, we
still sin sometimes and mess up, but if we ask, God will forgive us
and cleanse our sins.

A POWER NOTE

The next time you feel like doing something wrong, pray and ask
God for the strength to resist. Find a parent or trusted adult and
ask him or her to keep you on the right path. But if you mess up,
just remember how much God loves you. Ask Him to forgive you,
then try again.

SHINE LIKE THE SUN

Find It in the Bible

Commit your way to the LORD; trust in him and he will do this:
He will make your righteous reward shine like the dawn,
your vindication like the noonday sun.

PSALM 37:5–6

Have you ever gotten out of bed at dawn and watched the sun rise? The sky in the east slowly turns from black to grey to blue. It gets lighter and lighter as the sun comes up. The sun continues to travel across the sky, reaching its peak at noon, and then travels to the west where it sets. Did you know that the sun is really a star? It's a huge star measuring 875,000 miles across, which makes it 109 times bigger than the earth!

This verse says that if you commit your way to the Lord (meaning that you trust Him with your life and your future), He will take care of you and reward you. In fact, your reward will shine like the dawn. And if you have had lies told about you, your vindication (meaning the truth) will come out like the noonday sun.

God promises to take care of you. When you commit your life to God's will, you are telling Him that you trust Him.

Commit your way to the Lord today. Let the sun shine!

A POWER NOTE

Ask your mom or dad if some morning you can get up early enough to watch the sun rise. Thank God for His promise to reward you like the brightness of the sun.

A REAL RESCUE PARTY

Find It in the Bible

But I, with shouts of grateful praise, will sacrifice to you.
What I have vowed I will make good.
I will say, "Salvation comes from the LORD."

JONAH 2:9

The largest breed of fish in the world is the whale shark. One of these fish has been measured at over forty-one feet in length with a weight of over 47,000 pounds. It's large enough to swallow several people!

Jonah might have seen a fish like this up close and personal. He blew it big time by ignoring God's command to preach to the people of Nineveh. So God gave him a time-out in a large fish's stomach. Jonah called out to God for help. The verse above is part of Jonah's prayer. After Jonah's prayer, God rescued him from the fish. Jonah celebrated God's rescue *before* God actually rescued him because he knew that God would listen to him.

What do you want to talk about with God? Do you believe He wants to rescue you when you're in trouble? Do you believe He hears you and will help you? How do you celebrate when He does?

A POWER NOTE

Draw a picture of a fish on a piece of paper. Color it or decorate it as much as you like. Make it colorful or scary if you want. Cut out the fish and on the back write "Salvation comes from the Lord." Hang it in your bedroom to remind you that God hears all prayers, even the ones prayed inside the belly of a big fish.

ALL IN DUE TIME

Find It in the Bible

"For I know the plans I have for you," declares the LORD, "plans to prosper you and not to harm you, plans to give you hope and a future."

JEREMIAH 29:11

Many years ago, a young man took a job working at his father's small town newspaper. He dreamed of writing important news stories. But his father put him to work sweeping floors, answering the phone, and delivering the newspapers. After several months of this, the father had the boy start setting type for the printing of the newspaper. After that, he had him sell ads for the newspaper, then round up new subscriptions, and finally write some stories for each issue.

Frustrated, the boy asked his father, "Why have you waited more than three years before you let me write stories for the paper?"

His father answered, "Because my plan is for you to take over the newspaper one day, and I've been training you to know all of the jobs. I haven't been punishing you. I've been preparing you."

Sometimes we may think that God is slow in answering our prayers. In reality, He may be giving us time to gain the knowledge, experience, and wisdom we will need for great things in our future. We must rely on God's judgment, timing, and plan.

A POWER NOTE

Make a list of things you would like to do during your life. Share these hopes and desires with the Lord, and ask Him to prepare your mind, heart, and soul for all the good things He wants you to do.

A FORK IN THE ROAD

Find It in the Bible

There is a way that appears to be right,
but in the end it leads to death.

PROVERBS 14:12

Imagine that you are on a road trip and take a wrong turn. The sunny hills and highways turn into dark forests. After a few more miles, your family comes to a fork in the road. You don't know which way to go—the road on the left seems to go deeper into the forest, while the road on the right seems to head back into the sunshine—but you can't tell. Just as your dad decides to go right, someone finds a map. After studying it for a bit, you realize that, even though the road on the right looks better, it's the wrong way. You really should go to the left. The map clearly shows *that* road will get you back to the highway.

Life presents two ways to go: We can follow God, or we can follow the world. Sometimes following the world looks right to us and seems to make sense. Sometimes, following God doesn't make any sense at all. But that's where faith and trust come in. Following God will be challenging at times, but if you put your faith and trust in Him, He will guide you in the way you should go. Don't trust what "appears to be right." Trust God to guide you.

A POWER NOTE

Do you have to make an important decision? Draw a fork in the road on a piece of paper to represent your two choices. Talk to God about the decision, and write down the pros and cons of each choice. Ask God to guide you in the way He wants you to go.

TREASURES IN HEAVEN

Find It in the Bible

But store up for yourself treasures in heaven, where moths and
vermin do not destroy, and where thieves do not
break in and steal. For where your treasure is,
there your heart will be also.

MATTHEW 6:20–21

A pika is a furry little animal that lives on rocky mountainsides. About nine inches long, these tiny animals look sort of like bunnies with short ears. In the summer, the pika is busy storing up its treasure in a haystack. It builds big stacks of fresh grass, shoots, leaves, stems, and bright flowers. This treasure will be food in the cold, snowy months of winter.

Our "treasures" are the things we think about most. Have you ever seen something in a store and wanted to have it? It could be a new bike or a video game. You catch yourself thinking about the item all day, wondering what it would be like to have it.

God calls us to value what is in heaven, not on earth. On earth, the things we treasure are bound to fade, rust, be stolen, or get ruined. When we value God and our relationship with Jesus, we store up treasures that no one can take from us.

A POWER NOTE

Get a small box and make a treasure box. Every time you learn something new about God, Jesus, the Holy Spirit, or heaven, write it on a piece of paper and put it in your "Treasures in Heaven" box. It will be a constant reminder that where your treasure is, there your heart will be also.

THE GREATEST ARCHITECT

Find It in the Bible

So God created mankind in his own image, in the image of
God he created them; male and female he created them.

GENESIS 1:27

The famous architect Buckminster Fuller (he died in 1983 at age eighty-seven) designed homes, office buildings, and government structures the likes of which no one had ever seen before or even imagined. He was visionary and creative.

At one point in Fuller's career, he began to design tables, desks, and chairs that had no sharp edges. Everything was smooth and rounded. No one had ever thought to make furnishings less dangerous by changing the sharp edges for rounded ones. When people asked Mr. Fuller why he was making his furniture with no sharp edges, he said it was because he didn't like getting gouged and stabbed by sharp corners. So, he created furniture to fit his own body's needs. Everything was created in his own image.

Much more amazing, God created human beings in His image and likeness. We don't look like God, but we can imagine that He sees, hears, moves, touches, speaks, and thinks. Made in God's image, we have the ability to love and have joy and experience peace and care for others and worship and obey God. Because we're made in His image, we're very precious to Him.

A POWER NOTE

Spend some time online or in the library looking up the career achievements of Buckminster Fuller. Then read the first five chapters of Genesis and discover how much more creative God is.

OUR SPECIAL PROTECTOR

Find It in the Bible

The LORD will fight for you; you need only to be still.

EXODUS 14:14

Many years ago, *The Andy Griffith Show* was a popular TV program. In one episode, the town's skinny, nervous deputy, Barney Fife, was being bullied by some roughnecks who were strangers in town. Every time Barney gave them an order, they just laughed at him and continued to break the law. Finally, one day Barney made up his mind that if he was going to be a good law enforcement officer, he would have to stand up to those bullies. So, he went and found them. Then, he stood right in front of them and told them they had to obey the law or else he was going to arrest them. The two bullies immediately said yes, they would be law-abiding from then on.

What Barney did not know was that the sheriff, Andy Griffith, had walked up behind Barney for support, and *he* was carrying a shotgun. When the bullies saw that Barney had a protector, they were scared.

Many times we may feel like Barney Fife—small, vulnerable, and weak. But if we remind ourselves that God is there to defend us, we can be still, start to relax, and rely on God's protection.

A POWER NOTE

Make a list of things that are causing you to be afraid. Maybe your grandparents are sick, and you worry about them. Maybe you are worried about moving to a new school. Whatever your fears are, talk to God about them. Let Him be your defender and protector.

THANK GOD!

Find It in the Bible

Now the people complained about their hardships in the hearing of the LORD, and when he heard them his anger was aroused. Then fire from the LORD burned among them and consumed some of the outskirts of the camp.

NUMBERS 11:1

A fter leaving Egypt, the Israelites traveled through the desert toward the land God had promised them. The journey was uncomfortable because many of the Israelites were traveling by foot with all their belongings on their backs. After days of travel, they began to complain. This made God angry because the Israelites had forgotten that He had saved them from slavery in Egypt and promised to bring them somewhere better. Instead of being grateful to God for those good things, the Israelites focused only on the bad parts of their journey.

Think about a time when something has been difficult for you. You may have been tempted to complain about it. Complaining doesn't help because it means you're focusing on what is bad and forgetting all the good that God has done for you. Instead, God wants you to remember the good things and be thankful for them.

A POWER NOTE

Each morning for one week, before you start your activities for the day, write down three things you are thankful for. Each time you are tempted to complain during the day, remember one of the items on your list and thank God for what He has done for you.

GIVING THANKS

Find It in the Bible

Give thanks in all circumstances; for this is
God's will for you in Christ Jesus.

1 THESSALONIANS 5:18

What does it mean to give thanks in all circumstances? Don't some things happen that aren't happy at all? Do we have to be thankful when we lose our favorite bracelet or baseball mitt? How about when a person close to us dies or sad things happen to our family?

Notice that the verse doesn't say to be thankful *for* all circumstances; it says to be thankful *in* all circumstances. So, no, you don't have to be thankful for a bad thing—especially something sinful—that happens. That wouldn't make any sense.

But God does want us to be thankful *in* that circumstance, meaning we still have a thankful spirit before Him. We can be thankful during that difficult time because we know God is with us, He will never leave us alone, He will comfort us, He will guide us, and He will work all things together for good for us—because He promises all those things. When we give thanks in all things, we do God's will.

A POWER NOTE

Ask your mom or dad if you can have a blank thank-you card. The next time something happens that makes you feel sad or angry, write about it inside the card. Remember to thank God even in difficult times.

THANKFUL IN EVERYTHING

Find It in the Bible

And whatever you do, whether in word or deed, do it all in
the name of the Lord Jesus, giving thanks to
God the Father through him.

COLOSSIANS 3:17

W hat do you plan to do today? Like most kids, you probably have to go to school, do homework, and finish a couple of chores. Playing would be a lot more fun, but you know you have to get the important stuff done first.

Instead of grumbling and complaining when your teacher gives you homework or your parents ask you to clean your room, try to put a smile on your face and be thankful for all that God has done for you. As you do your homework, be thankful for all that you learn in your classes at school.

When you act that way, you honor Jesus. Every day is a gift from Him. If you grumble and complain your way through the day, you won't have time to be thankful. Jesus wants you to do everything—no matter what it is—in His name. That means you do homework, chores, and every other thing as though you were doing it for Him. He gave you the gift of this day. You can give Him the gift of a good attitude.

A POWER NOTE

Today as you do your household chores or your homework, pretend that Jesus is right there with you. Thank Him out loud for all the gifts He has given you—even the chores and homework—and do those tasks as though you were doing them for Him.

THANK YOU!

Find It in the Bible

He said: "LORD, the God of Israel, there is no God like you in heaven or on earth—you who keep your covenant of love with your servants who continue wholeheartedly in your way."

2 CHRONICLES 6:14

When Israel's first temple was completed after seven years of construction, the people of Israel had a huge celebration to express their gratitude. God had promised King David that his son would build a house for God—a temple. Solomon was that son. After God entered the temple in the form of a cloud, King Solomon prayed a prayer of thanks.

The biggest celebration of thanks we have in the United States is Thanksgiving, a national holiday occurring on the fourth Thursday in November. This holiday began in 1621, when the Plymouth Colony settlers and the Wampanoag Indians, the original inhabitants of the land, ate a meal together. But every day can be "Thanksgiving" if you remember what God has done for you and offer Him your thanks.

A POWER NOTE

Think of the promises God has made and kept in your life. (For example, He promised to help you and always be with you.) Show how thankful you are for what God has done in your life by first telling Him thank you. Go further by doing something kind for someone. When you do good things for others, you do them for God.

SHARING WITH OTHERS

Find It in the Bible

Nehemiah said, "Go and enjoy choice food and sweet drinks,
and send some to those who have nothing prepared.
This day is holy to our Lord. Do not grieve, for the
joy of the LORD is your strength."

NEHEMIAH 8:10

Close your eyes and imagine your last Thanksgiving. It was probably quite a feast, right? Thanksgiving, Christmas, Easter—something about these holidays makes us want to cook up all the food we have and eat it all in one sitting. Feasts are a way that people celebrate special days in the Bible, too. But we sometimes miss an important point.

In addition to feasting, the Bible encourages us to share our food with others. When we have plenty on the table we should share with those who don't have the food or money to celebrate.

Nehemiah explained that such joy in what God has done—joy in feasting and joy in sharing with others—gives us great strength.

Nothing is quite like joy, celebration, and sharing to make you know God is with you. And, with Him, you can accomplish anything.

A POWER NOTE

Talk to your parents about how you can share your food with others. If you could volunteer at a soup kitchen or at your church that would be a helpful way to show people that you and God care about them. Or, ask Mom and Dad if you can buy canned food to donate to a food pantry.

Remember Jesus

Find It in the Bible

For whenever you eat this bread and drink this cup,
you proclaim the Lord's death until he comes.

1 CORINTHIANS 11:26

What is your favorite food to eat at Thanksgiving? Do you like the turkey or mashed potatoes or rolls? Do you have a favorite dessert that you can't wait to eat, such as pumpkin pie or ice cream? Holidays like Thanksgiving can be fun because you can eat good food and spend time with family and friends you may not get to see very often.

Maybe Jesus had a favorite food at His holiday dinners, too. He celebrated the Passover dinner with His twelve disciples before He was taken away to be crucified. Jesus knew this would be His last holiday meal with them and one of His last days on earth. He told the disciples to always remember Him by getting together to share a meal and remember what He did for them.

Today, many churches celebrate Jesus' Last Supper by having Communion, The Lord's Supper. Because we believe in Jesus, we eat some special bread and drink grape juice in order to do just as Jesus said in this verse—to remember His death for us until He comes again. Now that's something to be thankful for!

A POWER NOTE

The next time your church celebrates Communion, pay careful attention to what your pastor says. As you take the bread and juice, remember all that Jesus did for you.

FOREVER THE SAME

Find It in the Bible

Jesus Christ is the same yesterday and today and forever.

HEBREWS 13:8

The desert locust goes through a lot of changes. It changes from a small egg, into a hopper, and then into a mature locust. When these locusts swarm, they change color. As they cluster together and touch each other, this triggers a chemical reaction. The young hoppers change from green to yellow, and the adult locusts change from brown to red. The desert locust also changes the place where it lives. Each year they migrate or swarm from North Africa to India. That's a lot of changes for one small insect!

People tend to change their minds often, about a lot of things. We change our minds about our favorite foods, or music, or clothes, or even our favorite friends. But Jesus never changes. He was the same thousands of years ago as He is today and as He will be a thousand years from now. He will always react in the same ways, think in the same ways. You never have to worry that He might change His mind.

Many things may change in your life, but one thing never will—Jesus.

A POWER NOTE

Look at some old pictures of you and your family. What has changed about you over the years? What about the other family members? Thank Jesus that even though lots of things in life change, He never does.

SING TO THE LORD

Find It in the Bible

With praise and thanksgiving they sang to the LORD: "He is good;
his love toward Israel endures forever." And all the people
gave a great shout of praise to the LORD, because the
foundation of the house of the LORD was laid.

EZRA 3:11

Have you heard of the emperor penguin? Emperor penguin
love to sing. When male and female penguins decide to
build a family together, they sing to each other. Her voice is soft
and his is loud. After the mother penguin lays her eggs, she leaves
for two weeks to eat fish in the ocean. While she is gone, the
father sits on the eggs and sings to them.

People who love God also love to sing and worship Him. The
Israelites sang to God because they had laid the foundation of
God's house. Why were they so happy? Well, they had spent
the last seventy years living in a foreign country because their
country had been taken over by foreign armies. But eventually,
just as God promised, they were able to return home. Ezra, the
priest, made sure that the first thing they did was to build an altar
and fix the foundation of the temple. They wanted to worship
and thank God for returning them to their homeland.

The Bible says that *we* are God's temple. You can praise Him and
sing to Him whenever you want to!

A POWER NOTE

Many of the psalms in the Bible were written as songs. Find one
verse in the Psalms and see if you can sing it to a tune you know.
This can be your own personal song to God.

GOD IS LISTENING

Find It in the Bible

"Lord, let your ear be attentive to the prayer of this your servant and to the prayer of your servants who delight in revering your name. Give your servant success today by granting him favor in the presence of this man."
I was cupbearer to the king.

NEHEMIAH 1:11

A baby monitor has two units—one goes in the baby's room and one goes in the kitchen or living room or with Mom or Dad, who can be in other parts of the house and still hear when the baby cries. The baby doesn't know it, but Mom or Dad is always listening. They want to take good care of their baby.

In this verse, Nehemiah asked God to be attentive to his prayer. In fact, throughout the book of Nehemiah, you'll often find him saying short, quick prayers that God would hear him and give him success in whatever he was doing for God at that moment.

Nehemiah knew that God was always listening—but these prayers, spoken in a moment of need, surely helped to calm his fears and remind him that God was with him.

God always hears you as well. He's never too busy or too distracted. Like Mom or Dad listening for the baby on the monitor, God is always listening for you.

A POWER NOTE

The next time something makes you feel anxious or afraid, write out Philippians 4:6–7. Now say it as a prayer to God. He is listening to your prayer.

JUST SAY NO!

Find It in the Bible

No temptation has overtaken you except what is common to mankind.
And God is faithful; he will not let you be tempted beyond
what you can bear. But when you are tempted,
he will also provide a way out so that you can endure it.

1 CORINTHIANS 10:13

People don't really know what fruit Adam and Eve ate from the Tree in the Garden of Eden. All we know is that the fruit looked good and tasted good. The problem was not the fruit. The problem was they got tempted and, instead of obeying God, they chose to give in to temptation.

Have you ever wanted to do something you knew you shouldn't? Like watching a movie that your parents don't like at a friend's house or gossiping about one of your friends with another friend? That's temptation. When you are tempted, Satan is trying to get you to do something wrong—just as he did with Adam and Eve in the Garden. He wants you to mess up and feel bad. When you stand up against temptation and choose *not* to do what's wrong, you choose to do what is right. People might make fun of you or stop being your friend, but doing the right thing is more important.

A POWER NOTE

The next time you are near a puddle or pond of water, throw a stone into the water and see what happens. Notice the circle of ripples that spreads out. Let that remind you that sin can spread negative effects into many areas of your life. It's best to say no to sin!

REMEMBER GOD

Find It in the Bible

Remember your Creator in the days of your youth.

ECCLESIASTES 12:1

What's the first event of your life that you remember? If you can't remember anything before the age of three, don't worry, you're normal! Most people can't remember anything before that age.

In the book of Ecclesiastes, King Solomon wrote about the things he had observed in his life and gave advice based on those observations. Here he says that it's important to think about God ("remember" Him) while you're still young. That way, as you try to live for Him and follow Him now, you'll avoid a lot of mistakes that could have bad consequences for the rest of your life.

Don't wait until you're older to start following God. Now is the time. You're not too young. In fact, as you start learning about Him now, you'll be stronger and wiser the older you get. You'll make smarter decisions. You'll know the path God wants you to follow, and you'll avoid some bad situations.

A POWER NOTE

See if you can unscramble the letters in this sentence:

sdiK anc vseer dGo hwti lal rtieh sthrea.

Is this what you want to do? Make a pledge to serve God with all your heart.

(Kids can serve God with all their hearts.)

DECEMBER

GOD KNOWS AND FORGIVES

Find It in the Bible

If we confess our sins, he is faithful and just and will forgive us our sins and purify us from all unrighteousness.

1 JOHN 1:9

God sees everything you do, and He knows why you do it. He is omniscient (pronounced *ahm-NI-shent*), which means He knows *everything*. Literally. He knows what you do when no one else is around. He even knows your thoughts! God is sad when we do wrong, and He is even sadder when we don't confess what we did.

So you might as well 'fess up to God—He's waiting for you to come. Don't worry; God won't get mad at you or be upset. He promises that when you confess your sins, He is "faithful and just" and will forgive you and help you do better next time.

God forgives all sins because Jesus died on the cross. When you tell God about your sins, He wipes them away forever. This helps you stay in a right relationship with Him.

A POWER NOTE

Ask an adult to help you fill a small bowl with cold water and then put about a cup of beans or other grain in the water. The beans represent the sins in our lives. Now pour the water through a sieve into another bowl. The water in the second bowl is clean. When we confess our sins, God takes them totally out of our lives.

CONSCIENCE CALLING

Find It in the Bible

Whoever conceals their sins does not prosper, but the one
who confesses and renounces them finds mercy.

PROVERBS 28:13

The Conscience Fund in Washington, DC has been receiving donations ever since the Civil War in the mid-1800s. It began when a check for $1,500 arrived from a citizen who felt guilty that he had spent government money in the wrong way and wanted to pay it back.

Thus began the Conscience Fund, and money continues to come in from people who feel guilty about cheating the government in some way. The donations are kept anonymous, and people who send the money probably feel better after they send it. They know they did something wrong, and paying the money back clears their conscience.

Everyone starts life with a conscience—that little voice in your head that makes you feel bad when you do something wrong. And if you keep what you did to yourself, your conscience will start to bother you (that's *good*). God gave you that little voice to help you know when you've done wrong so you can make things right.

A POWER NOTE

Do you feel guilty about something? Maybe you never told your mom about the glass you broke or the money you borrowed from her purse. What do you need to do to clear your conscience?

BeFORe THe BeGINNING

Find It in the Bible
In the beginning was the Word, and the Word
was with God, and the Word was God.

JOHN 1:1

How do you start an art project? Do you collect supplies lik
pencils, paper, and glue? Then do you try to find somethin
that will inspire you? If you were going to create an entire worl
out of nothing, how would you start?

In the beginning—before people like you existed—was nothing
But God was in that nothingness, and He created the univers
out of nothing. With God was the Word, Jesus, who was with Go
from the beginning and who, in fact, is God Himself.

That's a really difficult concept to understand, but you don't nee
to understand everything God is and does. If you could, then Go
wouldn't be God! What you do need to do is trust in this God wh
has existed for all time, and in Jesus, "the Word," who came to di
for you.

Our God is a powerful Creator—the only one who has bee
around since the very beginning and will continue to exist whe
time itself ends.

A POWER NOTE

What projects do you like to work on? Maybe you build mode
airplanes or make puzzles. Sit down and prepare to work on you
project. Take note of all the tools you need in order to work o
your craft. Then say thank you to God for creating the entir
world out of nothing at all!

SINGING ON THE ROAD

Find It in the Bible

Sing to the LORD, for he has done glorious things;
let this be known to all the world.

ISAIAH 12:5

Padam was just five years old when his mom died. The little boy grew up in Nepal with no parents and had to learn to take care of himself. Padam came from a group of people in Nepal who travel from city to city singing and playing music. So Padam learned how to play the Nepali violin to earn money. Can you imagine working for your food as a kid?

Padam's life wasn't easy, but it all changed when he learned about Jesus Christ. Now Padam is an adult, and he still travels all over South Asia. But these days, he sings about God's love. Padam can sing and play his music in villages that won't usually listen to the gospel. Several people have believed in Jesus because of Padam's music.

You don't need a great voice or amazing talent to praise God. Like Padam, you can sing wherever you go either out loud or in your heart. It tells God you are thinking about Him. The Lord delights when you let your love for Him come out in daily worship.

A POWER NOTE

Think of a few things you love about God. Then make up a song about why you love Him! Feel free to write down your song and sing it to a tune you already know. Praise to God is powerful!

GIANT FEAR

Find It in the Bible

David said to the Philistine, "You come against me with
sword and spear and javelin, but I come against you in
the name of the LORD Almighty, the God of the
armies of Israel, whom you have defied."

1 SAMUEL 17:45

Goliath was an enormous guy—as in, more than nine feet of
really big. Most of the men you know are probably about six
feet tall, so imagine a nine-foot-tall warrior in full armor and a
big sword coming toward you on the battlefield. What would you
do? Most people would run.

But not David. David must have been afraid. Maybe for a second
he thought, *What am I doing here? This is crazy.* But he stood his
ground. He knew what he was doing there. The giant man had
defied (meaning spoken against) God, and David wasn't going to
let that stand. So he stood up to the giant.

Some of our fears and problems can feel like giants. They're big
and looming and scary. When they come into our lives, we're
terrified. We want to run away. What if you just stood your
ground? What if you said, "God has told me I don't need to be
afraid of anything. So I'm not afraid of *you*."

A POWER NOTE

What are you most afraid of? Picture your fear as if it is dressed
in armor and has a weapon. Now imagine yourself, like David,
standing up to that fear. What do you think will happen with
God on your side?

FIVE SMOOTH STONES

Find It in the Bible

So David triumphed over the Philistine with a sling
and a stone; without a sword in his hand he
struck down the Philistine and killed him.

1 SAMUEL 17:50

It was just a sling and just a stone. No wonder the huge giant with all his armor laughed at the boy. But he didn't count on two facts: (1) David knew how to use that sling with great accuracy, and (2) David had God on his side.

David's greatest concern was God. When all of the seasoned soldiers refused to go to battle against the giant, David volunteered. When the king offered David his armor, David said no. He didn't need heavy armor. He just needed his sling, some stones, and God.

Maybe you don't feel as though you have much to offer. You're young, and you don't have much money or time. You're still trying to grow up! But God has given you special gifts and abilities that He will use. Now is the time for you to get better at those skills. Then, with those skills and your God, you will do amazing things!

A POWER NOTE

Go outside and pick up five smooth stones about the same size. With a marker, write on each stone one thing that you're good at. Maybe you can sing, or draw, or play sports. These are the things you have to offer to God. Ask God to help you use those abilities to honor Him.

THE MYSTERY OF GOD

Find It in the Bible

"For my thoughts are not your thoughts, neither are your ways my ways," declares the LORD. "As the heavens are higher than the earth, so are my ways higher than your ways and my thoughts than your thoughts."

ISAIAH 55:8–9

When you glance up at the night sky, sometimes the moon seems so close. Other times it seems farther away. Because of the moon's rotation around the earth, it is an average distance of 225,622 miles from earth. That's pretty far away!

Just as the moon can look so close yet is really thousands of miles away, God's plans can sometimes seem really easy to understand. Other times they seem as far away from our understanding as the moon is far from the earth.

In these verses, God was telling His people about His greatest plan, the plan of salvation. He was telling His people that if they would turn to God and follow Him, He would pardon their sins instead of punishing them as they deserved. It's easy to understand punishment for disobedience, but God's thoughts, which are higher than ours, are to offer forgiveness and salvation for those who will turn to Him and away from their sins.

A POWER NOTE

Try to memorize Isaiah 55:8–9. Print each phrase of the passage on a separate index card or small piece of paper. Read the verse through once, then flip over the cards or pieces of paper so that the words are face down. Scramble the cards or paper; then turn them over. Try to put the passage in order.

THE GOOD SHEPHERD

Find It in the Bible

The thief comes only to steal and kill and destroy; I have come
that they may have life, and have it to the full.

JOHN 10:10

If you've ever had something stolen, you know how upset it makes you—especially if the stolen item was really important to you, like your bike. Did you know that every year between 300,000 and 2,000,000 bicycles are stolen? That's a lot of missing bikes and a lot of sad people!

Jesus told a story that compared Himself to a good shepherd and Satan to a thief. While Jesus takes care of His sheep (us, His followers), Satan, the thief, comes only to kill and destroy.

That's what Satan is all about. He wants to destroy; he wants to make your life miserable. Satan is a joy thief who has come to ruin everything good and right in the world.

Jesus is just the opposite—the Good Shepherd. Jesus has come to give life—and not just any old boring life but life "to the full." That means He wants you to be joyous and full of life. Like a superhero, Jesus has come to save the day. He wants you to be joyful and to spread joy all around you.

A POWER NOTE

Make something out of building blocks or put a puzzle together. Then break down the building or break apart the puzzle. This is what Satan wants to do to your life. But God is powerful enough to protect you from all evil.

HELP THE HURTING

Find It in the Bible

The King will reply, "Truly I tell you, whatever you did for
one of the least of these brothers and
sisters of mine, you did for me."

MATTHEW 25:40

Did you know that animals and plants often help each other
Earthworms are important to trees because the worm
burrow into the soil around the tree roots and let oxygen into th
soil. How about the birds, bees, and other insects that pollinat
flowers? The flowers of the kapok tree release nectar at night s
that bats will transfer pollen from one flower to another on thei
tongues and noses!

Sometimes we decide to help others if we like the way they loo
or if they are popular. Or we help if others will notice what w
are doing. Jesus taught that we should be willing to help peopl
who are not easy to love. He wants us to care for people who ar
overlooked or poor or lonely or sick.

Would you be willing to help someone like that? This verse say
that when we do something for people who aren't easy to love, w
are doing it for God. This is pleasing to Him.

A POWER NOTE

Ask your parents to help you find information about a boy or gir
your age who needs help. It might be someone in your town o
someone in another country. Figure out at least one thing yo
can do to help that person and do it to please God. You will b
pleased, too!

STANDING IN THE GAP

Find It in the Bible

I looked for someone among them who would build up
the wall and stand before me in the gap on behalf of the
land so I would not have to destroy it, but I found no one.

Ezekiel 22:30

In Bible times, many cities had huge walls surrounding them. The walls protected the people in the city from their enemies. But sometimes enemy troops would attack and break through the wall. When that happened, soldiers would have to stand in the hole or gap of the wall to fight the enemy troops and keep them from entering the city. Those soldiers risked their lives to protect their people.

A person who prays for someone else is said to "stand in the gap." This is also known as *intercession*. The prophet Ezekiel was God's prophet while the people of Israel were captives in Babylon. That's where he lived, too. Ezekiel's job was to speak God's messages to the people. Even in captivity, He had the task of standing in the gap for God's people.

You also can stand in the gap for other people by praying for them. You can be God's helper!

A POWER NOTE

Make a list of people you know who need God to help them right now. Beside each name write the problem or responsibility each person is facing. Decide when you can take time every day this week to pray for each one. It is important to have people "standing in the gap" to pray for one another when there are needs.

OBSESSED BY LOVE

Find It in the Bible

Jesus replied: "'Love the Lord your God with all your heart and with all your soul and with all your mind.' This is the first and greatest commandment."

MATTHEW 22:37–38

Have you ever gotten so absorbed in a book or a game that you stayed up past your bedtime? Perhaps you got caught reading under your sheets or playing later than you were allowed. When you are absorbed in an activity, time flies by and nothing else seems to matter. Often it is unhealthy to become so absorbed in something that you forget about everything else.

Jesus names one healthy obsession—being obsessed with God. That's what loving Him with all your heart and soul and mind means. You love Him completely, with everything you are and have. You give Him your love and attention always. Jesus said this is the "first and greatest commandment" because loving God this way helps you to stay close to Him and turn away from sin.

Enjoying fun activities like reading and playing games is fine. But you must always remember that the most important thing in your life should be to love God.

A POWER NOTE

On a piece of paper draw a heart, a smile, and a brain (or at least what you think a brain looks like). Use these to represent loving God with your heart, your soul, and your mind.

A DEADLY SWIM

Find It in the Bible

I will give you a new heart and put a new spirit in you;
I will remove from you your heart of stone and
give you a heart of flesh.

EZEKIEL 36:26

Lake Natron, in Africa, has a frightening secret. Its water is full of minerals and salt. In fact, the lake has so many minerals that birds and other small animals that dip into it die . . . and are turned to stone. The salt and minerals dry around them, making them into statues, stiff and unmoving.

In today's verse, God used a word picture like that to describe His people's hearts. Something made of stone is hard and cold. It doesn't feel anything. It can't be changed or moved. That's what we are like without the Holy Spirit living in us. We make wrong choices over and over, and we don't want to change.

God knew that hearts made out of stone can't change themselves, in the same way that the stone animals of Lake Natron can't make themselves alive again. So He promised to give us new hearts: hearts that want to do good. All we have to do is let Him rescue us from our sin and breathe His life into us.

A POWER NOTE

Write out a list of bad habits you don't think you can change. ("I can't control my temper. I can't get my homework done on time. I can't stop lying to my parents.") Then cross out "I can't" and write "God can help me" in front of each item on your list. Ask the Holy Spirit to help you change and do what's right.

FOLLOW THE LEADER

Find It in the Bible

And I will put my Spirit in you and move you to follow my
decrees and be careful to keep my laws.

EZEKIEL 36:27

Australian Shepherd dogs can teach us a lot about obedience.
When it's time for the sheep to move to a new pasture, these
dogs work with the shepherd to guide the sheep in the right
direction. The shepherd rides on horseback while the dogs trot
happily alongside him. The shepherd can see the entire flock,
and he knows exactly what the dogs need to do to help. So he
gives a command, and the dogs begin to move among the sheep.
He whistles and calls, and the dogs respond with complete trust
in his decisions.

God is our trustworthy leader, and we obey His commands. When
He tells us to follow His decrees, we know that it's always for our
own good. That doesn't mean we'll always understand right away
why He gives us a certain rule or lets something happen. But He
will never lead us the wrong way.

Even though the Holy Spirit helps us follow God, that doesn't
mean we sit back and do nothing. We have to "be careful" to obey
God. That takes work on our part, too!

A POWER NOTE

Find more information about Australian Shepherd dogs in
library books or on the Internet. Read about the traits of these
dogs and how they are trained to be obedient. Think how you can
train yourself to be obedient to God.

THE LIMITLESS TREASURE

Find It in the Bible

If any of you lacks wisdom, you should ask God, who gives
generously to all without finding fault,
and it will be given to you.

JAMES 1:5

Our God gives generously. How do we know? Just look at this amazing world and see how generous He is. Did you know that a mature oak tree grows 250,000 leaves every year and 50,000 acorns? A fully grown birch tree can produce a million seeds in one year. And God provides millions of seeds each year for us to eat—like walnuts, peanuts, chestnuts, and pistachios. One of the most delicious foods from a seed is chocolate, which is made from the seeds inside the cocoa pod.

Yes, God is generous to provide for the needs of all creation. He is also generous to provide His children with wisdom. He has promised that if we ask Him for wisdom He will give it to us. We may get stuck and wonder what to do or how to live for Him. All we have to do is ask for His help. He will give us wisdom, not just a little bit but a generous amount.

A POWER NOTE

Ask your parents if you can make a chocolate dipping sauce for dessert. You will need a large bar of sweetened chocolate and half a cup of heavy cream. With an adult's help, melt the chocolate in a microwave oven for a few seconds or in a pan over very low heat. After the chocolate melts, add the cream and stir until it is smooth. Dip pieces of fruit, marshmallows, or nuts into the sauce.

ASK FOR ADVICE

Find It in the Bible

Plans fail for lack of counsel, but with many advisers they succeed.

PROVERBS 15:22

When do people need advice? Usually it's when they have a big decision to make. Maybe your big sister is thinking about going to college, and she needs to get advice about such a big decision. Maybe your parents are thinking about moving, and they get advice about where to move. Sometimes you need advice even for smaller decisions—like whether to join the baseball team.

Everyone needs advice sometimes. Big decisions, little decisions. When we trust God for guidance, often He sends people our way to give us advice we need. This verse says that it's wise to get advice from lots of people when you have to make a decision. Other people can ask good questions you haven't thought of or they can give insight that you don't have on your own.

Don't be afraid to ask for advice—especially from people older and wiser.

A POWER NOTE

Who do you seek counsel from? Make a list of all of the adults who love you and want you to succeed. Then thank God for giving you some good advisers to help you grow in your faith.

THE SPIRIT IN YOU

Find It in the Bible

I will put my Spirit in you and you will live, and I will
settle you in your own land. Then you will know that
I the LORD have spoken, and I have
done it, declares the LORD.

EZEKIEL 37:14

As a Christian it is important to know that the Holy Spirit
lives inside you. He gives you the courage and strength and
wisdom and understanding to please God. In the Old Testament,
God promised His people through the prophet Ezekiel that He
would put His Spirit within them.

When Jesus talked to His disciples the night before He died, He
told them, "I will ask the Father, and he will give you another
advocate to help you and be with you forever—the Spirit of
truth. . . . The Advocate, the Holy Spirit, whom the Father will
send in my name, will teach you all things and will remind you of
everything I have said to you" (John 14:16–17, 26).

When you ask Jesus to be your Savior, the Holy Spirit comes to
live in your heart. His presence gives you everything you need to
live a life that pleases God. He comforts you and guides you. Will
you listen to Him?

A POWER NOTE

Find a picture of yourself—maybe you have a few extra school
pictures lying around. Ask a parent if you can take one and write
on it. Across your shirt in the picture write the words, "The Holy
Spirit lives in me." Put the picture somewhere to remind you of
the Holy Spirit's presence in your life.

RULES OF LIFE

Find It in the Bible

Observe them carefully, for this will show your wisdom and understanding to the nations, who will hear about all these decrees and say, "Surely this great nation is a wise and understanding people."

DEUTERONOMY 4:6

Imagine a world without rules. Maybe it sounds wonderful. You could eat as much candy as you wanted or stay up late at night. But think about the bad side of a world without rules. Nothing would stop people from stealing your things or from driving on the wrong side of the road. The world could be crazy and scary!

God knows that human beings need structure and rules to survive. He knows the craziness that would happen without rules. He is the one who created us, so He also knows that your brain likes to have rules and limits in order to organize the world around you into something that makes sense. That is why God gave the Israelites the Ten Commandments and why those rules have survived for more than three thousand years.

A place with rules is stable, safe, and clean. It's the kind of place where you'd want to live. God wants you to follow His rules so that you can enjoy your life. When you follow the rules, you not only make yourself look like a wise, good person, but you also glorify God!

A POWER NOTE

Think of three rules that you are supposed to follow, and write them on a piece of paper. Next to each one, write down what might happen if no one followed that rule.

HOLY GROUND

Find It in the Bible

"Do not come any closer," God said. "Take off your sandals,
for the place where you are standing is holy ground."

EXODUS 3:5

One day, as Moses minded his own business, God showed up in the form of a fire in a bush. Moses went to investigate how a fire could be in a bush yet not burn it up, and that's when God spoke. "Take off your sandals, for the place where you are standing is holy ground," God said. Moses removed his sandals and bowed to show his respect for God.

You probably won't see a burning bush (that doesn't burn up), and you probably won't have to take off your shoes to show respect to God. But He expects His people to respect Him and remember how holy He is. For example, while God is with you anywhere you are, a church is a special place where you go to worship God and show Him respect.

When you're in church, listen to your leaders and learn the lessons. During the service, follow along in your Bible and take notes on what the pastor says. Remember to treat God with the honor and respect He deserves. Just like Moses did.

A POWER NOTE

Next Sunday before you go to church, make sure you have your Bible with you and a little notebook that you can use to write down prayer requests and take notes on what you learn during the service. You don't have to write a lot. Just write down things you learn.

GOD IS MY ROCK

Find It in the Bible

The LORD is my rock, my fortress and my deliverer; my God is
my rock, in whom I take my refuge, my shield and the
horn of my salvation, my stronghold.

PSALM 18:2

The writer of this psalm used many symbols to describe God such as rock, fortress, shield, horn. All these symbols are used frequently throughout the Old Testament. What do they have in common? They're all strong!

Rocks are solid and difficult to break through. A fortress, kind of like a giant castle, is a strong place of protection from enemies. Shields protect soldiers against sword or spear attacks and can save their lives. A horn may not seem like a normal symbol of strength, but the writer of this psalm was thinking of horned animals. Consider a rhinoceros or a bull. It probably would not be quite as strong-looking or scary without horns. Horns are a form of strength and protection for animals just as God is our strength and protection.

The psalm writer knew that God was strong enough to protect him in all things, and He is strong enough to protect you, too! He is your fortress!

A POWER NOTE

Go outside and find a rock with a smooth side. Use paint to write a phrase on it that reminds you of how strong God is. You could write, "God is my strength" or whatever you want! Let the rock remind you that God is strong enough to save you.

GOD'S SPECIAL FORCES

Find It in the Bible

This poor man called, and the LORD heard him; he saved him
out of all his troubles. The angel of the LORD encamps
around those who fear him, and he delivers them.

PSALM 34:6–7

What do you see in your mind when you hear the word *angel*? We often think of angels as looking like little babies floating on clouds with wings and harps. But the Bible makes clear that angels are super powerful beings. They are not little or sweet or soft. In fact, most of the times when angels appeared to humans in the Bible, the humans were terrified! The angels always had to say, "Don't be afraid!"

Angels are God's special forces. They come to serve Him— bringing messages, protecting, or even comforting. They fight off Satan and his demons and make important announcements about what God is doing. And in this verse, God promises that an angel will protect and deliver those who call to God for help.

Imagine having God's top warriors around you all the time to keep you safe—what an awesome thought! Sometimes we can't see God's protection in our lives. But it's there—in powerful ways!

A POWER NOTE

Can you think of some stories in the Bible where angels appeared? What did the angels do? What did they look like? Why did God send them? Here are some stories to get you started: Luke 1:11–20, 26–38.

EXACTLY WHAT YOU ASKED FOR

Find It in the Bible

Then Peter said, "Silver or gold I do not have, but what I do
have I give you. In the name of Jesus Christ of Nazareth, walk."

ACTS 3:6

How fun it is to open up a birthday present or a Christmas
present and it's exactly what you asked for! It's exciting to
get a new bike, a set of roller blades, a new videogame, or paints
and drawing pencils. You wrote what you wanted on your list,
starred it, circled it in red, and put exclamation points at the end
of it. When you did that, you said, "*This* is what I want."

The man in this story had stopped asking for what he really
wanted. He couldn't walk, and he didn't think he ever would.
Instead of asking to walk, he just sat and begged for money. When
Peter came along, he didn't have money to give to the man (which
is what the man wanted). Instead, he offered him a miracle—the
power of Jesus to heal him completely!

Sometimes you ask God for something and He gives it to you.
Other times, He says no or asks you to wait. There may even be
times when God knows what you need even if you don't ask.
That's how much He loves you! The point is, don't stop asking.
Believe God to give you what He knows is best for you.

A POWER NOTE

Write down a list of the times God has answered a prayer for
you or your family. Then write down things you have that maybe
you never asked for—things that are blessings from God. Circle
everything and write "Thank You" to God across the whole list.

THE ALWAYS FRIEND

Find It in the Bible

"The virgin will conceive and give birth to a son, and they will call him Immanuel" (which means "God with us").

MATTHEW 1:23

There are some interesting friendships in the animal world. The giant Galapagos tortoise is not able to reach the annoying ticks that gather on its body, but it has a friend who helps—a little bird called a finch. The finch will jump around in front of the tortoise to let her know it is ready to pick off the ticks. The tortoise stretches out her neck and the finch picks the insects off her skin with its tiny beak. The finch gets a delicious dinner, and the tortoise is relieved of the ticks. Now, that's a helpful friendship!

There are so many fun things to enjoy with friends, but sometimes our friends can't be with us. We can have a friend who is always with us—Jesus. When Jesus was born, angels said He would be called "Immanuel," which means "God with us." Instead of staying in heaven, Jesus came down to earth to walk and talk with us. He wants to be with us now. He wants to be our friend. Just like we talk with our friends, love them, and want to spend time with them, we can do the same with Jesus.

A POWER NOTE

See if you can unscramble this sentence. Is it true for you?

I tnwa sJues ot eb ym rrofvee rdifne.

(I want Jesus to be my forever friend.)

FINDING JESUS

Find It in the Bible

Where is the one who has been born king of the Jews? We saw his star when it rose and have come to worship him.

MATTHEW 2:2

When you look up at the sky at night, what do you see? The moon? Stars in a black sky? There are over 400 billion stars in our galaxy. Even if you counted them every day for many years, you would never be able to count them all. The largest star we know about is 1,800 times larger than the sun!

God used a special star to guide the wise men to Jesus. They came from a far country where they studied the stars. To these men, the new star in the sky meant that a king had been born. That's why they followed the star and traveled a long way to the country where Jesus was born. They wanted to worship Him and bring Him gifts.

You don't need a star to guide you to Jesus. If you believe in Him as your Savior, He lives inside your heart. You don't have to travel anywhere to worship Him. Just pray right where you are!

A POWER NOTE

You can always talk to Jesus, anytime, anywhere. Like the wise men, you can praise Him. Here is something fun to do. Draw a big star on a piece of paper. Write a prayer in the middle of it and say it out loud.

BORN IN A BARN

Find It in the Bible

While they were there, the time came for the baby to be born,
and she gave birth to her firstborn, a son. She wrapped
him in cloths and placed him in a manger, because there
was no guest room available for them.

LUKE 2:6–7

"Were you born in a barn?" Has anyone ever asked you that question? If they did, it probably came after you did something sloppy or forgot to close a door. When people read the story of Jesus' birth, they often picture a stable like a small barn. Others believe the stable was actually in a cave. Either way, this was a place where animals were kept. The manger where Mary laid the baby Jesus was an animal food trough.

So why was Jesus "born in a barn"? Because no other place was available for His parents to stay! The innkeeper had no guest rooms left, but he was kind enough to let Mary and Joseph stay in the stable. Jesus was born to a poor family in a smelly barn. He was God wrapped up in human skin.

He left the majesty of heaven to be born in a barn because He wanted to bring us salvation. He did it out of love.

A POWER NOTE

With your parents' permission, cut out pictures of animals from old magazines. On a piece of paper, draw a stable and baby Jesus in a manger. Then glue the animal pictures around the manger. When you pray, thank Jesus for coming into the world to save you.

GOOD NEWS!

Find It in the Bible

But the angel said to them, "Do not be afraid. I bring you
good news that will cause great joy for all the people.
Today in the town of David a Savior has been
born to you; he is the Messiah, the Lord."

LUKE 2:10–11

We get excited when someone says, "I've got good news!"
Your dad might be talking about a project at work, or
your big brother tells about making the wrestling team. You get
caught up in the excitement of the good news and you celebrate.

One night, a group of shepherds sat in the fields outside the
little village of Bethlehem. They expected a normal night. They
probably spread out their cloaks under the stars, maybe someone
played a flute, and they took turns watching the sheep.

Then suddenly the sky lit up, terrifying them. But an angel spoke
up and told them not to be afraid because he was bringing good
news. In fact, it was the best news of all time. The Savior was
born! Jesus Christ was born!

Now that's the best news of all! What can you do to spread the
word?

A POWER NOTE

As you sing Christmas hymns, listen carefully to the words and
what they say about Jesus. For instance, "Joy to the world, the
Lord is come, let earth receive her king" talks about the joy of the
birth of Jesus on the first Christmas.

SnOWMAGEDDON

Find It in the Bible

He got up and rebuked the wind and the raging waters;
the storm subsided, and all was calm.
"Where is your faith?" he asked his disciples.

LUKE 8:24-25

The winter of 2013–14 in the United States had record-breaking cold and snowfall in various parts of the country. This qualified it for the name "snowmageddon." The word is a combination of "snow" and "Armageddon"—the Bible's word for the battle at the end of the world. A "snowmageddon" is snowfall that is so bad and troublesome that it seems like the end of the world.

A bad storm can be scary. The disciples were in the middle of a storm in a tiny boat and were afraid they would sink. Jesus, however, simply got up, quieted the storm, and asked "Where is your faith?" He asked this because His disciples knew He was the Son of God. Why would they fear a storm? The Son of God was in the boat with them! And God can do anything!

No matter how many storms you experience in your life—whether this refers to weather or to difficult circumstances—Jesus stands up in your boat and asks you to have faith in Him. He will take care of you.

A POWER NOTE

Storms are no fun. Talk to your parents about how to prepare for storms in your house, and why it's important to have faith that God will protect you.

HUMBLE YOURSELF

Find It in the Bible

Humble yourselves before the Lord, and he will lift you up.

JAMES 4:10

Have you ever heard someone say, "He's as proud as a peacock?" That phrase is used to describe someone who struts around and is overly vain or proud. That's what peacocks do when they want to attract a mate. They raise their beautiful tail feathers into a magnificent fan shape and hope that their female friends will be impressed. The peacocks hold their heads high and show off their gorgeous feathers to the peahens.

God never instructs us to be proud. Instead, He teaches us to be humble. That doesn't mean He wants us to think we're worthless or that we don't matter. Instead, He wants us to know who He is and who we are in relation to Him—His beloved children.

Being humble also means thinking of others before yourself. It means you don't look for attention and praise. But being proud is just the opposite. Proud people want to be the center of attention all the time. God says that when you humble yourself, He will raise you up and honor you.

A POWER NOTE

Think about how you acted today. Were most of your actions proud or humble? Did you think of others first, or yourself first? Do you focus on other people or do you try to get all the attention? Now think about how you can strive to be humble. Ask God to help you act humbly.

378

Jesus: 1 Death: 0

Find It in the Bible

Jesus said to her, "I am the resurrection and the life.
The one who believes in me will live, even though they die."

JOHN 11:25

Jesus makes one of the most incredible claims in history here! Death, the first result of sin and one of the oldest enemies of life, is powerless before Him. Think about that! Death marks the end of . . . well, every living thing. Dogs, trees, fish, sheep, and people have to accept the fact of physical death. No one escapes. No one gets out alive. Eventually, everyone dies physically.

But Jesus said that people who believe in Him live even though they die. What does that mean? For Lazarus, it meant that he came to life after four days in the grave. Jesus displayed His power over death when Lazarus came back to life.

Jesus' power over death also means that those who love Jesus, even though they die physically, don't die spiritually. When their bodies die, their spirits go to heaven to be with Jesus. And one day, they will have new bodies like the body Jesus has.

Death will come to everyone, but death doesn't win. Jesus does!

A POWER NOTE

Make a resurrection banner. Fold ten sheets of paper in half and loop them over a piece of string in a row. Glue each paper to the string at the fold. Once the glue dries, write one letter on each piece of paper to spell out this: Jesus Wins! Hang it up in your room as a joyful reminder.

THE LAST TRUMPET

Find It in the Bible

In a flash, in the twinkling of an eye, at the last trumpet.
For the trumpet will sound, the dead will be
raised imperishable, and we will be changed.

1 CORINTHIANS 15:52

Did you know that the trumpet is among the oldest of the musical instruments? Trumpets made of bronze and silver were found in the grave of Tutankhamun, a pharaoh of Egypt who died around 1323 BC.

This verse describes a moment at the end of time when God will bring all His people (those who have died and those who are still alive) to heaven to be with Him. All of Jesus' followers, both living and dead in every part of the world, will hear the sound of the trumpet and will meet Jesus in the air.

At that time, everything will happen in "the twinkling of an eye," meaning so quickly that we won't even realize it—like blinking an eye! The point is that no one will have time to change his or her mind about following Jesus. The decision a person has already made will determine what will happen to that person when the final trumpet blows.

A POWER NOTE

Draw a trumpet. If you aren't sure what one looks like, find one in an encyclopedia or on the Internet. Write the verse above on the side of the trumpet to remind you of that great moment when the trumpet will sound.

BORN AGAIN

Find It in the Bible

Jesus replied, "Very truly I tell you, no one can see the
kingdom of God unless they are born again."

JOHN 3:3

Do you remember the fairy tales of Snow White or Cinderella?
Those fairy tales took place in far-off kingdoms. You knew
they were in kingdoms because they had castles and princes and
kings and queens. So what about the kingdom of God? What does
that look like, and how can you be "born again" in order to see it?

Someday the kingdom of God will be everything good that we can
imagine. It will be heaven. People can only guess what heaven is
like. The Bible describes streets paved with gold and gates made
from single pearls. But whatever heaven looks like, one thing
is for certain: A person must be "born again" to see it. How is a
person "born again"? You must believe that Jesus is God's Son,
that He lived a perfect life, and that He died and then came back
to life—and then give your life to Him in faith.

When you truly believe in Jesus Christ, He comes to live in you.
That's when you become part of the kingdom of God. Everyone
who loves Jesus will get to experience the final chapter of God's
kingdom in heaven.

A POWER NOTE

You can read about the throne of heaven in Revelation chapter 4.
Verse 4 says that twenty-four elders who surround the throne have
gold crowns on their heads. Try to design the gold crown you think
they might wear.

NO MORE TEARS

Find It in the Bible

He will wipe every tear from their eyes. There will be no
more death or mourning or crying or pain, for the old
order of things has passed away.

REVELATION 21:4

When was the last time you cried? Was it when a bigger
kid called you names at school? Was it when one of your
family members got really sick? Was it the time you tripped
and scraped your knees? Maybe you just felt sad and small and
alone. Even though tears help keep your eyes clean and having a
good cry can help you feel better, no one likes doing it because it
usually means that something is wrong.

Life here on earth gives us lots of reasons to cry. God promises
that one day we won't need to cry anymore. This will happen
when we join Him in heaven after a lifetime of serving Him. Until
that time, we can have hope even when we are sad and hurting.

We know that sorrow and pain and the things that make us cry
won't last forever. One day our heavenly Father will take away all
of our pain. In the meantime, we can lean on Him for strength
and comfort.

A POWER NOTE

Draw a teardrop on a piece of paper and cut it out. On it, list
things that have made you cry. Then rip up the piece of paper
because one day, we won't have any reasons to cry anymore!

SCRIPTURE INDEX

SCRIPTURE INDEX

Fire Bible for Kids
A One-of-a-Kind Bible Reading Experience for Kids

The first ever study Bible with an emphasis on the Holy Spirit written especially for kids ages 8–12.

Uses over 100 original illustrations to draw kids into the Word and builds family values while combating secular ideals. Also, children are taught to apply biblical truths for daily living.

Here are some of the many features:

- Complete Old and New Testaments
- Over 1,200 study notes
- 66 book introductions
- 12 articles on biblical teachings
- Plan of salvation

- Verses to help in times of need
- 8 pages of full-color maps
- Glossary and concordance
- Table of weights and measures
- Themefinders™ and Themefinders™ index

Bible Fact-Pak

If you want to help kids plant God's Word inside their hearts, then the *Bible Fact-Pak* makes it fun and easy.

This innovative Scripture memorization tool features 576 diverse questions covering people, places, events and teachings of the Bible. It effectively enables students to gain knowledge and confidence as they discover more about the Bible.

The *Bible Fact-Pak* can be used for family devotions, children's church, Sunday schools, home schools, and Christian schools.

Special Features
- Questions align with the *Fire Bible for Kids, NIV*.
- Select cards feature page numbers for further Bible reading.
- Scripture verse cards coordinate with select verses featured in the *Fire Bible for Kids Devotional.*

Bible Fact-Pak
Study Guide

Bible Fact-Pak
Audio CD

Bible Fact-Pak
Games and
Activities Book

For more information about these resources
please visit www.myhealthychurch.com